THE COMPLETE
BOOK OF
KNITTING
AND
CROCHETING

THE COMPLETE
BOOK OF
KNITTING
AND
CROCHETING

*

Revised Edition

Marguerite Maddox

Illustrated

Introduction by Rosamay Winston

GRAMERCY PUBLISHING COMPANY • NEW YORK

CONTENTS

INTRODUCTION

At the start of the 1970's a whole new way of life for America—and for that matter, the whole world—is taking shape. Many habits, techniques and traditions of the past are fading, to be replaced by new technologies and new forms of expression. However, some of mankind's earliest crafts and handiworks are assuming more and more importance in our society. In these times when the pressures of our mechanized society bear down heavily upon us, the return to a slower pace is a welcome change.

The simplest way is to pick up simple tools and create handmade objects with one's individual personality shining through. Indeed, one of the first evidences that the generation gap is being bridged is seen in the sudden dash of hordes of teenagers to yarn shops, variety and department stores and hobby shops to make "groovy" crocheted and knitted accessories to spark up their casual apparel. Mothers, grandmothers, aunts, and older sisters have been called upon to get these most desired and desirable vests, cardigans, pullovers, scarfs, caps and ponchos on the road and guided to completion.

There is a camaraderie to be found among the wielders of crochet and knitting needles from every generation who share the interest aroused by the humble skein of yarn.

We are all aware of the practicality of knits: for travel they are incomparable, never needing pressing or special care. For the busy young mother or career woman, the easy-care features of the new synthetics are taken for granted. And now, knits make the scene from early morn, through the day to cocktail time and dinner hours.

As Fashion Director of Columbia-Minerva Corporation for the past decade, I have seen fashions come and go, but never in my life have I witnessed such enthusiasm as has been evident in the past few seasons in all branches of handwork, especially in crochet and knitting.

It has been the purpose of our company as well as all members of our industry to create excitement for our products. For, to put it frankly, we create a useless commodity when we spin a skein of yarn—useless, that is, until we show you the multitude of things you can do with it, such as decorating the body and the home. And that is what we have been increasingly successful in doing year after year. Not only have we been designing easy and quick-to-make garments, but improving the quality of our worsted wools and synthetic yarns. Improved dyes and spinning processes and new synthetic fibers all add to the beauty and practicality of knitting and crochet yarns.

"Easy care" and "color fast" are words that go along with names like "Nantuk" "Wintuk" and "Orlon." They guarantee the machine launderability of these fibers.

Yet who will deny the beauty and luxury of pure wool. For if there were ever a miraculous fiber, it is the natural loveliness of pure wool, well worth the slight extra care it needs.

My enthusiasm for the business with which I have been associated for many years has never diminished. I must confess it grows greater with the passing of time, and I admit to being "hooked." My wish and hope is that "Maggie" Maddox and I have imparted some of this excitement to you.

Rosamay F. Winston
Fashion Director
Columbia-Minerva Corporation

EDITOR'S NOTE

We have sought, in this book, to use wool yarns and cotton threads available to knitters and crocheters in every part of the country. From east to west, north to south, you will find the yarns specifically used in the various designs, in big shops, in department stores, in many markets, in specialty shops. Should your local shop be temporarily out of stock, we have appended a list of the various manufacturers and their addresses so that your particular shop will be able to order the yarns you need for any of the designs given in this book. The readers should not, however, try to order them by mail directly from the manufacturer, as these concerns do not supply individuals, only the retail shops.

MARGUERITE MADDOX

YARN MANUFACTURERS

* The American Thread Co.
90 Park Avenue
New York, N.Y. 10016

Emile Bernat and Sons Co.
Uxbridge, Mass. 01569

Brunswick Worsted Mills, Inc.
Pickens, S.C. 29671

* Coats and Clark, Inc.
430 Park Avenue
New York, N.Y. 10022

* Columbia-Minerva Corp.
295 Fifth Avenue
New York, N.Y. 10016

D.M.C. Corp.
107 Trumbull Street
Elizabeth, N.J. 07206

LeJeune, Inc.
1060 W. Evelyn Avenue
Sunnyvale, Calif. 94086

* Lion Brand Yarn Co.
1270 Broadway
New York, N.Y. 10001

Mary Maxim, Inc.
2001 Holland Avenue
Port Huron, Mich. 48060

Merino Wool Co.
1225 Broadway
New York, N.Y. 10001

Paternayan Bros., Inc.
312 East 95th Street
New York, N.Y. 10028

Pic Corp.
15 Commerce Street
Norwalk, Conn. 06851

Reynolds Yarns, Inc.
215 Central Avenue
East Farmingdale, New York, N.Y. 11735

Spinnerin Yarn Co.
230 Fifth Avenue
New York, N.Y. 10001

Joan Toggitt, Ltd.
1170 Broadway
New York, N.Y. 10001

* Bernhard Ullmann Co.
30-20 Thompson Ave.
Long Island City, N.Y. 11101

* William Unger and Co.
230 Fifth Ave.
New York, N.Y. 10001

KNITTING NEEDLES, CROCHET HOOKS, AND ACCESSORIES

C. J. Bates and Son
Chester, Conn. 06412

Emile Bernat and Sons Co.
Uxbridge, Mass. 01569

Boye Needle Co.
4343 North Ravenswood Avenue
Chicago, Ill. 60613

Coats and Clark Inc.
430 Park Ave.
New York, N.Y. 10022
(Crochet hooks only)

Dritz, Scovill Mfg. Co.
350 Fifth Avenue
New York, N.Y. 10001

Henry Seligman Co., Inc.
25 West 25th Street
New York, N.Y. 10010

TO THE READER
Write to the manufacturer for the store nearest you.

* Manufacturer's yarn used in designs in this book.

YARN DEFINITIONS

YARN QUANTITIES—GENERAL USAGE: As a general rule, the following amounts of yarn are necessary for the corresponding articles. Specific amounts depend, of course, upon the size necessary and the exact yarn used.

Dress:	1¾ pounds of yarn on the average
Sweater:	¾ pound of yarn
Skirt:	1 pound of yarn
Stole:	8 to 10 ounces of yarn

Also, occasionally, a scarf will be knitted on a 10" needle and a sweater on a 14" needle. Sock needles are usually 7" long with double points; booties are done on 10" double-pointed needles. Cuffs are usually fashioned on an 11" circular needle, sleeves on a 16" circular needle, a skirt (for small hips) on a 24" circular needle, a skirt (for large hips) on a 29" circular needle.

YARN DEFINITIONS

YARN: A continuous strand of any kind of twisted material; less tightly twisted than thread.

THREAD: Smooth finished and uniform in size; several twisted strands of cotton, silk, or linen.

PLY YARN: Twisting together of yarns; 2, 3, 4 ply yarn refers to the number of strands twisted together to form the yarn.

WOOL: Has elasticity because of the varying length of fibers, each of which has distinct layers of cells. Wool also has resiliency and felting qualities; absorbs moisture without feeling clammy; is strong and durable; is thermostatic; is light in weight; is slow to oxidize; is long wearing. Wool from the shoulders of the sheep is best in length, quality, and strength with the quality decreasing toward the hindquarters of the sheep.

MERCERIZED COTTON: Cotton yarn which is given a silky finish before dyeing has increased luster (the main feature), a soft feel, more strength, and better dyeing qualities.

ORLON YARN: A synthetic fiber produced by chemical and mechanical processes of different types. The raw material is acrylic. Orlon and its variations are durable; often machine washable and dryable and are in special demand for sensitive and allergic people. Almost any texture and effect of wool yarn may be duplicated in orlon.

KNITTING WORSTED: A sturdy 4 ply, loosely twisted yarn, moderate in price, and excellent for rough usage. A utility yarn suitable for heavy sweaters, socks, caps, scarfs, mittens, gloves, sportswear for men, women, and children, and heavy afghans. Usually takes #4 to #6 American standard needles of aluminum or steel or a set of #10 or #11 steel needles.

ZEPHYR GERMANTOWN: A very soft, heavy 4 ply Zephyr yarn, usually made from pure Australian wool or a similar type wool. Smooth in texture, due to the long staple wool used, and lightweight, and warm. One of the finest yarns for blankets, robes, afghans, and baby garments. Usually takes #4 to #6 American standard needles of aluminum or steel or a set of #10 or #11 needles.

SPORTS YARN: A tightly twisted 3 or 4 ply worsted yarn of fine quality. A utility yarn excellent for garments and accessories of hard wear, but the finished product does not look as coarse or heavy as knitting worsted. Uses include sportswear for men, women, and children, socks, stockings, mittens, gloves, women's suits and coats and children's coats, dresses, and sweaters. Suitable needles are steel or aluminum American standard #3 to #5 or a set of #12 or #13 for mittens, gloves, and stockings.

FINGERING YARN: A 2 or 3 ply worsted yarn spun more loosely than sports yarn, and of a better quality.

SHETLAND FLOSS: A fine 2 ply worsted, loosely spun, of a hairy nature, and fine but strong fibers. Suitable for lighter wearing apparel for women and children, infants' wear, shawls, scarfs, etc. Not suitable for garments with a lace stitch, nor for sweaters which require hard wear. Suitable needles are steel, aluminum, or composition (depending upon the purpose) from #2 to #5 American standard.

SOCK & STOCKING YARN: Ideal for sweaters, mittens, stockings, and anything needing good, hard wear. Needles: steel or aluminum American standard #3 or #4 and set of #12 and #13 for stockings, mittens, gloves.

ANGORA: Hair from the Angora rabbit, of 2 or 3 ply thickness, very soft and fluffy yarn usually mixed with other fibers. Needles: real Angora on American standard needles of #4 and up; mixtures on varying sizes from #2 depending on the weight of the yarn.

BOUCLÉ YARN: A novelty yarn made by twisting at one time 2 or more fine yarns held at different tensions. One yarn is made of a stiff fiber, loosely twisted. Loops are formed.

MOHAIR: A brushed yarn spun from goat's hair. For light yet bulky knits. The softness of the yarn depends on the amount of kid mohair blended with adult, tougher fibers. Very often it is blended with wool or orlon fibers, for additional strength and luster. Variations also include "loop" mohair where the effect is not as "furry" as it is more "bouclé" in appearance.

CREPE BOUCLÉ: Wool and rayon bouclé heavily crinkled. Suitable for women's dresses and suits and girls' lightweight coats and dresses. Should be knitted fairly tight on #2 or #3 American standard needles.

NUB OR SEED YARN: Formed with 2 ply heavier core yarn and 1 to 3 finer yarns. The fine yarn twists around the core yarn to form a knot or nub. A novelty yarn.

SLUB YARN: Has raised slubs or thick sections which are not twisted as much as the rest of the yarn.

COVERED CORE YARN: Of spiral type. The twisting together of 2 yarns, one soft and heavy and one fine. The heavy one is fed faster and winds around the fine one in spiral formation. The core yarn is entirely or partly covered; the covering yarn wraps around the ground yarn.

ELASTIC YARN: Rubber covered with cotton, rayon, nylon, etc., which is wound around it. Yarn has stretching powers.

METAL THREAD: Made with cotton, rayon, or silk core, around which is wound flat copper or brass wire coated with gold or silver.

RATINÉ YARN: Fine and thick yarn twisted together. Then the resulting yarn is twisted with a fine yarn producing nubs.

CORDÉ: Soft spun cotton covered with rayon.

CHENILLE: Fine cotton spun with 80% rayon; each side of rayon winding is cut, giving the yarn a velvety texture.

STRAW YARN: 100% viscose-process rayon yarn with a strawlike texture.

HOW TO KNIT

Knitting is a very adaptable needle art; articles produced range from the most delicate lingerie trimmings and highly styled outer garments through numerous household articles to the most intricate designs for laces. Articles can be made heavy and warm (afghans and sweaters), or light and porous (laces), according to the size of needles and size of thread or yarn used.

STITCH GAUGE: The tightness or looseness of each stitch (and thus of the finished article) is determined by the size of needles used; and this is always chosen in relation to the size of thread or yarn to be used, modified somewhat by the tightness or looseness desired. This tightness or looseness is called **Gauge,** and is influenced by one other factor—**Tension,** which is the strain put upon the thread or yarn by the knitter. Tension is a matter of nervous and muscular control of the fingers and is best regulated by always holding the work in the position which is most comfortable for your hands.

At the beginning of every set of instructions the proper **Stitch Gauge** for that piece of work is given, i.e., the number of stitches to the inch (a width measurement), and the number of rows to the inch (a length measurement). It is necessary that you get the same **Stitch Gauge** if your finished article is to be the size specified. Knit a 3″ square, using the pattern stitch, size of needles, thread or yarn specified in your instructions, press, then count number of stitches to the inch and number of rows to the inch. If you are knitting more stitches to the inch or more rows to the inch, use larger needles; if less use smaller needles. As the work progresses some people automatically tighten or loosen the tension on their work. Check your **Stitch Gauge** frequently.

ABBREVIATIONS

K—Knit	**St**—Stitch	**Inc**—Increase
P—Purl	**Tog**—Together	**Dec**—Decrease
Yo—Yarn Over	**Beg**—Beginning	**Incl**—Inclusive
O—Over	**Rnd**—Round	**Sl**—Slip
		Sk—Skip

Slip a St—Slip a stitch from one needle to the other without working it

Psso—Pass slip stitch over knit stitch

Dp—Double-pointed needle

* Repeat everything after asterisk (*) as many times as specified in instructions.

( ) Repeat everything within parentheses ( ) as many times as specified in instructions.

Abbreviations are usually listed at the beginning of every set of instructions.

The presence of one or more asterisks [*] in the instructions indicates that the instructions following the symbol will be repeated a specified number of times, i.e., repeat from * 6 times (means repeat 6 times in all), or repeat from * across row (or round). Occasionally, due to long and intricate directions, the instructions will read: repeat from * to * 6 times in all. For many and varied repetitions, one [*], two [**] or three [***] asterisks are sometimes used.

Parentheses in the instructions indicate that the instructions within the parentheses are to be repeated a number of times, i.e., (k 2, p 6) 4 times means to do everything within the parentheses 4 times in all.

.   .   .

YARNS: There are various types of yarn differing in twist, size and texture. The yarn specified in the instructions has been chosen to suit the article. Unless you are an expert knitter it is inadvisable to change the size or type of yarn recommended.

WINDING YARN: A majority of yarn comes already wound; the end to start usually comes out of the center of the ball and unwinds evenly and easily with very little effort.

Those yarns such as knitting worsted, dress yarns, rug yarns, etc. that are sold in skeins are wound into balls before knitting. Yarn should *never be wound tightly*, as this stretches the yarn and results in a garment or article with no spring or stretch. When winding keep 2 or 3 fingers under the yarn on ball, wind several strands of yarn over fingers, remove fingers and place fingers on top of ball again, wind several strands over fingers and remove fingers. Continue in this manner.

KNITTING NEEDLES: There are also various types of needles made up of a variety of materials. Instructions specify the type to use. Any change from those specified should be done carefully as the size of needles has a definite effect on finished size of article (see **Stitch Gauge**).

TYPES OF NEEDLES

STRAIGHT NEEDLES have one pointed end. When working with a pair of straight needles, the work is done flat and in rows. Work across all the stitches on one needle, then turn work to other side and work across all the stitches on other needle. They are usually 10″, 12″, or 14″ long, the sizes start: 1, 2, 3, 4, etc. The smaller the number, the finer the needle.

A CIRCULAR NEEDLE is made circular with 2 pointed ends of flexible nylon. The circular part is made with metal points which are thicker than the nylon section, enabling the knitting to be moved easily around needle. They are used for knitting circular skirts, collars, sleeves, V-necks, etc., or whenever a seam is not to be used. The stitches are knitted from one needle point to the other needle point continuously, going around and around in one direction.

DOUBLE-POINTED NEEDLES come in sets of 4 or 5 and are used for doilies, gloves, mittens, round necklines, socks, etc. or whenever a seam is not used. The stitches are cast on as in ordinary knitting and then divided on 3 or 4 needles as instructions specify. The ends of each needle cross each other and form a triangle or square (finished knitting is tubular). The needle following the end of yarn is usually specified in instructions as the first needle; the 4th or 5th needle is used to knit with. When all the stitches from one needle have been knitted onto a spare needle, that needle is then used to knit the stitches off the next needle, etc. Bone and plastic needles come in same sizes as straight needles *but* steel double-pointed needles are numbered in the opposite way; the *larger* the number, the *finer* the needle.

KNITTING AIDS

MARKERS may be purchased in packages in yarn shops and department stores. They are small plastic circles in various sizes for small and large needles. They are placed wherever increases begin to form a continuous angle, or placed after a specified number of stitches in intricate patterns. Place on needle where designated in instructions and slip them from one needle to another while working.

STITCH HOLDERS are made of plastic, bone, or metal in the shape of a large safety pin. When instructions specify to place stitches on a stitch holder, the specified stitches are *slipped* on the holder. These stitches are picked up and worked later on. A large safety pin or an extra knitting needle can be used in place of a holder. The stitches may also be slipped onto a thread.

STITCH COUNTERS are handy little gadgets, usually made of plastic, with little dials of numbers that turn easily. The counter is slipped on the needle first in front of work; when keeping count of rows the dial is turned to the next number as each row is finished.

CABLE NEEDLES are hairpin shaped, made of aluminum to hold cable stitches from sliding off. They come in thin size for fine yarns and heavy size for bulky yarns.

YARN BOBBINS are made in several shapes and sizes, in plastic, to hold small amounts of colored yarns used in Fair Isle and Argyle knitting.

JOINING YARN: Whenever possible, start a new ball of yarn at the edge of an article or garment by tying the new yarn to the end of the old yarn.

Where it cannot be done, splice the yarn by threading the end of old yarn into a needle and weaving it into the beginning of new yarn for 2″ or 3″, having on the Wrong Side the short end, which can be cut off after you have worked past the spliced yarn.

For yarns that cannot be spliced, start working with new yarn, leaving a 3″ or 4″ length on the Wrong Side, and after 1 or 2 rows have been worked, tie ends close to work. Using a crochet hook, weave ends in and out of stitches on the Wrong Side making sure they do not show on the Right Side of work.

BLOCKING refers to the pressing of the shape and size of each piece of knitting and is very important to the finished result of an article. Always block before sewing pieces together. When 2 pieces have the same shape, block them together at one time so they will be exactly alike. Place pieces on a flat padded surface Wrong Side up, using rust-proof pins; pin straight edges in a straight line, having pins ⅛″ apart and inserting pins in last stitch of each row. *Never* stretch ribbing. Pin shaped pieces into their proper shapes, taking care to have same shape on identical pieces (instructions usually specify measurements). When piece has been pinned into proper shape all around, press very *lightly* with a hot iron through a damp cloth, being careful not to *iron* the knitting—just steam it. Allow to dry thoroughly before removing pins.

JOINING: Always sew pieces together using a blunt-pointed needle and same yarn as knitting. Pick up one stitch on each side so that edges meet evenly; match corresponding rows whenever possible, *never* drawing these stitches *tightly*. When setting in sleeves always ease in any extra fullness towards top of sleeve.

Another method of joining is pinning edges together, easing in any extra fullness, using a backstitch to sew a narrow seam. Press seams open.

On articles made of finer yarns, the seams may be machine-stitched and then pressed open.

Sewing seam binding over edges of shoulder seams will prevent these seams from stretching.

WEAVING: When 2 pieces of knitting are joined together by weaving it is usually done so that there is no seam line. There are usually the same amount of stitches on each needle. Break off the yarn in a long length and thread it into a large-eyed blunt-pointed needle, with the 2 needles parallel to each other. Insert the needle from right to left through *front* of first stitch on back needle, pull yarn through, insert needle from right to left in *back* of corresponding stitch on front needle, * pull yarn through, insert needle from right to left through *front* of next stitch on back needle, pull yarn through, insert needle in back of next stitch on *front* needle, repeat from * until all stitches have been woven together, then remove needles. Stitches can be pulled as close together as desired by pulling end of yarn; weave end of yarn into Wrong Side of work, using a crochet hook.

MULTIPLE OF STS: This expression is used when working a pattern; if the pattern is to work out correctly, the number of "cast on" stitches must be divisible by the multiple given at the beginning of instructions. **Ex:** Multiple of 3 would be 12, 24, 36, or any number that can be divided evenly by 3. A multiple of 3+2 would be 14, 26, 38, or any number that has 2 extra stitches after being divided by 3.

CASTING ON

This is the first step in knitting and refers to putting the first set of stitches on a needle before you can begin to work.

Note: For practicing, use a thick yarn and large needle so that the formation of stitches and where the yarn goes and emerges will show clearly. Practice until you can knit easily, relaxed, and your work has acquired evenness and accuracy.

Method #1 is simple and fast and is usually used at the start of an article; the finished edge is fairly loose.

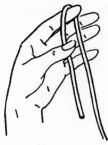

Illus. 1

Step 1: Grasp end of yarn as shown in Illus. 1, make a slip knot as shown in Illus. 2 and 3, pull long yarn gently to tighten loop (Illus. 4), slip loop of knot onto point of one needle (Illus. 5), pull on yarn attached to ball to tighten loop. You are now ready to "cast on" stitches.

Method #1: Make a loop around left thumb with yarn attached to ball as shown in Illus. 6. * Insert point of needle with

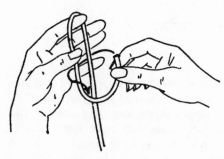

Illus. 2

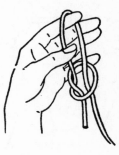

Illus. 3

CASTING ON (cont.)

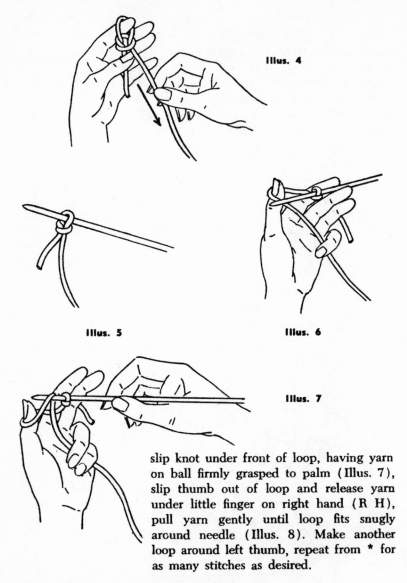

Illus. 4

Illus. 5

Illus. 6

Illus. 7

slip knot under front of loop, having yarn on ball firmly grasped to palm (Illus. 7), slip thumb out of loop and release yarn under little finger on right hand (R H), pull yarn gently until loop fits snugly around needle (Illus. 8). Make another loop around left thumb, repeat from * for as many stitches as desired.

Note: Stitches should fit closely but not tightly around needle, loose enough to move back and forth freely but not so loose as to allow needle to fall out.

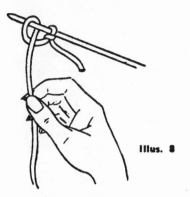

Illus. 8

Method #2 is more complicated, as the stitches are knitted on at start of article, and is most always used when stitches are to be cast on for buttonholes or when a sleeve is worked at the same time as garment. The finished edge is much firmer.

Illus. 9

Illus. 10

Method #2: Make a slip knot and place on needle in same manner as in Step 1. Holding this needle in left hand (L H) between thumb and forefinger about ¾″ from point, insert empty needle with R H into *back* of slip knot (Illus. 9). Hold crossed tips of needles and slip knot between L thumb and forefinger, with R H wrap yarn around point of R H needle from back (Illus. 10). Still holding needles and loop in same position with L H, place yarn fairly taut over R H forefinger and between middle finger and ring finger. Holding R H needle with thumb and the 3 other fingers, gently move tip of R H needle (with yarn around it) down against L H

[11]

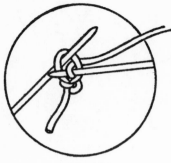

Illus. 11

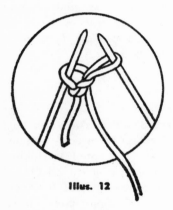

Illus. 12

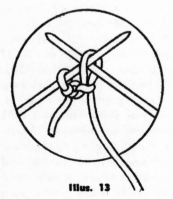

Illus. 13

needle until tip and yarn emerge on R H needle thru the slip knot (Illus. 11).

* Pull this loop out until it is long enough to be slipped over onto L H needle (Illus. 12), then slip the loop from the R H needle onto the L H needle (Illus. 13). Insert point of R H needle into back of stitch just slipped onto L H needle (Illus. 14), wrap yarn around tip of R H needle from back, and gently pull R H needle and yarn thru same as before. Repeat from * for as many stitches as desired (Illus. 14).

Note: Slip knot is first stitch, next stitch is second stitch, etc.

You are now ready to knit on these "cast on" stitches.

KNITTING

Holding L H needle (with cast-on stitches) in L H and yarn in *back* of needle, insert R H needle into back of first stitch (Illus. 15). Wrap yarn around tip of R H needle from back (Illus. 16), pull tip of R H needle gently down against L H needle until tip and yarn emerge thru first stitch (Illus. 17), draw a loop thru. With this loop on R H needle slip the

Illus. 14

Illus. 15

Illus. 16

Illus. 17

stitch thru which this stitch was made off the point of L H needle (Illus. 18). This completes the first stitch and is the beginning of the first row of knitting on R H needle. * Insert R H needle into back of next stitch, wrap yarn around point of R H needle from back, pull tip of needle against tip of L H needle until tip and yarn emerge thru next stitch. With this stitch on R H needle, slip the stitch thru which this stitch was made off the L H needle. Repeat from * across all the cast-on stitches. Place this needle in L H, and with other needle in R H, knit the second row in same manner as before, always knitting through *front* of stitches on second and all subsequent rows. Knitting every row produces the Garter Stitch, which has the same appearance on both sides and has a great deal of stretch or elasticity.

Illus. 18

PURLING

With yarn in front of needle, insert point of R H needle into front of first stitch (Illus. 19), wrap yarn around point of R H needle from back (Illus. 20), gently draw point and yarn down against L H needle until yarn and tip of needle emerge thru the back of first stitch (Illus. 21). * With this loop on R H needle, slip the stitch thru which this loop was made off the point of L H needle (Illus. 22), insert R H needle into front of next stitch, wrap yarn around point from back, gently draw point and yarn down against L H needle until yarn and tip of needle emerge thru the back of this stitch. Repeat from * across row.

Illus. 19

Note: Purling differs in two ways from *knitting:* first, the yarn is kept in *front* of the work and, second, the needle is inserted in the *front* of each stitch. It is seldom used alone but is combined with knitting to produce ribbing and pattern stitches.

Illus. 20

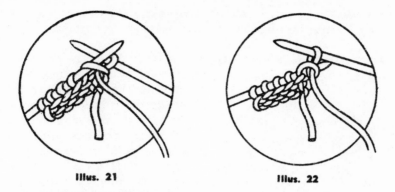

Illus. 21   **Illus. 22**

STOCKINETTE STITCH: Cast on as many stitches as are desired. Knit every stitch on the first row. Insert R H needle into the front of the first stitch on L H needle and slip this stitch onto R H needle (this is known as "slipping the first st"). Bring yarn in front of needle and purl all remaining stitches. On next row insert R H needle into back of first stitch and slip this stitch onto R H needle, bring yarn to back of work, and knit all the remaining stitches. **Note:** When working on a straight piece of knitting always slip the first stitch at the beginning of each row; this produces a flat, even edge. The smooth, even surface is usually the Right Side of work; the knotty surface is the Wrong Side of work. When working in Stockinette Stitch always knit the knit rows (knot of each stitch is in *back*), always purl the purl rows (knot of each stitch is in *front*).

RIBBING is usually used where a great deal of elasticity is required. **Ex:** Hat, cap, waistband, cuffs, necklines, tops of socks, etc. It is made by alternating a set number of knit stitches with a set number of purl stitches. In a ribbing of k 2, p 2, the number of stitches cast on should be divisible by 4 so that if you begin with k 2 you end with p 2. When work is turned the first 2 stitches now (which were purled on last row) will be knitted on this row, the next 2 stitches, which were knitted on last row, will be purled on this row, etc. In ribbing, the knit stitches (those with the knots in the *back*) are always knitted, the purl stitches (those with the knots in the *front*) are always purled.

INCREASING & DECREASING

In order to make your work larger or smaller in places, you will have to increase or decrease usually in the first or last stitch of a row. **Ex:** On a sweater, you will increase on the part over the hips, decrease at the waistline and increase again at the bustline.

INCREASING IN KNITTING Method #1: Insert needle from back into next st, wrap yarn around point of needle from back and bring thru the same st. Do not slip this st off. Insert needle into back of same st (Illus. 23) and bring yarn thru, then slip the st off needle. You will have 2 sts on R H needle over 1 st below. On the next row, work each loop as if it were 1 st, being careful that the st that was increased is not slipped off the needle with the original st.

Illus. 23

Method #2: Yarn over (bring yarn under and over needle), knit the next st (there are now 2 sts over the 1 st below). This method of increasing makes a hole in the work. It is used for lace, openwork patterns, beading, etc.

Illus. 24

INCREASING IN PURLING: Purl into the front of st, leave this st on needle, purl into the back of the same st. (Illus. 24), then slip this st off needle. There are 2 purled sts on R H needle over the 1 purled st below.

DECREASING IN KNITTING Method # 1: Knit 2 sts together (insert needle in back of next 2 sts at one time, then knit the 2 sts off together as 1 st). There is 1 st on R H needle over the 2 sts below.

Method #2: Slip 1, knit 1, and pass slip st over knit st (slip the next st from L H needle onto R H needle without knitting it, knit the next st, now slip these 2 sts back onto L H needle, insert R H needle into slip st as if to purl and under the knit st, twisting tip of needle gently until knit st is thru the slip st, now slip the 2 sts off together). There is 1 st on R H needle over the 2 sts below.

DECREASING IN PURLING: Purl 2 sts together (insert needle in front of next 2 sts at one time, then purl the 2 sts together as 1 st). There is 1 st on R H needle over the 2 sts below.

SLIPPING A STITCH (Slip St): Insert R H needle thru st on L H needle from R to L and slip onto R H needle without working it.

To pass a slip st over a knit st (psso), slip 1 st, knit the next st, pass the slip st thru the knit st as in Binding Off Method #1. The slip st is used in working openwork patterns, laces, etc.

YARN OVER (Yo): In knitting, yarn over means to bring the yarn under to front of needle and over to back of needle. There is an extra st on R H needle and you are ready to knit the next st off.

In purling, yarn over means to take the yarn back over top of needle and forward under needle. There is an extra st on R H needle and you are ready to purl the next st off.

BINDING OFF

When work is finished, the stitches must be fastened together to prevent them from "running." This is referred to as *binding off*.

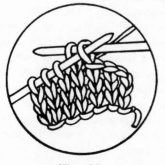

Illus. 25

Note: Binding off should *always* be done *loosely*. If you have a tendency to bind off tightly, use a larger needle in R H. When binding off, *always* knit the knit stitches, purl the purl stitches.

Method #1: Knit the first 2 sts *loosely*, * insert tip of L H needle into the front of the first knitted st (Illus. 25), gently

Illus. 26

pull point of R H needle and second knit st along L H needle until point and st emerge thru the first st (Illus. 26), slip the first st off of L H needle, and then knit the next st on the L H needle onto the R H needle. Repeat from * for as many sts as specified or until 1 st remains, break yarn, and draw thru the remaining loop.

Method #2: Knit the first st, * put this st back on L H needle, insert R H needle in back of this st and in back of the next st at one time. Knit these 2 sts together as one, slip the 2 sts off the L H needle (there is 1 st on R H needle), knit the next st from L H needle. Repeat from * for as many sts as specified or until 1 st remains, break yarn, and draw thru remaining loop.

PICKING UP DROPPED STITCHES

When you accidentally drop a stitch (this stitch is off the needle and has "run" down the row on which it belongs), it must be picked up correctly and put back on the needle by using a crochet hook.

PICKING UP A KNIT STITCH

Illus. 27

Insert crochet hook from front of work thru the loop of the dropped stitch and thru the next crossbar of yarn that belongs in this st (Illus. 27). Pull the yarn thru the loop on hook and, keeping this loop on hook, insert hook under next crossbar of yarn and pull this thru loop on hook. Continue in this manner until the stitch has been worked up to needle; then put stitch back on needle in proper position.

Illus. 28

PICKING UP A PURL STITCH

Insert crochet hook from back of work thru loop of dropped stitch and over cross-bar of yarn (Illus. 28). Pull yarn thru. Continue in this manner until the stitch has been worked up to needle; then put the stitch back on needle.

PICKING UP STITCHES that have been unraveled or have accidentally slipped off the needle. When you have made a mistake that should be corrected, your work can easily be unraveled back to that row. This row of stitches must be placed back on the needle correctly or there will be a row of twisted stitches that will show on the Right Side of the work. Whenever possible, pick up on the Right Side of the work and start at the edge opposite the ball of yarn, so that after all the stitches have been picked up, you can continue to work over these stitches without any further transferring. Use a slightly smaller needle to pick up stitches.

KNIT ST: Pick up knit stitches as shown in Illus. 29.

PURL ST: Pick up purl stitches as shown in Illus. 30.

On **GARTER STITCH** alternate the 2 movements.

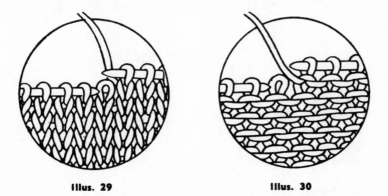

Illus. 29   **Illus. 30**

Note: If a stitch has not been picked up properly it is easily noticed when working the stitch, as it will not be laying right and the needle will not be in the same position in that stitch as it has been in others. When this happens, insert the point of the R H needle from left to right in front of this stitch, slip it onto the R H needle, then back onto the L H needle (you will have twisted the stitch back to its correct position on needle).

PICKING UP STITCHES

When a sleeve is knitted into a garment or when a neckline is finished by working ribbing around a neck edge, you will have to "pick up" a specified number of stitches around the armhole or neck edge.

Always pick up stitches on the Right Side of work from right to left with a slightly smaller needle.

Illus. 31

Method #1: Hold free end of yarn against edge of garment with L H until several sts have been picked up; leave a 3" or 4" end of yarn dangling (this can be woven into work on Wrong Side later). Insert R H needle into center from front to back of last st on first row, pull a loop of the free yarn thru (this first st can be put on easily with a crochet hook). * Insert R H needle into center from front to back of next st, bring yarn around to front of needle and towards back, gently pull point of needle and yarn thru center of this st. Repeat from * for as many sts as specified (Illus. 31).

Method #2: Hold yarn and pull a loop thru on R H needle in same manner as Method #1. Using L H needle, * insert point from L to R into the side of next st on article or garment. With R H needle knit this st onto R H needle. Repeat from * for as many sts as specified.

Note: Always pick up each st in *same manner*.

Instructions specify the number of sts to be picked up; sometimes you will have to pick up on every row; other times you will have to skip 1 st here and there in order to get the specified amount. When picking up an *irregular* edge made by increases or decreases, pick up a st *in every row*.

BUTTONHOLES

On a garment where buttonholes are needed, an opening is made to form a buttonhole.

Work to the st specified, bind off the number of sts specified for buttonhole in instructions (Illus. 32), continue working to the end of row. On the next row, work to the sts that were bound off; turn work to other side and cast on the specified amount of sts (see Casting On, Method #2); turn work back and continue working across row. On the next row, work the cast-on sts (Illus. 33).

Illus. 32   **Illus. 33**

KNITTING ON 4 NEEDLES

Round knitting is worked using 4 or 5 double-pointed needles. **Casting-on Method #1 (on 4 Needles):** Cast on ⅓ of the number of sts required on one needle, place a 2nd needle to the left and slightly forward of first needle, cast on the same amount of sts on this needle, place 3rd needle to the left and slightly forward of 2nd needle, cast on the same amount of sts on 3rd needle (Illus. 34). Arrange the needles to form a triangle, insert 4th needle into first st of first needle (Illus. 35). (The needle following end of yarn is first needle unless otherwise specified.)

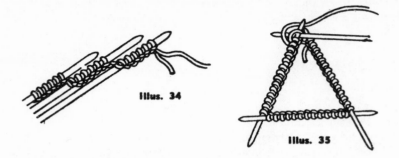

Illus. 34

Illus. 35

Method #2: Cast on the required amount of sts on one Dp needle, divide sts in thirds, slip ⅓ of the sts on one needle, slip the next ⅓ on 2nd needle, slip ⅓ on 3rd needle, insert 4th needle into first st of first needle (Illus. 35). Knit all the sts from the first needle onto spare needle (4th needle). Using the spare needle, knit all the sts from 2nd needle, then knit all the sts from 3rd needle. Continue in this manner in *rounds;* after all 3 needles have been knitted 1 round has been completed, unless otherwise specified.

The rounds are knitted continuously in one direction and automatically produce a Stockinette Stitch.

Illus. 36

KNITTED PATCHES

A patch can be easily knitted at a worn-out elbow or a tear on a knitted garment or article. Cut a neat square around the hole to be patched, slash the yarn by separating 3 sts (Illus. 36) at top and bottom of 3 side rows on each side. Next, carefully pick up *all* the free sts along top that belong on that row and place on holder; pick up all the free sts on bottom that belong on that row and place on another holder or needle. Then, turn the side edges of the 3 separated sts back to Wrong Side and slip st to article or garment on all 3 sides (Illus. 37). Put the bottom sts on a needle from L to R (Illus. 38). Attach matching yarn and knit in Stockinette Stitch (or Pattern Stitch) until the new strip is long enough to be woven to top free sts. Now weave these sts together, then weave the rows together along sides.

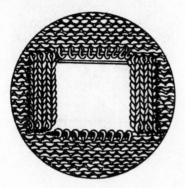

Illus. 37

Illus. 38

POPULAR PATTERN STITCHES

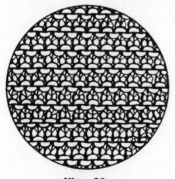

Illus. 39
Garter st

GARTER STITCH

(Illus. 39) On any number of sts. Work has same appearance on both sides (there is no Right or Wrong Side).

Row 1: K each st across row. Repeat this row throughout.

STOCKINETTE STITCH

(Illus. 40) On any number of sts.

Row 1: K each st across.
Row 2: P each st across.
Repeat Rows 1 and 2 alternately for Pattern.

Illus. 40
Stockinette st

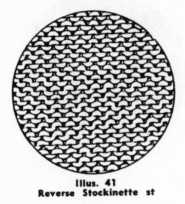

Illus. 41
Reverse Stockinette st

REVERSE STOCKINETTE STITCH

(Illus. 41) On any number of sts.

Row 1 (Right Side of work): P each st across.
Row 2: K each st across.
Repeat Rows 1 and 2 alternately for Pattern.

MOSS, RICE, OR SEED STITCH

(Illus. 42) On an *uneven* number of sts. Work has same appearance on both sides.

Row 1: * K 1, p 1, repeat from * across, end with k 1.
Repeat this row for Pattern.

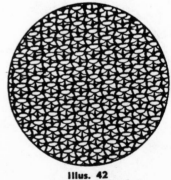

Illus. 42
Moss, Rice, or Seed st

DOUBLE MOSS STITCH

(Illus. 43) On a multiple of 4 plus 2.

Ex: 16 (which is divisible by 4) plus 2 = 18 sts.

Row 1: * K 2, p 2, repeat from * across, end with k 2.
Row 2: * P 2, k 2, repeat from * across, end with p 2.
Row 3: * P 2, k 2, repeat from * across, end with p 2.
Row 4: * K 2, p 2, repeat from * across, end with k 2.
Repeat Row 1 thru Row 4 for Pattern.

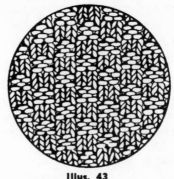

Illus. 43
Double Moss st

OPENWORK STITCH

(Illus. 44) On an *even* number of sts.

Row 1: K 1, * yo, k 2 tog, repeat from * across, end with k 1.
Row 2: P each st across.
Repeat Rows 1 and 2 alternately for Pattern.

Illus. 44
Openwork st

FAGGOTING STITCH

(Illus. 45) On an *even* number of sts.

Row 1: K 1, * yo, slip 1 st (as if to purl), k 1, psso, repeat from * across, end with k 1.
Repeat this row for Pattern.

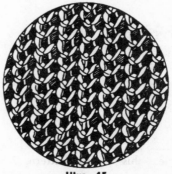

Illus. 45
Faggoting st

[25]

HONEYCOMB STITCH

(Illus. 46) On an *uneven* number of sts.

Row 1 (Wrong Side): K each st across.
Row 2: * K 1, insert needle from R to L under R H loop of next st on row below and knit this st, then slip corresponding st off L H needle. Repeat from * across.
Row 3: K each st across.

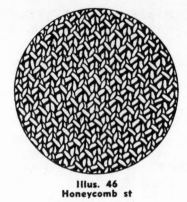

Illus. 46
Honeycomb st

Row 4: K 2, * insert needle in next st on row below and knit this st, then slip corresponding st off L H needle, k 1. Repeat from * across row.
Repeat Row 1 thru Row 4 for Pattern.

RIBBING PATTERNS

RIBBING OF K 1, P 1

(Illus. 47) On an *even* number of sts.

Row 1: * K 1, p 1, repeat from * across, end with p 1.
Repeat this row throughout.

Illus. 47
K 1, P 1 Ribbing

CROSSED K RIBBING

(Illus. 48) On an *even* number of sts.

Row 1: * K 1 into back of st, p 1, repeat from * across, end with p 1.
Repeat this row throughout.

Illus. 48
Crossed K Ribbing

RIBBING OF K 2, P 2

(Illus. 49) On a multiple of 4.

Row 1: * K 2, p 2, repeat from * across, end with p 2.
Repeat this row throughout.
Either side can be shown as Right Side.

Illus. 49
K 2, P 2 Ribbing

RIBBING OF K 1, P 3

(Illus. 50) On a multiple of 4.

Row 1: * K 1, p 3, repeat from * across, end with p 3.
Row 2: * K 3, p 1, repeat from * across, end with p 1.
Repeat these 2 rows for Pattern. Either side can be shown as Right •
Side (Illus. 51 is other side).

Illus. 50
K 1, P 3 Ribbing

Illus. 51
Other side

Illus. 52

Note: When changing colors on a Ribbed Band, always *knit all* the sts of the first row of New Color with the new color, then change to Ribbing Pattern on next row; otherwise the purled sts of new color will show on Right Side of work (Illus. 52).

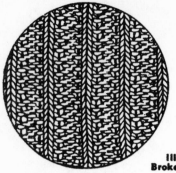

BROKEN RIB STITCH

(Illus. 53) On an *uneven* number of sts.

Row 1: * K 2, p 2, repeat from * across ending with k 1, or p 1.
Repeat Row 1 for Pattern.

Illus. 53
Broken Rib st

FANCY MOSS RIB STITCH
(Illus. 54) On a multiple of 4.

Row 1 (Right Side): * K 1, p 3, repeat from * across.
Row 2: K 2, * p 1, k 3, repeat from * across.
Repeat Rows 1 and 2 alternately for Pattern.

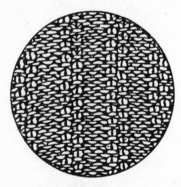

Illus. 54
Fancy Moss Rib st

Illus. 55
Pennant st

PENNANT STITCH
(Illus. 55) On a multiple of 10.

Row 1: * P 2, k 8, repeat from * across.
Row 2: * P 7, k 3, repeat from * across.
Row 3: * P 4, k 6, repeat from * across.
Row 4: * P 5, k 5, repeat from * across.
Row 5: * P 6, k 4, repeat from * across.

Row 6: * P 3, k 7, repeat from * across.
Row 7: * P 8, k 2, repeat from * across.
Row 8: Repeat Row 6.
Row 9: Repeat Row 5.
Row 10: Repeat Row 4.
Row 11: Repeat Row 3.
Row 12: Repeat Row 2.
Repeat Row 1 thru Row 12 as many times as desired for Pattern.

FANCY PATTERN STITCHES

ZIG-ZAG OR LITTLE CHEVRON PATTERN STITCH
(Illus. 56) Multiple of 12 plus 1.

Row 1: * P 1, k 3, p 5, k 3, repeat from * across, end with p 1.
Row 2: K 1, * p 3, k 5, p 3, k 1, repeat from * across.
Row 3: P 2, * k 3, p 3, repeat from * across, end with k 3, p 2.
Row 4: K 2, * p 3, k 3, repeat from * across, end with p 3, k 2.
Row 5: P 3, * k 3, p 1, k 3, p 5, repeat from * across, end with k 3, p 1, k 3, p 3.
Row 6: K 3, * p 3, k 1, p 3; k 5, repeat from * across, end with p 3, k 1, p 3, k 3.

Illus. 56
Ziz-Zag or
Little Chevron st

Row 7: * K 1, p 3, k 5, p 3, repeat from * across, end with k 1.
Row 8: P 1, * k 3, p 5, k 3, p 1, repeat from * across.
Row 9: K 2, * p 3, k 3, repeat from * across, end with p 3, k 2.
Row 10: P 2, * k 3, p 3, repeat from * across, end with k 3, p 2.
Row 11: K 3, * p 3, k 1, p 3, k 5, repeat from * across, end with p 3, k 1, p 3, k 3.
Row 12: P 3, * k 3, p 1, k 3, p 5, repeat from * across, end with p 1, k 3, p 3.
Repeat Row 1 thru Row 12 for Pattern.

BUTTERFLY STITCH
(Illus. 57) Multiple of 10 plus 9.

Row 1: K 2, * yarn in front, sl the next 5 sts, yarn in back, k 5, repeat from * across row, end with sl 5, k 2.
Row 2: Purl.
Row 3: Repeat Row 1.
Row 4: Purl.
Row 5: Repeat Row 1.
Row 6: Purl.
Row 7: Repeat Row 1.
Row 8: Purl.
Row 9: Repeat Row 1.
Row 10 (Wrong Side): P 4, * on the next st (which is the center st of the 5 slipped-st group) insert the R H needle down thru the 5 loose strands, bring needle up and transfer the 5 strands to L H needle, purl these 5 strands and the next st tog as 1 st, p 9, repeat from * across, end with p 4.
Row 11: K 7, * yarn in front, sl the next 5 sts, yarn in back, k 5, repeat from * across row, end with sl 5, k 7.

Illus. 57
Butterfly st

Row 12: Purl
Row 13: Repeat Row 11.
Row 14: Purl.
Row 15: Repeat Row 11.
Row 16: Purl.
Row 17: Repeat Row 11.
Row 18: Purl.
Row 19: Repeat Row 11.
Row 20: P 9, * on the next st (which is the center st of the 5 slipped-st group), insert the R H needle down thru the 5 loose strands, bring needle up and transfer the 5 strands to L H needle, purl these 5 strands and the next st tog as 1 st, p 9, repeat from * across, end with p 9.
Repeat these 20 rows for Pattern.

BOWKNOT STITCH

(Illus. 58) Multiple of 18 plus 9.

Row 1: * K 9, p 9, repeat from * across, end with k 9.
Row 2: * P 9, k 9, repeat from * across, end with p 9.
Row 3: Knit.
Row 4: Purl.
Row 5: Knit.
Row 6: Purl.
Row 7: Repeat Row 1.
Row 8: Repeat Row 2.
Row 9: K 13, * insert needle thru next st 9 rows below and draw loop thru as if to knit, hold yarn tightly and sl this loop onto L H needle, knit this loop and the next st tog as 1 st, k 17, repeat from * across, end with k 13.
Row 10: Purl.
Row 11: Repeat Row 2.
Row 12: Repeat Row 1.
Row 13: Knit.
Row 14: Purl.
Row 15: Knit.
Row 16: Purl.
Row 17: Repeat Row 2.
Row 18: Repeat Row 1.

Illus. 58
Bowknot st

Row 19: K 4, * insert needle thru next st 9 rows below and draw loop thru as if to knit, hold yarn tightly and sl this loop on L H needle, knit this loop and the next st tog as 1 st, k 17, repeat from * across, end with k 4.
Row 20: Purl.
Repeat these 20 rows for Pattern.

SMOCKING STITCH

(Illus. 59) Multiple of 8 plus 2.

Row 1: * P 2, k 2, repeat from * across, end with p 2.
Row 2: * K 2, p 2, repeat from * across, end with k 2.
Row 3: * P 2, insert the R H needle between the 7th and 8th

sts on L H needle and pull thru a loop; sl the loop on the R H needle, k 2 tog, k 1, p 2, k 2, repeat from * across, end with p 2.

Row 4: Repeat Row 2.
Row 5: Repeat Row 1.
Row 6: Repeat Row 2.
Row 7: P 2, k 2, repeat from * of Row 3, end with p 2, k 2, p 2.
Row 8: Repeat Row 2.
Repeat these 8 rows for Pattern.

Illus. 59
Smocking st

WOVEN STITCH

(Illus. 60) On an *uneven* number of sts.

Row 1: * K 1, yarn in front, sl 1 st as if to purl, yarn in back, repeat from * across, end with yarn in front, sl 1.
Row 2: Purl.
Row 3: * Yarn in front, sl 1 as if to purl, yarn in back, k 1, repeat from * across, end with k 1.
Row 4: Purl.
Repeat these 4 rows for Pattern.

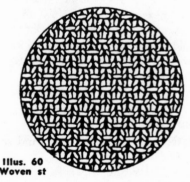

Illus. 60
Woven st

FABRIC STITCH

(Illus. 61) On an *uneven* number of sts.

Note: This stitch gives a close woven appearance with little stretch and must be worked with large needles.

Row 1: * K 1, yarn in front, sl 1 st as if to purl, yarn in back, repeat from * across, end with yarn in front, sl 1.
Row 2: * P 1, yarn in back, sl 1 st as if to purl, yarn in front, repeat from * across, end with p 2.
Repeat these 2 rows for Pattern.

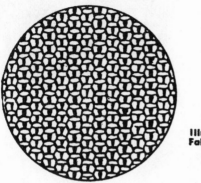

Illus. 61
Fabric st

WOVEN RIB STITCH
(Illus. 62) Multiple of 6 plus 3.

Row 1: * P 3, yarn in back, sl 1 st as if to purl, k 1, yarn in back, sl 1 st as if to purl, repeat from * across, end with p 3.
Row 2: Knit.
Repeat these 2 rows for Pattern.

BRAMBLE STITCH
(Illus. 63) Multiple of 4 sts plus 4 edge sts.

Note: For dresses, blouses, and scarves.

Row 1 (Wrong Side): K 2, * (k 1, p 1, k 1) into the next st (making 3 sts from 1), yarn to front, p 3 tog, yarn to back, repeat from * across, end with k 2.
Row 2: Purl.
Row 3: K 2, * p 3 tog (k 1, p 1, k 1) into the next st, yarn to front, repeat from * across, end with k 2.
Row 4: Purl.
Repeat these 4 rows for Pattern.

[33]

Illus. 62
Woven Rib st

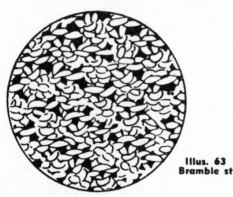

Illus. 63
Bramble st

REPEAT BELL MOTIF

(Illus. 64) Multiple of 4 sts plus 4 edge sts.

Row 1: P 4, * cast on 8 sts, p 4, repeat from * across.

Row 2: * K 4, p 8, repeat from * across, end with k 4.

Row 3: P 4, * k 8, p 4, repeat from * across.

Row 4: * K 4, p 8, repeat from * across, end with k 4.

Row 5: P 4, sl 1 (as if to knit), k 1, psso, k 4, k 2 tog, p 4, repeat from * across.

Row 6: * K 4, p 6, repeat from * across, end with k 4.

Row 7: P 4, * sl 1, (as if to knit), k 1, psso, k 2, k 2 tog, p 4, repeat from * across.

Row 8: *K 4, p 4, repeat from * across, end with k 4.

Row 9: P 4, * sl 1 (as if to knit), k 1, psso, k 2 tog, p 4, repeat from * across.

Row 10: * K 4, p 2, repeat from * across, end with k 4.

Row 11: P 4, * k 2 tog, p 4, repeat from * across.
Row 12: * K 4, p 1, repeat from * across, end with k 4.
Row 13: P 4, * k 2 tog, p 3, repeat from * across, end with p 3.
Row 14: Knit.
Work 2 rows of Garter or Stockinette Stitch, then repeat from Row 1.
To alternate Pattern, start with p 6 and end with p 6.

Illus. 64
Repeat Bell Motif

FEATHER & FAN STITCH
(Illus. 65) Multiple of 18 sts.

Row 1: K each st across row.
Row 2: P each st across row.
Row 3: (K 2 tog) 3 times, * (yo, k 1) 6 times, (k 2 tog) 6 times, repeat from * across row, end with (k 2 tog) 3 times.
Row 4: K each st across row.
Repeat row 1 thru row 4 for Pattern.

Illus. 65
Feather & Fan st

HERRINGBONE LACE STITCH
(Illus. 66) Multiple of 6 sts.

Row 1: * K 2 tog, k 2, yo, k 2, repeat from * across, end with yo, k 2.
Row 2: P each st across.
Row 3: Repeat Row 1.

Row 4: P each st across.
Row 5: Repeat Row 1.
Row 6: P each st across.
Row 7: K 1, * k 2, yo, k 2, k 2 tog, repeat from * across, end with yo, k 2 tog, k 1.
Row 8: P each st across.
Row 9: Repeat Row 7.
Row 10: P each st across.
Row 11: Repeat Row 7.
Row 12: P each st across.
Repeat Row 1 thru Row 12 for Pattern.

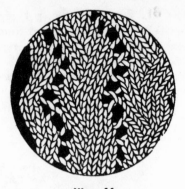

Illus. 66
Herringbone Lace st

EDGINGS & BORDERS

GARTER STITCH
(Illus. 67)

Work the required depth in Garter St, then change to Stockinette St, keeping the required number of sts at beg (or end) of row in Garter St.

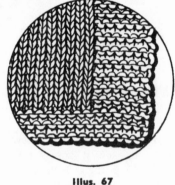

Illus. 67
Garter st

SEED STITCH
(Illus. 68)

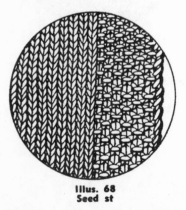

Illus. 68
Seed st

Work the required depth in Seed St, then change to Stockinette St, keeping the required number of sts at beg (or end) of row in Seed St.

RIBBING OF P 1, K 1
(Illus. 69)

Any desired ribbing may be used. By using a novelty edging, the edges of the fabric do not "curl" as in plain Stockinette St.

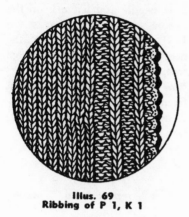

Illus. 69
Ribbing of P 1, K 1

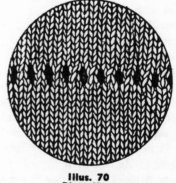

Illus. 70
Picot Hem

PICOT HEM
(Illus. 70)

Work in Stockinette St for desired depth, ending with a purl row.
Next Row: K 1, * yo, k 2 tog. Repeat from * across row, end with k 1. Continue in Stockinette or Pattern St. Hem turnback is on openwork row.

CABLE STITCHES

Illus. 71
Mock Cable

MOCK CABLE
(Illus. 71) Multiple of 5 plus 3.

Row 1: * P 3, k the 2nd st on L H needle and leave it on the needle, then k the first st on L H needle, sl both sts off the needle, repeat from * across row, end with p 3.
Row 2: K 3, * p 2, k 3, repeat from * across.
Repeat these 2 rows for Pattern.

MOCK CABLE & RIB
(Illus. 72) Multiple of 10 plus 5.

Row 1: K 2, * p 1, k 2, p 2, k 1, p 2, k 2, repeat from * across, end with p 1, k 2.
Row 2: P 2, k 1, * p 2, k 2, p 1, k 2, p 2, k 1, repeat from * across, end with k 1, p 2.
Row 3: Repeat Row 1.
Row 4: Repeat Row 2.
Row 5: K 2, * p 1, k the 2nd st on L H needle and leave this st on L H needle, k the first st on L H needle, sl both sts off L H needle, p 2, k 1, p 2, k the 2nd st on L H needle and leave this st on L H needle, k the first st on L H needle, sl both sts off L H needle, repeat from * across, end with p 1, k 2.
Row 6: Repeat Row 2.
Repeat these 6 rows for Pattern.

Illus. 72
Mock Cable & Rib

SIMPLE CABLE
(Illus. 73) Multiple of 10 plus 4.

Row 1: * P 4, k 6, repeat from * across, end with p 4.
Row 2: * K 4, p 6, repeat from * across, end with k 4.
Row 3: Repeat Row 1.
Row 4: Repeat Row 2.
Row 5: Repeat Row 1.
Row 6: Repeat Row 2.
Row 7: * P 4, sl next 3 sts off L H needle onto a Dp needle and drop to *back* of work, k the next 3 sts on L H needle, then k the 3 sts from Dp needle, repeat from * across, end with p 4.
Row 8: Repeat Row 2.
Repeat these 8 rows for Pattern.

Illus. 73
Simple Cable

CABLE & RIB
(Illus. 74) Multiple of 11 plus 1.

Row 1: * K 1, p 2, k 6, p 2, repeat from * across, end with k 1.
Row 2: * P 1, k 2, p 6, k 2, repeat from * across, end with p 1.
Row 3: Repeat Row 1.
Row 4: Repeat Row 2.
Row 5: Repeat Row 1.
Row 6: Repeat Row 2.
Row 7: * K 1, p 2, sl the next 3 sts to a Dp needle and drop to *front* of work, k to the next 3 sts, then k the 3 sts from Dp needle, p 2, repeat from * across, end with k 1.

[39]

Row 8: Repeat Row 2.

Repeat these 8 rows for Pattern.

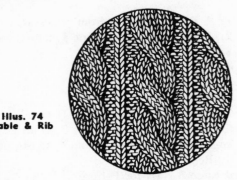

**Illus. 74
Cable & Rib**

HORSESHOE CABLE & MOSS STITCH
(Illus. 75) Multiple of 13 plus 1.

Row 1: K 1, p 1, * k 10, p 1, k 1, p 1, repeat from * across, end with k 10, p 1, k 1.

Row 2: K 1, p 1, k 1, * p 8, k 1, p 1, k 1, p 1, k 1, repeat from * across, end with p 8, k 1, p 1, k 1.

Row 3: Repeat Row 1.

Row 4: Repeat Row 2.

Row 5: Repeat Row 1.

Row 6: Repeat Row 2.

Row 7: K 1, p 1, k 1, * sl the next 2 sts to a Dp needle and drop to *back* of work, k 2, then k the 2 sts from Dp needle, sl the next 2 sts to Dp needle and drop to *front* of work, k 2, then k the 2 sts from Dp needle, k 1, p 1, k 1, p 1, k 1, repeat from * across, end with cable, k 1, p 1, k 1.

Row 8: Repeat Row 2.

Repeat Rows 2 thru 8 for Pattern.

PLAITED RIB CABLE
(Illus. 76) Multiple of 10 plus 4.

Row 1: * P 4, k 6, repeat from * across, end with p 4.

Row 2: K 4, * p 6, k 4, repeat from * across, end with k 4.

Row 3: * P 4, k 6, repeat from * across, end with p 4.

Row 4: K 4, * p 6, k 4, repeat from * across, end with k 4.

Row 5: * P 4, sl next 2 sts on a Dp needle and drop to *back* of work, k 2, then k the 2 sts from Dp needle, k 2, repeat from * across, end with p 4.

Row 6: Repeat Row 2.
Row 7: Repeat Row 1.
Row 8: Repeat Row 2.
Row 9: * P 4, k 2, sl 2 sts on a Dp needle and drop to *front* of work, k 2, then k the 2 sts from Dp needle, repeat from * across, end with p 4.
Row 10: Repeat Row 2.
Repeat Row 3 thru Row 10 for Pattern.

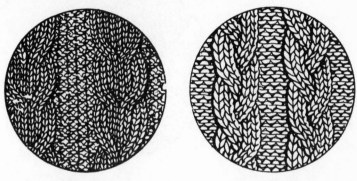

Illus. 75
Horseshoe Cable & Moss st

Illus. 76
Plaited Rib Cable

LATTICE CABLE
(Illus. 77) Multiple of 4 plus 2.

Row 1: * K 2, p 2, repeat from * across, end with k 2.
Row 2: * P 2, k 2, repeat from * across, end with p 2.
Row 3: * K 2, p 2, repeat from * across, end with k 2.
Row 4: * P 2, k 2, repeat from * across, end with p 2.
Row 5: * K 2, p 2, repeat from * across, end with k 2.
Row 6: * P 2, k 2, repeat from * across, end with p 2.
Row 7: * K 2, p 2, repeat from * across, end with k 2.
Row 8: * P 2, sl next 4 sts to a Dp needle and drop to *back* of work, k 2 sts from L H needle, sl the 2 p sts from Dp needle back to L H needle and p these 2 sts, k 2 from Dp needle, repeat from * across, end with p 2.
Row 9: Repeat Row 1.
Row 10: Repeat Row 2.
Row 11: Repeat Row 1.
Row 12: Repeat Row 2.
Row 13: Repeat Row 1.
Row 14: Repeat Row 2.
Row 15: Repeat Row 1.

Row 16: P 2, k 2, * p 2, sl the next 4 sts to a Dp needle and drop to *front* of work, k 2 sts from L H needle, sl the 2 p sts from Dp needle back to L H needle and p these 2 sts, k 2 from Dp needle, repeat from * across, end with p 2.
Repeat these 16 rows for Pattern.

Illus. 77
Lattice Cable

CORN ON THE COB STITCH

(No Illus.) On an *even* number of sts. Worked with 1 Light (L) and 1 Dark (D) Color.

Row 1 (L): Knit. This is the Wrong Side.
Row 2 (D): * K 1, sl 1 as if to purl, repeat from * across, end with k 2.
Row 3 (D): * Yarn in front, sl 1, yarn in back, k 1, repeat from * across. The dark sts of previous row are all knitted, the light sts are all slipped.
Row 4 (L): * Sl 1, k 1, repeat from * across. All light sts are knitted, all dark sts are slipped, and yarn is kept in back throughout.
Row 5 (L): * K 1, yarn in front, sl 1, yarn in back, repeat from * across row. Light sts are knitted, dark sts are slipped. Repeat from Row 2 for Pattern.

HEXAGON PATTERN STITCH

(No Illus.) Multiple of 8 sts plus 6. Worked with 1 L and 1 D Color.

Row 1 (D): Knit. This is the Right Side.
Row 2 (D): Knit.

Row 3 (L): K 2, * sl 2 (dark sts of last row) as if to purl, k 6, repeat from * across, end with sl 2, k 2.
Row 4 (L): P 2, * sl 2 (same sts as last row), p 6, repeat from * across, end sl 2, p 2.
Row 5 (L): Repeat Row 3.
Row 6 (L): Repeat Row 4.
Row 7 (L): Repeat Row 3.
Row 8 (L): Repeat Row 4.
Row 9 (D): Knit all sts, including the slipped sts.
Row 10 (D): Knit.
Row 11 (D): Knit.
Row 12 (D): Knit.
Row 13 (L): K 6, * sl 2, k 6, repeat from * across.
Row 14 (L): P 6, * sl 2, p 6, repeat from * across.
Row 15 (L): Repeat Row 13.
Row 16 (L): Repeat Row 14.
Row 17 (L): Repeat Row 13.
Row 18 (L): Repeat Row 14.
Row 19 (D): Repeat Row 9.
Row 20 (D): Knit.
Row 21 (D): Knit.
Row 22 (D): Knit.
Repeat from Row 3 to Row 22 for Pattern.

HOUNDS TOOTH CHECK STITCH

(No Illus.) Multiple of 4 sts. Worked with 1 L and 1 D Color.

Row 1: K 1 D, * k 1 L, k 3 D, repeat from * to last 3 sts, end with k 1 L, k 2 D.
Row 2: * P 3 L, p 1 D, repeat from * across.
Row 3: * K 3 L, k 1 D, repeat from * across.
Row 4: P 1 D, * p 1 L, p 3 D, repeat from * to last 3 sts, end with p 1 L, p 2 D.
Repeat these 4 rows for Pattern.

ZIG-ZAG BANDS

(No Illus.) Multiple of 10 sts plus 1. Worked with Red (R) and White (W).

Row 1: * K 1 R, k 3 W, k 3 R, k 3 W, repeat from * across, end with k 1 R.
Row 2: P 1 R, * p 1 R, p 3 W, p 1 R, p 3 W, p 2 R, repeat from * across.

Row 3: * K 3 R, k 5 W, k 2 R, repeat from * across, end with k 3 R.

Row 4: P 1 W, * p 3 R, p 3, W, p 3 R, p 1 W, repeat from * across.

Row 5: * K 2 W, k 3 R, k 1 W, k 3 R, k 1 W, repeat from * across, end with k 2 W.

Row 6: P 1 W, * p 2 W, p 5 R, p 3 W, repeat from * across. Repeat these 6 rows for Pattern.

DUPLICATE STITCH

The Duplicate Stitch is an embroidery stitch devised especially for knitting. The Knit Stitch is duplicated, using yarn or 6-strand embroidery cotton and an embroidery needle.

On a **Charted Motif** (see pp. 46 and 47) each square equals 1 stitch; follow **Chart,** using colors as specified or as desired.

DUPLICATE STITCH: Working from bottom to top, bring needle thru center of st from Wrong Side of work to Right Side. Insert needle from right to left under the 2 strands of next st (Diag 1), draw yarn thru. Insert needle back into same st where needle was brought out at beg (Diag 2), * bring needle up thru center of st just completed. Insert needle from right to left under the 2 strands of next st (Diag 3), draw yarn thru, insert needle back into same st where needle was brought out, repeat from * for specified amount of sts. At top of row, weave yarn back down on Wrong Side under sts just made, and bring needle out in position to work first st of next row.

#1 Motif: Goose—White and Orange with Black eye.

#2 Motif: Lamb—White or Gray with a Pink nose, or Black with a Pink nose.

#3 Motif: Flower Border—Yellow center, White around center, Pink around outside edges, Green stem and leaves.

#4 Motif: Flower (Use alone or repeat for border)—Colors same as #3 Motif or as desired.

#5 Motif: Masks—Black masks with a White ribbon (or any Colors desired).

#6 Motif: Figure—Blue dress, Pink arms, legs, and face, Black or Brown hair and shoes.

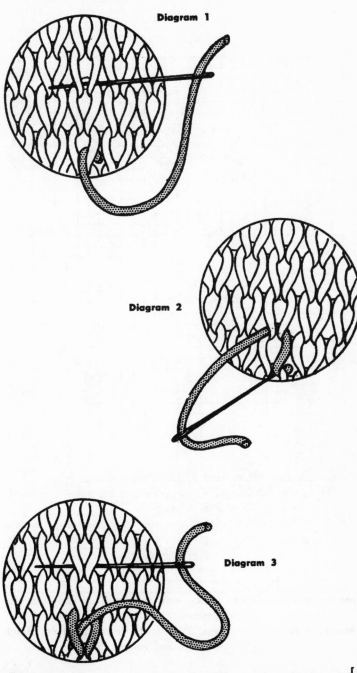

Diagram 1

Diagram 2

Diagram 3

NOTE: Designs are elongated because they have been adapted to knitting which is not square.

GOOSE -- GIRL --

-- MOTIFS
for
Duplicate St

LAMB --

FLOWER --

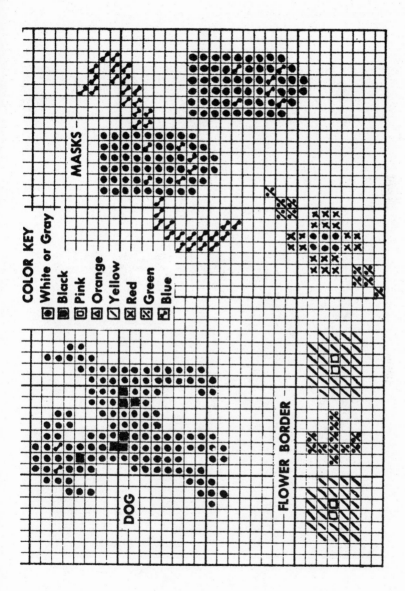

COLOR KEY
◉ White or Gray
▣ Black
▢ Pink
◭ Orange
▨ Yellow
⊠ Red
⊠ Green
⬒ Blue

MASKS --

DOG

FLOWER BORDER

PONCHOS PLUS
(Knitted Style at Left, Crochet Style at Right)

DESIGNS FOR KNITTING

PONCHOS PLUS (One Knitted, One Crocheted)
One size fits all

MATERIALS REQUIRED:
Columbia-Minerva Nantuk Sweater & Afghan Yarn (2 oz. pull skein)
- 3 skeins of Color A
- 2 skeins each of Colors B & C for each style
- #J crochet hook for crochet style
- #10 knitting needles
- Size J hook for knitted style

CROCHET STYLE (Shown at Right)

STITCH GAUGE: 5 sts = 2"

CROCHETING INSTRUCTIONS: With Color A ch 93.

Row 1: 1 sc in 2nd ch from hook, 1 dc in next ch, * 1 sc in next ch, 1 dc in next ch, repeat from * across, ch 1, turn.

Row 2: * 1 sc in next dc, 1 dc in next sc, repeat from * across, ch 1, turn.

Repeat Row 2 for pattern working 2 more rows to complete first Color A stripe, working off last 2 loops of last dc on last row with Color B, ch 1, turn. Continue in pattern working 4 rows each of Colors B, C and A until 3rd stripe of Color C has been completed. Fasten off.

Make other half the same.

Sew last row of first half to side edge of other half, starting at first row. Sew last row of other half to side of first half.

EDGING: Join Color A at seam at neck edge. * Ch 1, 1 sc in st, repeat from * around, holding in to fit. Join with sl st.

Row 2: * Ch 1, 1 sc in ch-1 space, repeat from * around, skipping st at corners. Join with sl st and fasten off. Join yarn at lower edge, * ch 2, skip ½", 1 sc in st, repeat from * around. Join and fasten off.

FRINGE: Cut three 14" strands of Color A. Fold in half and draw through space at lower edge then draw ends through loop and tighten. Repeat in every loop, rotating Colors B, C & A.

KNITTED STYLE (Shown at Left)

STITCH GAUGE: 7 sts = 2"   6 rows = 1"

KNITTING INSTRUCTIONS: With Color A, cast on 133 sts. P 1 row.
Row 2: K 1, * P 1, K 1, repeat from * across.
Row 3: P.
Row 4: P 1, * K 1, P 1, repeat from * across.

Repeat these 4 rows for pattern, working 10 more rows to complete first Color A stripe. Continue in pattern, working 14 rows each of Colors B, C and A until 3rd A stripe has been completed. Bind off.

Make other half the same.

Sew bound-off edge of first half to side edge of other half, starting at first row. Sew bound-off edge of other half to side edge of first half.

EDGING AND FRINGE: Same as for crocheted poncho.

FOR THE MAN IN YOUR LIFE
(Cardigan and Pullover Knits)

Directions are for Size 38. Changes for Sizes 40, 42 and 44 are in parentheses.

MATERIALS REQUIRED:
Columbia-Minerva Yarn for Fisherman's Knit or Knitting Worsted (4 oz. skein)
5 (5-6-6) skeins for each
#6 and #9 Knitting Needles for Sizes 38 and 40
#7 and #10 Knitting Needles for Sizes 42 and 44
Cable Needle

STITCH GAUGE: Pattern Stitch on #9 needles based on overall measurement—5 sts = 1"   13 rows = 2"

Pattern Stitch on #10 needles based on overall measurement—9 sts = 2"   6 rows = 1"

PATTERN STITCH FOR SIZES 38 AND 42:

Row 1 (Right Side): [P 2, k 2] twice, p 1, k 2, p 3, k 2, p 1, * k 2, p 2, k 2, p 1, k 2, p 1, k 6, p 1, k 2, p 1, k 2, p 2, k 2, p 1, k 2, p 3, k 2, p 1 *, repeat from * to * once, end [k 2 and p 2] twice.

Row 2 and All Even Rows: K the k sts and p the p sts as they face you.

Row 3: [K 2 and p 2] twice for double moss stitch; p 1, k 2nd st through back but do not drop from needle then k the first st in front and drop both sts from left-hand needle to twist 2 sts, p 1, work popcorn in next st as follows: [K in front and back of st] 3 times, skipping first st from point of right-hand needle, pass 2nd, 3rd, 4th, 5th and 6th st over first st one at a time, p 1, twist 2, p 1; * p 2, k 2, p 2; p 1, twist 2, p 1, k 6, p 1, twist 2, p 1; p 2, k 2, p 2; p 1, twist 2, p 1, popcorn, p 1, twist 2, p 1 *, repeat from * to * once, end [p 2 and k 2] twice.

Row 5: [P 2 and k 2] twice, p 1, twist 2, p 3, twist 2, p 1, * k 2, p 2, k 2, p 1, twist 2, p 1, sl next 2 sts to cable needle and hold in front, k 2 then k the 2 sts from cable needle for *front twist*, k 2, p 1, twist 2, p 1, k 2, p 2, k 2, p 1, twist 2, p 3, twist 2, p 1 *, repeat from * to * once, end [k 2 and p 2] twice.

Row 7: Repeat Row 3.

Row 9: [P 2 and k 2] twice, p 1, twist 2, p 3, twist 2, p 1, * k 2, p 2, k 2, p 1, twist 2, p 1, k 2, sl next 2 sts to cable needle and hold in back, k 2 then k the 2 sts from needle for *back twist*, p 1, twist 2, p 1, k 2, p 2, k 2, p 1, twist 2, p 3, twist 2, p 1 *, repeat from * to * once, end [k 2 and p 2] twice.

Row 10: K the k sts and p the p sts as they face you.

Repeat Rows 3 through 10 for pattern.

PATTERN STITCH FOR SIZES 40 AND 44:

Row 1 (Right Side): [P 2 and k 2] twice, p 1, k 2, p 3, k 2, p 1, * k 2, p 2, k 2, p 1, k 2, p 1, k 9, p 1, k 2, p 1, k 2, p 2, k 2, p 1, k 2, p 3, k 2, p 1 *, repeat from * to * once, end [k 2 and p 2] twice.

Row 2 and All Even Rows: K the k sts and p the p sts as they face you.

Row 3: [K 2 and p 2] twice for double Moss Stitch: p 1, k 2nd st through back but do not drop from needle, k the first st in front then drop both sts from left-hand needle to twist 2 sts, p 1, work

FOR THE MAN IN YOUR LIFE (Cardigan and Pullover Knits)

popcorn in next st as follows: [K in front and back of st] 3 times, skipping first st from point of right-hand needle, pass 2nd, 3rd, 4th, 5th and 6th st over first st one at a time, p 1, twist 2, p 1, * p 2, k 2, p 2; p 1, twist 2, p 1, k 9, p 1, twist 2, p 1; p 2, k 2, p 2; p 1, twist 2, p 1, popcorn, p 1, twist 2, p 1 *, repeat from * to * once, end [p 2 and k 2] twice.

Row 5: [P 2 and k 2] twice, p 1, twist 2, p 3, twist 2, p 1, * k 2, p 2, k 2, p 1, twist 2, p 1, sl next 3 sts to cable needle and hold in front, k 3 then k the 3 sts from cable needle for *front twist,* k 3, p 1, twist 2, p 1, k 2, p 2, k 2, p 1, twist 2, p 3, twist 2, p 1 *, repeat from * to * once, end [k 2 and p 2] twice.

Row 7: Repeat Row 3.

Row 9: [P 2 and k 2] twice, p 1, twist 2, p 3, twist 2, p 1, * k 2, p 2, k 2, p 1, twist 2, p 1, k 3, sl next 3 sts to cable needle and hold in back, k 3 then k the 3 sts from cable needle for *back twist,* p 1, twist 2, p 1, k 2, p 2, k 2, p 1, twist 2, p 3, twist 2, p 1 *, repeat from * to * once, end [k 2 and p 2] twice.

Row 10: K the k sts and p the p sts as they face you.

Repeat Rows 3 through 10 for pattern.

CARDIGAN (Shown at Left)

KNITTING INSTRUCTIONS:

BACK: With #6 (6-7-7) needles cast on 86 (92-86-92) sts. K 1 and p 1 in ribbing for 16 rows, inc'ing 9 sts evenly spaced across last row. Change to #9 (9-10-10) needles. Work in pattern on the 95 (101-95-101) sts to 16" from start. Width across back is 19 (20-21-22¼) inches.

ARMHOLES: Bind off 4 sts at beg of next 2 rows. Dec 1 st each side every other row 4 times. Work on the remaining 79 (85-79-85) sts to 9 (9½-10-10½) inches straight above underarm. Width across shoulders is 16¾ (17-17-19) inches.

SHOULDERS: Bind off 9 (10-9-10) sts at beg of next 4 rows then 7 (8-7-8) sts at beg of next 2 rows. Bind off the 29 sts for back of neck.

RIGHT FRONT: With #6 (6-7-7) needles cast on 49 (53-49-53) sts.

Row 1 (Right Side): K 1, * p 1, k 1, repeat from * across.

Row 2: P 1, * k 1, p 1, repeat from * across.

Repeat these 2 rows for 15 rows.

Next Row: Continue ribbing, inc'ing 1 st in every 7th (9th-7th-9th) st 5 (4-5-4) times, work to last 9 sts then sl the 9 sts to a holder for front band. Change to #9 (9-10-10) needles. Start pattern on the 45 (48-45-48) sts.

Row 1 (Right Side): [P 2 and k 2] twice, p 1, k 2, p 1, k 6 (9-6-9), p 1, k 2, p 1, k 2, p 2, k 2, p 1, k 2, p 3, k 2, p 1, [k 2 and p 2] twice.

Row 2 and All Even Rows: K the k sts and p the p sts as they face you.

Row 3: [K 2 and p 2] twice, p 1, twist 2, p 1, k 6 (9-6-9), p 1, twist 2, p 1; p 2, k 2, p 2; p 1, twist 2, p 1, popcorn, p 1, twist 2, p 1; [p 2 and k 2] twice.

Continue in pattern, twisting cables as on back to same length as back to underarm, end on Right Side.

Width across front, not including band, is 9 (9½-10-10½) inches.

ARMHOLE, NECK AND SHOULDER: Bind off 4 sts at side edge, work to end of row.

Dec Row: K 2 tog for neck dec, work last 2 sts, k 2 tog for armhole dec.

Dec 1 st at armhole every other row 3 times more and dec 1 st at neck every 6th row 6 times then every 4th row 5 times more *and at the same time* when armhole matches back armhole, bind off 9 (10-9-10) sts at armhole edge twice then 7 (8-7-8) sts at same edge once.

FRONT BAND: Sew shoulder seam. With #6 (6-7-7) needles work in ribbing on the 9 sts to fit to center back of neck when band is slightly stretched. Sl sts to a holder. Sew in place to shoulder seam. Place markers for 6 buttons evenly spaced on front edge with first marker on 6th row of ribbing and 6th marker at start of neck shaping.

LEFT FRONT: With #6 (6-7-7) needles cast on 49 (53-49-53) sts. Work ribbing same as on right front for 5 rows.

BUTTONHOLE: Starting at front edge, work 2 sts, bind off next 3 sts, work to end of row. Next row cast on 3 sts over buttonhole. Work 8 more rows, end at front edge. Next row work 9 sts and sl them to a holder for front band.

Continue in ribbing, inc'ing 1 st in every 7th (9th-7th-9th) st 5 (4-5-4) times, work to end.

Change to #9 (9-10-10) needles. Start pattern as follows:

Row 1 (Right Side): [P 2 and k 2] twice, p 1, k 2, p 3, k 2, p 1, k 2, p 2, k 2, p 1, k 2, p 1, k 6 (9-6-9), p 1, k 2, p 1, [k 2 and p 2] twice.

Row 2 and All Even Rows: K the k sts and p the p sts as they face you.

Finish to correspond to Right Front.

FRONT BAND: Sew shoulder seam. With #6 (6-7-7) needles work to correspond to right band, repeating buttonholes opposite markers.

SLEEVES: With #6 (6-7-7) needles cast on 44 (46-44-46) sts. K 1 and p 1 in ribbing for 3", inc'ing 8 (9-8-9) sts across last row. Change to #9 (9-10-10) needles. Start pattern on the 52 (55-52-55) sts as follows:

Row 1 (Right Side): P 2, k 2, p 1, k 2, p 3, k 2, p 1, k 2, p 2, k 2, p 1, k 2, p 1, k 6 (9-6-9), p 1, k 2, p 1, k 2, p 2, k 2, p 1, k 2, p 3, k 2, p 1, k 2, p 2.

Row 2 and All Even Rows: K the k sts and p the p sts as they face you.

Row 3: K 2, p 2; p 1, twist 2, p 1, work popcorn in next st, p 1, twist 2, p 1; p 2, k 2, p 2; p 1, twist 2, p 1, k 6 (9-6-9), p 1, twist 2, p 1; p 2, k 2, p 2; p 1, twist 2, p 1, popcorn in next st, p 1, twist 2, p 1; p 2, k 2. Work 1 more row. Working added sts in double Moss St, inc 1 st each side on next row then every 10th row 9 (9-8-6) times more, then on *Size 44 only* inc 1 st each side every 8th row 3 times. Work on the 72 (75-70-75) sts to 19" from start. Width across sleeve is 14½ (15-15½-16½) inches.

SLEEVE CAP: Bind off 4 sts at beg of next 2 rows. Dec 1 st each side every other row 2 (3-2-4) times. Bind off 2 sts at beg of next 20 rows. Bind off the 20 (21-18-19) sts.

Sew or weave neckband sts then sew band to neck. Sew sleeves in place then sew underarm and sleeve seams. If desired, face fronts with ribbon, working around buttonholes.

PULLOVER (Shown at Right)

KNITTING INSTRUCTIONS:

BACK: Work same as back of cardigan until armholes measure 9 (9½-10-10½) inches straight above underarm.

SHOULDERS: Bind off 8 sts at beg of next 2 (4-2-4) rows then 7 (9-7-9) sts at beg of next 4 (2-4-2) rows. Sl the 35 sts to a holder for back of neck.

FRONT: Work same as back until armholes measure 6½ (7-7½-8) inches straight above underarm, end on Right Side.

NECK AND SHOULDER: Work 31 (34-31-34) sts and sl them to a holder, work center 17 sts and sl them to 2nd holder for neck, work to end of row. Dec 1 st at neck every row 6 times, every other row 3 times, and when armhole measures same as on back, bind off 8 sts at armhole edge 1 (2-1-2) times then 7 (9-7-9) sts at same edge 2 (1-2-1) times. Starting at neck, work other side to correspond.

SLEEVES: Same as sleeves of cardigan.

NECKBAND: Sew left shoulder seam. Starting at open seam with #6 (6-7-7) needles, k across the 35 sts on back, pick up and k 16 sts along side, k the 17 center sts, pick up and k 16 sts on other side. K 1 and p 1 in ribbing on the 84 sts for 6 rows. Bind off in ribbing. Sew open shoulder seam, joining neckband.

Sew sleeves in place then sew underarm and sleeve seams.

KNITTED STOLE

KNITTED STOLE

(Approximately 20" x 64")

MATERIALS REQUIRED:

9 Balls of Bear Brand or Fleisher or Botany Supra Mohair

or

8 Balls of Bucilla Mist Air

(All these yarns are manufactured by Bernhard Ullman and Company, 230 Fifth Avenue, New York, N.Y. If not obtainable in your local shops, a postcard addressed to the manufacturer will obtain the name of the shop nearest you which stocks these yarns.)

Aluminum Crochet Hook

Plastic Knitting Needles—size 11 or the size which you require to obtain gauge.

STITCH GAUGE: 6 sts = 2"   9 rows = 2"

KNITTING INSTRUCTIONS:

Cast on 61 sts.

Row 1: K 1, * p 1, k 1; repeat from * to end.

Repeat this row for Seed St until 64" from beginning (about 288 rows). Bind off in Seed St.

FRINGE: Using #1 hook, from Right Side, join yarn at corner, insert hook in first st, * ch 20, sk 1 st, work 1 sl st in next st; repeat from * across end of stole. Fasten off.

Work same fringe on other end.

THE MODERN MISS

Directions are for Size 4. Changes for Sizes 6 and 8 are in parentheses.

MATERIALS REQUIRED:

Columbia-Minerva Nantuk 4-Ply Yarn (4 oz. skein)
2 (3-3) skeins in Color A for each dress
1 skein in Color B for each dress
#8 Knitting Needles
6 Buttons

STITCH GAUGE: Stockinette st on #8 needles
9 sts = 2"   6 rows = 1"

MODERN MISS WITH POCKETS (Shown at Left)

Suggested Colors: Hunter Green and Tangerine

Note: Directions are for a 19¾ (21-23¾) inches dress measured from lower edge to shoulder allowing ½" for blocking.

KNITTING INSTRUCTIONS:

BACK: With Color A cast on 70 (72-76) sts. Work in Stockinette St for 2½", end on Wrong Side.

Dec Row: K 7 (8-10), * k 2 tog, k 16, repeat from * twice more, k 2 tog, k to end. Work on the 66 (68-72) sts for 9 (11-13) rows.

Dec Row: K 6 (7-9), * k 2 tog, k 15, repeat from * twice, k 2 tog, k to end. Work on the 62 (64-68) sts for 9 (11-13) rows.

Dec Row: K 6 (7-9), * k 2 tog, k 14, repeat from * twice, k 2 tog k to end. Work on the 58 (60-64) sts to 13½ (15¼-17) inches or ½" less than desired length to underarm, end on Wrong Side.
Width across back is 12¾ (13¼-14¼) inches.

ARMHOLES: Bind off 3 sts at beg of next 2 rows. Dec 1 st each side every other row 3 (3-4) times. Work on the 46 (48-50) sts to 4½ (4¾-5) inches above underarm, end on Right Side.
Width across shoulder is 10¼ (10¾-11) inches.

NECK: Work across 15 (16-16) sts and sl them to a holder, bind off center 16 (16-18) sts, work to end. Dec 1 st at neck edge every other row 3 times, place a marker at each end of last row. Work on the 12 (13-13) sts to 6¼ (6½-6¾) inches above underarm, end on Wrong Side. Bind off for shoulder. Starting at neck, work other side to correspond.

FRONT: Work same as back.

SLEEVES: With Color A cast on 28 (30-32) sts. Work in Stockinette St for 1". Inc 1 st each side on next row, then every 6th (6th-8th) row 4 (4-5) times, then every 8th (8th-10th) row 3 (3-2) times more. Work on the 44 (46-48) sts to 11 (12-13) inches above start, end on Wrong Side.

Width across sleeve is 9¾ (10¼-10¾) inches.

SLEEVE CAP: Bind off 3 sts at beg of next 2 rows. Dec 1 st each side every other row until 24 sts remain. Bind off 3 sts at beg of next 4 rows. Bind off. Split yarn for sewing. Sew side seams.

POCKETS: (Make 2.) With Color A cast on 7 sts. P 1 row. Work in Stockinette St inc'ing 1 st each side *every* row 6 (7-7) times. Work on the 19 (21-21) sts to 2" from start, end with a k row. K 1 row and p 1 row for 2¾ (3-3) inches. Dec 1 st each side *every* row 6 (7-7) times. Bind off.

BIAS TRIM: (Make 10 pieces.) With Color B cast on 5 sts. P 1 row. Next row inc 1 in first st, k to last 2 sts, k 2 tog. Repeat last 2 rows. Bind off at end of each piece. Make pieces to fit around lower edge, around hipline 6 (7-8) inches above lower edge, around pockets, pocket flaps, sleeves, one piece for back of neck and another across front of neck and shoulders.

Placing bias trim on knitted fabric, sew to back of neck. Sew trim on front neck and across shoulders. Lap front shoulder over back shoulder matching markers, tack at armhole edge. Sew in sleeves. Sew sleeve seams. Sew bias on sleeve edges. Sew bias at hipline about 6 (7-8) inches above lower edge. Trim pockets with bias and sew to skirt as shown. Sew buttons to pocket flaps and front shoulders. Close with snaps.

MODERN MISS WITH BELT (Shown at Right)

Suggested Colors: Sapphire and Kelly Green

Directions are for a 19½ (21½-23½) inch dress measured from lower edge to back of neck allowing ½" for blocking.

KNITTING INSTRUCTIONS:

BACK: With Color A cast on 78 (80-84) sts. K 1 row, p 1 row and k 1 row. K next row for turn. K 1 row and p 1 row for 4 rows. Break off A and attach B. K 2 rows. P 1 row, k 1 row and p 1 row. * Break off B and attach A. P 1 row and k 1 row for 5 rows. Break off A and attach B. K 2 rows. P 1 row, k 1 row and p 1 row. Repeat from * once more. Break off B and continue with A only.

Starting with a p row work in Stockinette St. Dec 1 st each side on next k row then every 4th (6th-6th) row 3 times more. Work 2 (4-6) rows on the 70 (72-76) sts. Next row p 23 (23-25) sts, place a marker, p 24 (26-26) sts, place a marker, p to end. Sl markers every row.

DARTS: Next row k 2 tog, k to 2 sts before marker, k 2 tog, k to next marker, sl 1, k 1, psso, k to last 2 sts, k 2 tog. Work 3 (5-7) rows. Repeat last 4 (6-8) rows twice more—58 (60-64) sts remaining. Remove markers and continue in Stockinette St to 13 (14¾-16½) inches above turn or ½" less than desired length to underarm, end on Wrong Side. Width across back is 12¾ (13¼-14) inches.

ARMHOLES: Bind off 3 sts at beg of next 2 rows. Dec 1 st each side every other row 3 (3-4) times. Work on the 46 (48-50) sts to 5½ (5¾-6) inches above underarm, end on Wrong Side. Width across shoulders is 10¼ (10¾-11) inches.

NECK AND SHOULDERS: Bind off 5 (5-6) sts, work to end. Work 1 row. Bind off 6 sts at same edge, k 23 (25-25) sts more and sl the 24 (26-26) sts to a holder for neck, place a marker, work to end. Work 4 rows on the 11 (11-12) sts. Bind off.

FRONT: Work same as back until armholes measure 4 (4¼-4½) inches above underarm, end on Wrong Side.

THE MODERN MISS

NECK: Work across 15 (15-16) sts and sl them to a holder, work across center 16 (18-18) sts and sl them to 2nd holder, work to end. Dec 1 st at edge *every* row 4 times. Work on the 11 (11-12) sts until armhole matches back armhole, end at armhole edge.

SHOULDERS: Bind off 5 (5-6) sts at beg of next row. Work 1 row. Bind off 6 sts. Starting at neck edge, work other side as follows:
Dec 1 st at neck edge *every* row 4 times. Work on the 11 (11-12) sts to 5½ (5¾-6) inches above underarm, end at armhole edge. Next row, k 2 (2-3), k 2 tog, yo, k 3, k 2 tog, yo, k 2, place a marker at the end of row. Work 1 row on the 11 (11-12) sts. Bind off.

SLEEVES: With Color B cast on 32 (34-36) sts. K 1 row and p 1 row for 4 rows. P next row for turn, place a marker at each end. K 1 row and p 1 row for 4 rows. Break off B and continue with A. Starting with a p row work in Stockinette St, inc'ing 1 st each side on next row, then every 4th (4th-6th) row 4 (1-5) times, then every 6th (6th-8th) row 1 (4-1) times more. Work on the 44 (46-48) sts to 7 (8-9) inches above markers, end on Wrong Side. Width across sleeve is 9¾ (10¼-10¾) inches.

SLEEVE CAP: Bind off 3 sts at beg of next 2 rows. Dec 1 st each side every other row until 24 sts remain. Bind off 3 sts at beg of next 4 rows. Bind off 12 sts.

BELT: With Color A cast on 12 sts.
Row 1: P.
Row 2: K 1, sl 1, k 8, sl 1, k 1.
Repeat these 2 rows to 27½ (28½-29½) inches, end with Row 1.
Next Row: Work 5 sts, bind off next 2 for buttonhole, work to end.
Next Row: Cast on 2 sts over buttonhole. Work 3 more inches, end on Wrong Side. Work a buttonhole on next 2 rows.
Next Row: K 1, sl 1, k 2 tog, k to last 4 sts, sl 1, k 1, psso, sl 1, k 1. Work 1 row. Repeat last 2 rows until 6 sts remain, end with p row. K 1, k 2 tog, sl 1, k 1, psso, k 1.
Next Row: P 2 tog twice. K 2 tog and fasten off.

BELT LOOPS: (Make 4.) With Color B cast on 20 sts. Work 4 rows in Stockinette St. Bind off tightly.

Split yarn for sewing. Sew right shoulder seam.

NECKBAND: With Color B and Right Side facing, starting at marker pick up and k 9 sts, k across 16 (18-18) sts on front holder, pick up and k 9 sts on other side, k across 24 (26-26) sts. K 1 row and p 1 row for 4 rows on the 58 (62-62) sts. P 1 row and k 1 row. Bind off.

Lap left front shoulder over back about ½" and tack at armhole edge. Sew in sleeves. Sew sleeve and underarm seam. Turn up hems and sew in place.

Sew on belt loops as shown about 8 (10-11) inches from lower edge. Turn in neck facing and sew in place. Sew on buttons.

CLASSIC SWEATER SET FOR CHILDREN AND WOMEN

CLASSIC SWEATER SET

For Children and Women

MATERIALS REQUIRED:

Coats & Clark's "Red Heart" Super Fingering, 3 Ply, Art. E.239 (1 oz. "Tangle-Proof" Pull-Out Skeins)

	CHILDREN					WOMEN				
Sizes	4	6	8	10	11	12	14	16	18	20
Skeins										
Pullover with Long Sleeves	5	6	7	8	8	9	10	12	13	14
Pullover with Short Sleeves	4	5	6	6	7	8	9	10	11	12
Cardigan with Long Sleeves	6	7	8	8	9	10	11	13	14	15

#1 and #2 Knitting Needles
#1 Double-pointed Sock Needles
Buttons

STITCH GAUGE: 8 sts = 1"   11 rows = 1"

BLOCKING MEASUREMENTS:

Sizes	4	6	8	10	11	12	14	16	18	20
Body Chest Size (in Inches)	23	24	26	28	30	32	34	36	38	40

Pullover—Actual Knitting Measurements (Easy-Fit)

Chest (in inches)									
24	26	28	30	32	34	36	38	40	42

Width across back or front at underarm (in inches)

12	13	14	15	16	17	18	19	20	21

Width across back or front above armhole shaping (in inches)

10	10½	11½	12	12½	13	13½	14	14½	15

Length from shoulder seam to lower edge (in inches)

14	15	16½	18	19	20	21	22	22½	23

Length of side seam (in inches)

9¼	10	11	12	12½	13	13½	14	14	14

Length of sleeve seam
Long Sleeves (in inches)

11	12	13	14	15	17	17½	18	18	18½

Short Sleeves (in inches)

2	2½	3	3	3½	3½	4	4½	4½	5

Width across sleeve at upper arm (in inches)

9½	10½	11	12	12½	12½	13	13½	14	14½

Cardigan—Actual Knitting Measurements

Chest (Buttoned) (in inches)									
25	27	29	31	33	35	37	39	41	43

Width across back at underarm (in inches)

12	13	14	15	16	17	18	19	20	21

Width across back above armhole shaping (in inches)

10½ 11 12 12½ 13 13½ 14 14½ 15 15½

Width across each front at underarm—including folded band (in inches)

7 7½ 8 8½ 9 9½ 10 10½ 11 11½

Length from shoulder seam to lower edge (in inches)

15 16 17½ 19 20 21 22 23 23½ 24

Length of side seam (in inches)

10 10½ 11½ 12½ 13 13½ 14 14½ 14½ 14½

Length of sleeve seam (in inches)

11½ 12½ 13½ 14½ 15½ 17½ 18 18½ 18½ 19

Width across sleeve at upper arm (in inches)

10 11 11½ 12½ 13 13 13½ 14 14½ 15

PULLOVER

BACK: Starting at lower edge with #1 needles, cast on

96 104 112 120 128 136 144 152 160 168 sts

Work in desired ribbing of k 1, p 1, or k 2, p 2 for

2" 2" 2½" 2½" 2½" 3" 3" 3½" 3½" 3½"

Change to #2 needles and work in Stockinette St (knit 1 row, purl 1 row) ending with a p row, until total length is

9¼" 10" 11" 12" 12½" 13" 13½" 14" 14" 14"

ARMHOLE SHAPING: Bind off

| 4 | 5 | 5 | 6 | 7 | 8 | 9 | 10 | 11 | 11 sts |

at beginning of next 2 rows. Dec 1 st at both ends of every other row until there remain

| 80 | 84 | 92 | 96 | 100 | 104 | 108 | 112 | 116 | 120 sts |

Work even, ending with a p row, until length from first row of armhole shaping is

| 4¾" | 5" | 5½" | 6" | 6½" | 7" | 7½" | 8" | 8½" | 9" |

SHOULDER SHAPING: Bind off

| 6 | 7 | 7 | 6 | 6 | 7 | 7 | 7 | 6 | 6 sts |

at beginning of next

| 6 | 6 | 6 | 10 | 8 | 8 | 8 | 10 | 12 | 10 rows |

then at beginning of next 2 rows, bind off

| 7 | 8 | 5 | 8 | 8 | 8 | 5 | 6 | 0 | 8 sts |

Slip remaining

| 30 | 32 | 34 | 36 | 36 | 38 | 40 | 42 | 44 | 44 sts |

on a stitch holder to be worked later for back of neck.

FRONT: Work exactly as for back until piece measures from first row of armhole shaping, ending with a p row

| 3¼" | 3½" | 3¾" | 4¼" | 4½" | 5" | 5½" | 5¾" | 6" | 6¼" |

NECK SHAPING: K across first

| 30 | 32 | 34 | 36 | 38 | 40 | 41 | 43 | 44 | 46 sts |

Place on a stitch holder the remaining

| 50 | 52 | 58 | 60 | 62 | 64 | 67 | 69 | 72 | 74 sts |

Turn and work over the first set of sts only, decreasing 1 st at neck edge on every other row until there remain

25 26 29 30 32 33 34 35 36 38 sts

Work even, ending at side edge, until length from first row of armhole shaping is

4¾" 5" 5½" 6" 6½" 7" 7½" 8" 8½" 9"

SHOULDER SHAPING: Bind off

6 7 6 6 7 7 7 6 6 sts

at beg of next row and every other row for a total of

3 3 5 4 4 4 5 6 5 times

Bind off at same edge the remaining

7 8 0 8 6 5 0 0 8 sts

Slip the last

30 32 34 36 38 40 41 43 44 46 sts

from stitch holder onto needle. There remain on stitch holder the center

20 20 24 24 24 26 26 28 28 sts

Attach yarn to first st at neck edge and work other side of neck to correspond, reversing shapings.

SLEEVES: Starting at cuff with #1 needles, cast on
for long sleeves

48 52 52 56 60 60 64 68 72 76 sts

for short sleeves

72 76 80 84 88 88 92 96 100 104 sts

Work in ribbing as for back
for long sleeves

2" 2" 2¼" 2½" 2½" 2½" 2½" 2½" 2½" 3"

for short sleeves

3/4"   1"   1"   1"   1½"   1½"   1½"   1½"

increasing 4 sts evenly spaced on last row. Change to #2 needles and work in Stockinette St, increasing 1 st at both ends of every

for long sleeves

7th   7th   7th   6th   7th   8th   8th   9th   9th row

for short sleeves

0   6th   7th   5th   5th   6th   6th   6th   7th row

until there are on the needle

76   84   88   96   100   100   104   108   112   116 sts

Work even, ending with a p row, until total length is

for long sleeves

11"   12"   13"   14"   15"   17"   17½"   18"   18"   18½"

for short sleeves

2"   2½"   3"   3"   3½"   3½"   4"   4½"   4½"   5"

Cap of Sleeve Shaping: Bind off at beg of next 2 rows

4   5   5   6   7   8   9   10   11   11 sts

Dec 1 st at both ends of every other row until length from first row of shaping is

2"   2"   2½"   3"   3"   3½"   4"   4½"   5"   5½"   6"

Bind off 5 sts at beg of next 4 rows. Bind off remaining sts.

NECKBAND: Sew shoulder seams. With #1 Dp needles and Right Side facing, pick up and k around entire neck, including sts on stitch holders,

100   104   112   120   124   128   132   140   144   148 sts

Work in ribbing as before for 1". Bind off loosely in ribbing.

FINISHING: Block to measurements. Sew side and sleeve seams. Sew in sleeves.

CARDIGAN

BACK: Work as for Pullover until total length is, ending with a p row,

10"	10½"	11½"	12½"	13"	13½"	14"	14½"	14½"	14½"

ARMHOLE SHAPING: Work as for Pullover until there remain

84	88	96	100	104	108	112	116	120	124 sts

Work even until length from first row of armhole shaping, ending with a p row, is

5"	5½"	6"	6½"	7"	7½"	8"	8½"	9"	9½"

SHOULDER SHAPING: Bind off

7	7	8	7	7	7	8	6	7 sts

at beginning of next

8	6	8	8	10	8	8	8	10 rows

Then at beginning of next 2 rows, bind off

0	8	0	5	0	8	9	6	6 sts

Slip remaining sts on a stitch holder to be worked later for back of neck.

Note: Buttonholes are made on left front for boys, on right front for girls and women. Make right front first for boys and left front first for girls.

LEFT FRONT: Starting at lower edge with #1 needles, cast on

64	68	72	76	80	84	88	92	96	100 sts

Row 1: Work in ribbing as for back to within last 16 sts, k 16 (front band).
Row 2: P 16, complete row in ribbing. Repeat these 2 rows until piece measures, ending with Row 2,

2"	2"	2½"	2½"	3"	3"	3½"	3½"	3½"

Change to #2 needles and work in Stockinette St until piece measures in all, ending at side edge,

10"	10½"	11½"	12½"	13"	13½"	14"	14½"	14½"	14½"

ARMHOLE SHAPING: Row 1: Bind off

4	5	5	6	7	8	9	10	11	11 sts

Dec 1 st at armhole edge every other row until there remain

58	60	64	66	68	70	72	74	76	78 sts

Work even until length from first row of armhole shaping is, ending at front edge,

3½"	4"	4½"	5"	5¼"	5½"	6"	6½"	7"	7"

NECK SHAPING: At beg of next row, bind off

24	26	26	28	28	28	28	28	28	28 sts

and complete row. Dec 1 st at neck edge on every other row until there remain

28	29	32	33	35	36	37	38	39	41 sts

Work even until length from first row of armhole shaping is, ending at side edge,

5"	5½"	6"	6½"	7"	7½"	8"	8½"	9"	9½"

SHOULDER SHAPING: Bind off

7	7	8	7	7	8	7	7	8	6	7 sts

at beg of next row and every other row

4	3	4	4	5	4	4	4	5 times

At same edge, bind off remaining

0	8	0	5	0	8	6	6	9	9	6 sts

LEFT-FRONT BORDER: With pins mark the position of buttons on front band:

6	6	7	7	8	8	8	9	9

evenly spaced, having the first pin ½" up from lower edge and the last one on the center row of neckband (½" above neck edge).

To make a set of buttonholes: **Row 1:** Starting at front edge, work first 2 sts, bind off next 3 sts, work over next 6 sts, bind off next 3 sts, and complete row.

Row 2: Work across, casting on 3 sts over each set of bound-off sts.

RIGHT FRONT: Work as for left front, reversing position of front band and shapings.

SLEEVES: Starting at cuff with #1 needles, cast on

48	52	52	56	60	60	64	68	72	76 sts

Work in ribbing as for back for

2½"	2½"	2¾"	3"	3"	3"	3"	3"	3"	3½"

increasing 8 sts evenly spaced on last row. Change to #2 needles and work as for long sleeves of pullover until there are on the needle

80	88	92	100	104	104	108	112	116	120 sts

Work even until piece measures in all

11½" 12½" 13½" 14½" 15½" 17½" 18" 18½" 18½" 19"

Cap of Sleeve Shaping: Work as for cap of sleeve of pullover until length from first row of shaping is 2½" 3" 3½" 4" 4½" 5" 5½" 6" 6½"

Bind off 5 sts at beg of next 4 rows. Bind off remaining sts.

NECKBAND: Sew shoulder seams. With Right Side facing and using #1 needles, leave 8 sts free at each front edge, and pick up and k around entire neck edge, including sts on stitch holder,

104 112 116 124 124 128 132 140 148 **152 sts**

Work in ribbing as before for 1", making a buttonhole in line with previous buttonholes when length is ½". Bind off in ribbing.

FINISHING: Block to measurements. Sew side and sleeve seams. Sew in sleeves. Fold under 8 sts at each front edge and sew to Wrong Side. Work buttonhole stitch around buttonholes. Sew on buttons.

TURTLENECK CABLE-KNIT DRESS

TURTLENECK CABLE-KNIT DRESS

Directions are for Size 10. Changes for Sizes 12, 14, 16 and 18 are in parentheses.

MATERIALS REQUIRED:

Columbia-Minerva Knitting Worsted or Nantuk 4-Ply Knitting Yarn (4 oz. skein)—6 (6-7-7-7) skeins
#9 Knitting Needles
#0 Crochet Hook
Cable Needle

STITCH GAUGE: Overall gauge allowing for "take-in" of patterns
                6 sts = 1"   6 rows = 1"

Note: Dress measures 35 (35¼-35½-35¾-36) inches from hemline to back of neck.

KNITTING INSTRUCTIONS:

BACK: With #9 needles cast on 120 (124-128-134-142) sts. P 1 row. Start pattern as follows:

Row 1 (Right Side): K 8 (8-8-9-9), * p 1 (1-1-2-3), skip 1 st and k in *front loop* of 2nd st but do not drop from needle, k the skipped st then drop both sts from left-hand needle for a *front twist*, skip 1 st, k in *back* of 2nd st but do not drop from needle k in front of skipped st and drop both from left-hand needle for a *back twist*, p 1, (1-2-2-2), k 9, p 1 (1-2-2-2), front twist, back twist, p 1 (1-1-2-3) *. ** K 2, p 3, in front of next st k 1, p 1, k 1 and p 1 for a cluster st, p 1, cluster st in next st, p 3, k 2 **, p 1 (2-2-2-3), front twist, back twist, p 1 (2-2-2-3), [with yarn at back sl 1 as if to p, k 4, sl 1] 4 times, p 1 (2-2-2-3), front twist, back twist, p 1 (2-2-2-3), repeat from ** to ** once then repeat from * to * once, k 8 (8-8-9-9).

Row 2: P 8 (8-8-9-9), * k 1 (1-1-2-3), p 4, k 1 (1-2-2-2), p 9, k 1 (1-2-2-2), p 4, k 1 (1-1-2-3) *. ** P 2, k 3, p 4, k 1, p 4, k 3, p 2 **, k 1 (2-2-2-3), p 4, k 1 (2-2-2-3), [with yarn in front sl 1 as if to p, p 4, sl 1] 4 times, k 1 (2-2-2-3), p 4, k 1 (2-2-2-3), repeat from ** to ** once then repeat from * to * once, p 8 (8-8-9-9).

Row 3: K 8 (8-8-9-9), * p 1 (1-1-2-3), front twist, back twist, p 1 (1-2-2-2), k 9, p 1 (1-2-2-2), front twist, back twist, p 1

(1-1-2-3) * ** K 2, p 3, k 4, p 1, k 4, p 3, k 2 **, p 1 (2-2-2-3), front twist, back twist, p 1 (2-2-2-3), [sl next st to cable needle and hold in front, k next 2 sts and k the st from cable needle, sl next 2 to cable needle and hold in back, k next st then k the 2 from cable needle] 4 times, p 1 (2-2-2-3), front twist, back twist, p 1 (2-2-2-3), repeat from ** to ** once then repeat from * to * once, k 8 (8-8-9-9).

Row 4: P 8 (8-8-9-9), repeat from * to * of Row 2 once, ** p 2, k 3, p 4 tog, k 1, p 4 tog, k 3, p 2 **, k 1 (2-2-2-3), p 4, k 1 (2-2-2-3), p 24, k 1 (2-2-2-3), p 4, k 1 (2-2-2-3), repeat from ** to ** once, then repeat from * to * of Row 2 once, p 8 (8-8-9-9).

Row 5: K 8 (8-8-9-9), repeat from * to * of Row 3 once, ** k 2, p 4, cluster st in next st, p 4, k 2 **, p 1 (2-2-2-3), front twist, back twist, p 1 (2-2-2-3), [k 2, with yarn in back sl 2, k 2] 4 times, p 1 (2-2-2-3), front twist, back twist, p 1 (2-2-2-3), repeat from ** to ** once, then repeat from * to * of Row 3 once, k 8 (8-8-9-9).

Row 6: P 8 (8-8-9-9), repeat from * to * of Row 2 once, ** p 2, k 4, p 4, k 4, p 2 **, k 1 (2-2-2-3), p 4, k 1 (2-2-2-3), [p 2, with yarn in front sl 2, p 2] 4 times, k 1 (2-2-2-3), p 4, k 1 (2-2-2-3), repeat from ** to ** once, then repeat from * to * of Row 2 once, p 8 (8-8-9-9).

Row 7: K 8 (8-8-9-9), * p 1 (1-1-2-3), front twist, back twist, p 1 (1-2-2-2), sl next 3 sts to cable needle and hold in front, k next 3, pass cable needle with 3 sts to back, k next 3 then k the 3 from cable needle for a *braided cable*, p 1 (1-2-2-2), front twist, back twist, p 1 (1-1-2-3) *—**Sl next 2 sts to a cable needle and hold in front, p next st then k the 2 from cable needle for a *left twist*, p 3, k 4, p 3, sl next st to a cable needle and hold in back, k next 2 then p the st from cable needle for a *right twist* **, p 1 (2-2-2-3), front twist, back twist, p 1 (2-2-2-3), [sl next 2 to cable needle and hold in back, k next st then k the 2 from cable needle, sl next st to cable needle and hold in front, k next 2 sts, then k the st from cable needle] 4 times, p 1 (2-2-2-3), front twist, back twist, p 1 (2-2-2-3), repeat from ** to ** once, then repeat from * to * once, k 8 (8-8-9-9).

Row 8: P 8 (8-8-9-9), repeat from * to * of Row 2, ** k 1, p 2, k 3, p 4 tog, k 3, p 2, k 1 **, k 1 (2-2-2-3), p 4, k 1 (2-2-2-3), p 24, k 1 (2-2-2-3), p 4, k 1 (2-2-2-3), repeat from ** to ** once, then repeat from * to * of Row 2 once, p 8 (8-8-9-9).

Row 9: K 8 (8-8-9-9), repeat from * to * of Row 3, ** p 1, left twist, p 5, right twist, p 1 **, p 1 (2-2-2-3), front twist, back twist, p 1 (2-2-2-3), [with yarn at back sl 1, k 4, sl 1] 4 times, p 1 (2-2-2-3), front twist, back twist, p 1 (2-2-2-3), repeat from ** to ** once, then repeat from * to * of Row 3, k 8 (8-8-9-9).

Row 10: P 8 (8-8-8-9-9), repeat from * to * of Row 2, ** k 2, p 2, k 5, p 2, k 2 **, k 1 (2-2-2-3), p 4, k 1 (2-2-2-3), [with yarn in front sl 1, p 4, sl 1] 4 times, k 1 (2-2-2-3), p 4, k 1 (2-2-2-3), repeat from ** to ** once, then repeat from * to * of Row 2 once, p 8 (8-8-9-9).

Row 11: K 8 (8-8-9-9), repeat from * to * of Row 3 once, ** p 2, left twist, p 3, right twist, p 2 **, p 1 (2-2-2-3), front twist, back twist, p 1 (2-2-2-3), [sl next st to a cable needle and hold in front, k next 2 sts, then k the st from cable needle, sl next 2 to cable needle and hold in back, k next st then k the 2 from cable needle] 4 times, p 1 (2-2-2-3), front twist, back twist, p 1 (2-2-2-3), repeat from ** to ** once, then repeat from * to * of Row 3 once, k 8 (8-8-9-9).

Row 12: P 8 (8-8-9-9), repeat from * to * of Row 2 once, ** [k 3, p 2] twice, k 3 **, k 1 (2-2-2-3), p 4, k 1 (2-2-2-3), p 24, k 1 (2-2-2-3), p 4, k 1 (2-2-2-3), repeat from ** to ** once, then repeat from * to * of Row 2 once, p 8 (8-8-9-9).

Row 13: K 8 (8-8-9-9), repeat from * to * of Row 3 once, ** p 3, left twist, p 1, right twist, p 3 **, p 1 (2-2-2-3), front twist, back twist, p 1 (2-2-2-3), [k 2, with yarn in back sl 2, k 2] 4 times, p 1 (2-2-2-3), front twist, back twist, p 1 (2-2-2-3), repeat from ** to ** once, then repeat from * to * of Row 3 once, k 8 (8-8-9-9).

Row 14: P 8 (8-8-9-9), repeat from * to * of Row 2 once, ** k 4, p 2, k 1, p 2, k 4 **, k 1 (2-2-2-3), p 4, k 1 (2-2-2-3), [p 2, with yarn in front sl 2, p 2] 4 times, k 1 (2-2-2-3), p 4, k 1 (2-2-2-3), repeat from ** to ** once, then repeat from * to * of Row 2 once, p 8 (8-8-9-9).

Row 15: K 8 (8-8-9-9), repeat from * to * of Row 3 once, ** p 4, sl next 2 to cable needle and hold in front, k 2, p 1, then k the 2 from cable needle, p 4 **, p 1. (2-2-2-3), front twist, back twist, p 1 (2-2-2-3), [sl next 2 to a cable needle and hold in back, k next st then k the 2 from cable needle, sl next st to cable needle and hold in front, k next 2 then k the st from cable needle] 4 times, p 1 (2-2-2-3), front twist, back twist, p 1 (2-2-2-3), repeat from ** to ** once, then repeat from * to * of Row 3 once, k 8 (8-8-9-9).

Row 16: P 8 (8-8-9-9), repeat from * to * of Row 2 once, k 13, k 1 (2-2-2-3), p 4, k 1 (2-2-2-3), p 24, k 1 (2-2-2-3), p 4, k 1 (2-2-2-3), k 13, repeat from * to * of Row 2 once, p 8 (8-8-9-9).

Repeat these 16 rows for pattern working to 9" from start. Dec 1 st each side on next row then every 1½ (1½-2-2-1½) inches 4 (4-3-3-4) times more—110 (114-120-126-132) sts. Width across hipline is 18¼ (19-20-21-22) inches.

Dec 1 each side every 2 (2-1½-1¼-1½) inches 3 times. Work on the 104 (108-114-120-126) sts to 28" or desired length to underarm. Width across back is 17¼ (18-19-20-21) inches.

ARMHOLES: Bind off 3 (3-4-5-5) sts at beg of next 2 rows, Dec 1 st each side every other row 3 (3-4-5-5) times.

Note: Continue to work cable at armhole edges.

Work on the 92 (96-98-100-106) sts until armholes measure 6 (6¼-6½-7-7¼) inches straight above underarm.

SHOULDERS: Bind off 10 sts at beg of next 4 (4-6-6-2) rows, then *on Sizes 10 (12-18) only,* bind off 8 (9-11) sts at beg of next 2 (2-4) rows. Sl remaining 36 (38-38-40-42) sts to a holder for neck.

FRONT: Work same as back until armholes measure 4¼ (4½-4¾-5-5¼) inches straight above underarm.

NECK AND SHOULDERS: Work across 34 (35-36-36-38) and sl them to a holder, work center 24 (26-26-28-30) sts and sl them to 2nd holder for neck, work to end. Dec 1 at neck every other row 6 times *and at the same time* when armhole matches back armhole, bind off 10 sts at armhole edge 2 (2-3-3-1) times, then *on Sizes 10 (12-18) only,* bind off 8 (9-11) sts at the same edge 1 (1-2) times. Starting at neck, work other side to correspond.

COLLAR: Sew right shoulder seam. On Right Side, starting at open shoulder, pick up and k 14 sts along side of neck, k the 24 (26-26-28-30) of center front, pick up and k 14 on other side, k the 36 (38-38-40-42) sts of back. K 1 and p 1 in ribbing on the 88 (92-92-96-100) sts for 6". Bind off loosely in ribbing. Sew left shoulder and collar reversing for turn.

Sew side seams. On Right Side starting at side seam crochet 1 row of sc around armholes and hemline. Turn in ¼" hemline around armholes.

A YOUNG "LONGIE"

Directions are for Small Size (10 to 12). Changes for Medium (14 to 16) and Large (18) are in parentheses.

MATERIALS REQUIRED:

Columbia-Minerva Knitting Worsted or Nantuk 4-Ply Knitting Yarn (4 oz. skein)—3 skeins

Small Size—#8 Knitting Needles
Gauge 17 sts = 4"
Medium Size—#9 Knitting Needles
Gauge 4 sts = 1"
Large Size—#10 Knitting Needles
Gauge 7 sts = 2"

PATTERN STITCH: Multiple of 8 sts plus 1.

Row 1 (Right Side): P.

Row 2: K.

Row 3: K 1, * yo, k 1, [work a long st in next st as follows: insert needle in st and wrap yarn around needle twice then k the st] 5 times, k 1, yo, k 1, repeat from * across.

Row 4: P 3, * [with yarn in front sl long st as to p, dropping extra loop] 5 times, p 5, repeat from * across, end p 3 instead of p 5.

Row 5: K 2, * yo, k 1, with yarn in back sl 5 as to p, k 1, yo, k 3, repeat from * across, end k 2 instead of k 3.

Row 6: P 4, * p 5 tog, p 7, repeat from * across, end p 4 instead of p 7.

Repeat these 6 rows for pattern.

Note: Needle Sizes account for changes in sizes of garment.

KNITTING INSTRUCTIONS:

BACK: With #8 (9-10) needles cast on 73 sts. Work in pattern for 26 patterns then work Row 1 of next pattern. Bind off as to k. Width across back is 17 (18¼-20¼) inches.

FRONT: Work same as back.

JOINING: Seam lightly, stretching slightly in length. Sew shoulder to 4 (4¾-5¼) inches from each side edge, leaving a 9¼ (9¼-9¾)

A YOUNG "LONGIE"

inches opening at center for neck. Starting 7" above lower edge, sew side seams to 6½ (7-7½) inches below shoulder.

TWISTED CORD: Cut three 6-yard strands of yarn, tie at one end and fasten tied end to a stationary object *or* have another person hold end. Twist strands tightly. Bring the 2 ends together, allowing yarn to twist upon itself. Tie a knot on free end. Trim ends. Draw cord through waistline as shown.

FAIR ISLE WINTER SPORTS SET

FAIR ISLE WINTER SPORTS SET

Directions are for Size 12. Changes for Sizes 14 and 16 are in parentheses.

MATERIALS REQUIRED:

Unger's Les Bouquets (50 gram ball)
6 (7-7) White, 4 (5-5) Black, 2 (3-3) Orange, and 2 Green.
#6 and #8 Knitting Needles, *or size required to obtain the given stitch gauge*
3 Stitch Holders
6 buttons and bobbins

STITCH GAUGE: #8 needles   9 sts = 2"

Note: Do not carry yarn across back of work. Use a separate bobbin for each pattern and always twist yarn in back of work to prevent holes.

KNITTING INSTRUCTIONS:

BACK: Using #6 needles and White, cast on 81 (87-91) sts. Knit 1 row, purl 1 row for 5 rows (for hem). Knit 1 row on Wrong Side (for hemline).

Change to #8 needles and continue in Stockinette St, following chart for design. Work even until 16" from hemline.

ARMHOLE SHAPING: Dec 1 st each end of every other row 7 times—67 (73-77) sts.

Work even until armhole is 8 (8-8½) inches.

SHOULDER SHAPING: Bind off 7 (8-5) sts at beg of next 6 (6-10) rows—25 (25-27) sts.

Bind off remaining sts.

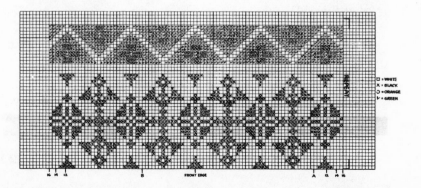

LEFT FRONT: Using #6 needles and White, cast on 41 (44-46) sts. Work hem and hemline as for back.

Change to #8 needles and continue in Stockinette St, following chart: start at seam edge for each size and work to the 41st (44th-46th) st.

Work to underarm as for back.

ARMHOLE SHAPING: At arm edge, dec 1 st every other row 7 times—34 (37-39) sts.

Work even until armhole is 6 (6-6½) inches.

NECK SHAPING: At front edge, bind off 10 (10-11) sts, dec 1 st every other row 3 times—21 (24-25) sts.

Work even until armhole is same as for back.

SHOULDER SHAPING: At arm edge, bind off 7 (8-5) sts every other row 3 (3-5) times.

RIGHT FRONT: Work to correspond to left front. Start at the 41st (44th-46th) st on chart (front edge) and work to the desired seam edge.

SLEEVE (Make 2): Using #6 needles and White, cast on 41 (47-51) sts. Work hem and hemline as for back. Change to #8 needles and continue in Stockinette St, following chart for pattern: **For Size 12,** start at Size 12 on chart and work across 41 sts, **For Size 14,** k 3 White, then start at Size 12 on chart and work across 41 sts, and end with k 3 White, **For Size 16,** k 5 White, then start at Size 12 on chart and work across 41 sts, and end with k 5 White.

As you inc, work in Fair Isle pattern. Inc 1 st each end every 1½", 10 (8-7) times—61 (63-65) sts.

Work even until about 17" from hemline (end with completion of Row 30).

SLEEVE CAP: Dec 1 st each end of every other row 7 times—47 (49-51) sts. Bind off.

COLLAR: Using #6 needles and Black, cast on 65 sts. K 1, p 1 ribbing for 4 rows. Next row, rib across first 6 sts and place onto a holder, change to #8 needles and work Stockinette St, following chart, starting at A and working across to B (53 sts between A and B), slip last 6 sts onto a 2nd holder. Work pattern on 53 sts for 30 rows. Bind off (neck edge).

Attach Black and, using #6 needles, work ribbing on each of the 6 sts for 30 rows. Bind off. Sew each side strip to collar.

LEFT-FRONT BAND: Using #6 needles and Black, cast on 8 st: Work k 1, p 1 ribbing to measure from lower edge (measure fror hemline) to neck shaping. Bind off.

Sew onto left front. Mark for 6 buttons evenly spaced, placir.₀ the first ½" from lower edge and the last ½" below neck shaping.

RIGHT-FRONT BAND: Work to correspond to left-front band, working in buttonholes to match markings for buttons.

BUTTONHOLE: Rib across 3 sts, bind off 2 sts, and complete the row.
Next Row: Cast on 3 sts above those bound off on previous row. Sew onto right front.

FINISHING: Pin pieces to measurements and block. Sew shoulder, side, and sleeve seams. Sew in sleeves. Turn under hems and sew. Sew on collar to within 1" from each front edge. Sew on buttons.

CAP: Using #6 needles and Black, cast on 81 sts. Work in ribbing of k 1, p 1 for 8 rows. Change to #8 needles and work in Stockinette St for 30 rows, following chart as for Size 12.

Change to White and work in Stockinette St as follows:
Next Row: K 5, k 2 tog, * k 8, k 2 tog; repeat from * to last 4 sts, k 4.
Purl 1 row, knit 1 row, purl 1 row.
Next Row: K 4, k 2 tog, * k 7, k 2 tog; repeat from * to last 4 sts, k 4.
Purl 1 row.
Next Row: K 3, k 2 tog, * k 6, k 2 tog; repeat from * to last 4 sts, k 4.
Purl 1 row.
Continue in this manner to dec 8 sts on every other row until 41 sts remain, ending with a p row.

Next Row: * K 2 tog; repeat from * to last st, k 1.
Purl 1 row. Leave a 12" strand and break off.
Draw yarn through remaining sts, pull tog and tack.

FINISHING: Block. Sew back seam. Turn half of ribbing at lower edge to inside and sew.

POMPON: Wind Black 50 times over 4 fingers. Remove from fingers and tie securely in center (over all strands). Cut each side and trim. Sew to top of hat as shown.

KNITTED NECK TUCKER

NECK TUCKER

MATERIALS REQUIRED:
   3 (1 oz.) balls of Columbia-Minerva Reverie Mohair
   #6 Knitting Needles
   #6 Double-pointed Needles

STITCH GAUGE: 6 sts = 1"   7 rows = 1"

KNITTING INSTRUCTIONS: Using #6 needles, cast on 63 sts.
Row 1 (Right Side): K 1, * p 1, k 1, repeat from * across.
Row 2: P 1, * k 1, p 1, repeat from * across.
   Repeat Rows 1 and 2, working until piece measures 14".

NECK: Row 1: Work across 20 sts, join another ball of yarn and
bind off center 23 sts for neck, work to end of row.
Next 4 Rows: Working on sts of both sides, dec 1 st at neck edge
every other row twice.
   Work on the 18 sts of each side until Tucker measures 16½"
from start.
Next Row: Work across first 18 sts, cast on 27 sts for back of neck,
work across last 18 sts.
   Work on the 63 sts for 3½". Bind off loosely in ribbing.

TURTLENECK: Using Dp needles, starting at left shoulder, pick
up and k 13 sts along side of neck, 23 sts across front of neck, 13
sts on other side, 27 sts across back of neck.
   Divide sts onto 3 needles and work around in ribbing on the
76 sts until collar measures 5".
   Bind off loosely in ribbing.

FINISHING: No blocking is necessary.

SMART AND INEXPENSIVE

SMART AND INEXPENSIVE

Directions are for Small Size (10 to 12). Changes for Large Size (14 to 16) are in parentheses.

MATERIALS REQUIRED:

Columbia-Minerva Knitting Worsted or Nantuk 4-Ply Knitting Yarn (4 oz. skein)—2 skeins for each design
#10 and #13 Knitting Needles for each design
#6 or H Crochet Hook for each design

STITCH GAUGE: Pattern stitch on #13 needles
                  5 sts = 2"   9 rows = 2"

PULLOVER (Shown at Right)

KNITTING INSTRUCTIONS:

BACK: With #13 needles cast on 45 (49) sts. Change to #10 needles and k 10 rows in Garter St. Change to #13 needles. Work in pattern as follows:

Row 1 (Wrong Side): K 3 (5), * p 3, k 3, repeat from * across, ending p 3, k 3 (5).

Row 2 and All Even Rows: P 3 (5), * k 3, p 3, repeat from * across, ending k 3, p 3 (5).

Rows 3, 5 and 7: Repeat Row 1.

Row 8: P 3 (5), * k 1, drop next st 5 rows down, k the dropped st under the 5 strands and sl onto left-hand needle and k this st again, k 1, p 3, repeat from * across, ending k 3, p 3 (5).

Repeat these 8 rows for pattern, working to about 12" from start ending with Row 1.

ARMHOLES: Bind off 2 (3) sts at beg of next 2 rows. Continue in pattern on the 41 (43) sts until armholes measure about 7", ending with Row 8. Change to #10 needles. Knit in Garter St for 8 rows (4 ridges).

SHOULDERS: Bind off 4 sts at beg of next 4 rows. With #13 needle, bind off remaining 25 (27) sts loosely for neck.

FRONT: Same as back.

Sew side and shoulder seams. Crochet one row of single crochet around armholes.

PULLOVER (Shown at Left)

PATTERN STITCH: Multiple of 8 sts plus 1.
Row 1 (Right Side): P 1, * k 1, p 5, k 1, p 1, repeat from * across.
Row 2: K 1, * p 1, k 5, p 1, k 1, repeat from * across.
Row 3: K 1, * yo, sl 1, k 1, psso, p 3, k 2 tog, yo, k 1, repeat from * across.
Row 4: P 3, * k 3, p 5, repeat from * across, ending k 3, p 3.
Row 5: K 2, * yo, sl 1, k 1, psso, p 1, k 2 tog, yo, k 3, repeat from * across, ending k 2 instead of k 3.
Row 6: P 4, * k 1, p 7, repeat from * across, ending k 1, p 4.
Row 7: Repeat Row 4.
Row 8: K 3, * p 3, k 5, repeat from * across, ending p 3, k 3.
Row 9: P 2, * k 2 tog, yo, k 1, yo, sl 1, k 1, psso, p 3, repeat from * across, ending p 2 instead of p 3.
Row 10: K 2, * p 5, k 3, repeat from * across, ending k 2 instead of k 3.
Row 11: P 1, * k 2 tog, yo, k 3, yo, sl 1, k 1, psso, p 1, repeat from * across.
Row 12: K 1, * p 7, k 1, repeat from * across.
      Repeat these 12 rows for pattern.

KNITTING INSTRUCTIONS:
BODY: With #10 needles cast on 89 (97) sts. K 8 rows in Garter St. Change to #13 needles and work in pattern to 11th row of 5th pattern.

ARMHOLES: Bind off 1 st then work in pattern until there are 47 sts on right-hand needle and sl these sts to a holder for front, bind off next st, work to end of row. Next row bind off 1 st, work to end of row.

BACK: Inc 1 st in first st, work in pattern to last st, inc 1 st in last st. Work in pattern on the 41 (49) sts until there are 7 complete patterns from start. Change to #10 needles. *Small Size only:* K 5, inc 1 st in next st, * k 9, inc 1 st in next st, repeat from * twice more, k to end of row. *All Sizes:* K in garter st on the 45 (49) sts for 5 (8) rows.

SHOULDERS: Bind off 5 sts at beg of next 4 rows. With #13 needle, bind off remaining 25 (29) sts for neck.

FRONT: Sl the 47 sts to #13 needle. Inc 1 st in first st, work in pattern to last st, inc 1 st in last st. Work in pattern on the 49 sts until there are 7 complete patterns from start. Change to #10 needles. K 6 (8) rows.

SHOULDERS: Bind off 5 sts at beg of next 4 rows. With #13 needle, bind off remaining 29 sts for neck.

Sew side seam from lower edge to bound-off st at underarm. Sew shoulder seams. Starting at underarm edge on right side of work, crochet 1 row of sc around armholes.

COLORFUL RAGLAN COAT

KNITTED RAGLAN COAT

Directions are given for Small Size. Changes for Medium and Large Sizes are in parentheses.

MATERIALS REQUIRED:
Coats & Clark's "Red Heart" Knitting Worsted (4-Ply "Tangle-Proof" Pull-Out Skeins)
   40 (44–48) ozs. of No. 625 Flame
   #7—29" Circular Needle
   3 Stitch Holders
STITCH GAUGE: 4 sts = 1"   8 rows = 1"

BLOCKING MEASUREMENTS:

Sizes	Small	Medium	Large
Body Bust Size (in Inches)	30-32	34-36	38-40
Actual Knitting Measurements:			
Bust	**43**	**47**	**51**
Length from center back of neck to hemline	**41**	**42**	**43**
Length from underarm to lower edge	**31**	**31**	**31**
Length of sleeve seam	**11**	**12**	**13**
Width across sleeve at upper arm	**16**	**17½**	**19**

KNITTING INSTRUCTIONS:
Starting at neck edge, cast on 35 sts for all sizes. *Do not* join, work in rows as follows:
Row 1 (Wrong Side): K 3—front, place a marker on needle; p 2—seam, place a marker on needle; k 3—sleeve, place a marker; p 2 —seam, place a marker; k 15—back, place a marker; p 2—seam, place a marker; k 3—sleeve, place a marker; p 2—seam, place a marker; k 3—front.
Row 2: (*K 1 by inserting needle in next st of the row below, then k the st on needle—a double-knit st made;* k 1, make a double-knit st, slip marker, k 2, slip marker) twice; double-k st 7 times; (slip marker, k 2, slip marker double-k st, k 1, double-k st) twice.
Row 3: (K the 2 sts of the double-k tog, k 1, k 2 tog, slip marker, p 2, slip marker) twice; k 2 tog, (k 1, k 2 tog) 7 times; (slip marker, p 2, slip marker, k 2 tog, k 1, k 2 tog) twice. *Note: Always slip markers.*
Row 4: (K in front and back of next st—one st increased; double-k,

[93]

inc in next st; k 2) twice; inc in next st, double-k, (k 1, double k) 6 times; inc in next st; (k 2; inc in next st, double-k, inc in next st) twice—10 sts increased, counting each double-k st as 1 st.

Row 5: (K 2, k 2 tog, k 2, p 2) twice; k 2, k 2 tog, (k 1, k 2 tog) 6 times; k 2, (p 2, k 2, k 2 tog, k 2) twice—45 sts on row.

Row 6: (K 1, * double-k, k 1; repeat from * to next marker, k 2) 4 times; work in pattern of k 1, double-k, to end of row, ending with k 1.

Row 7: (K 1, * k 2 tog, k 1; repeat from * to next marker, p 2) 4 times; work in pattern of k 1, k 2 tog, to end of row, ending with k 1.

Row 8: (Inc in next st, k 1, double-k, k 1, inc in next st, k 2) twice; inc in next st, k 1, * double-k, k 1. Repeat from * across to within 1 st before next marker, inc in next st, (k 2, inc in next st, k 1, double-k, k 1, inc in next st) twice—10 sts increased.

Row 9: (K 3, k 2 tog, k 3, p 2) twice: k 3, (k 2 tog, k 1) 7 times, k 2, (p 2, k 3, k 2 tog, k 3) twice—55 sts.

Row 10: Inc in next st, (K 1, * double-k, k 1; repeat from * to within 1 st before next marker, inc in next st, k 2, inc in next st) 4 times; k 1, work in pattern to end of row, increasing in last st—10 sts increased.

Row 11: K 3, (work in pattern of k 2 tog, k 1, to within 2 sts of next marker, k 2, p 2, k 3) 4 times; work in pattern of k 2 tog, k 1, to last 2 sts, k 2—65 sts.

Row 12: (Double-k, * k 1, double-k; repeat from * to next marker, k 2) 4 times; work in pattern of double-k, k 1, to end of row, ending with a double-k.

Row 13: (K 2 tog, * k 1, k 2 tog; repeat from * to next marker, p 2) 4 times; work in pattern to end of row.

Row 14: Inc in next st, (double-k, * k 1, double-k; repeat from * to within 1 st before next marker, inc in next st, k 2, inc in next st) 4 times; work in pattern to end_ of row, increasing in last st—*10 sts increased.*

Row 15: K 2, (k 2 tog, * k 1, k 2 tog; repeat from * to within 2 sts before next marker, k 2, p 2, k 2) 4 times; work in pattern to end of row, ending with k 2—75 sts.

Rows 16 through 21: Repeat 14th, 15th, 6th, 7th, 10th and 11th rows. At end of last row, cast on 10 sts—105 sts.

Now work as follows:

Row 22: K 2—*front edge;* * double-k, k 1. Repeat from * across to within 1 st before next marker, inc in next st, k 2, inc in next st, (work in pattern of k 1, double-k, across to within 2 sts before next marker, k 1, inc in next st, k 2, inc in next st) 3 times; work in pattern of k 1, double-k, to end of row—8 *sts increased*. At end of row, cast on 10 sts.

Row 23: Starting with k 10 (instead of k 3), work as for Row 11, ending with k 2 (*front edge*)—123 sts on needle.

Neck shaping has been completed.

Row 24: K 2—front edge; work in pattern of k 1, double-k, to next marker, k 2, (double-k, * k 1, double-k; repeat from * to next marker, k 2) 3 times; work in pattern of double-k, k 1, to within last 2 sts, k 2—*front edge.*

Row 25: K 3, then work as for Row 13, ending with k 3 instead of k 1.

Row 26: Starting with k 2 (instead of an inc), work as for Row 14, ending with k 2 (do not inc in last st)—8 *sts increased.*

Row 27: Repeat Row 15—131 sts.

Row 28: Starting and ending with k 3 (instead of inc in next st), work as for Row 14—8 *sts increased.*

Row 29: Starting and ending with k 3 (instead of k 2), repeat Row 15—139 sts.

Row 30: K 2 (work in pattern of double-k, k 1, to next marker, k 3) 4 times; work in pattern to end of row, ending with k 2.

Row 31 and Every Uneven Row: Keeping the first and last 2 sts in Garter St (k each row), work in pattern to next marker, being careful to always k the 2 sts of each double-k tog; p 2, complete row as before.

Row 32: Starting and ending with k 3, repeat Row 22, omitting the cast-on sts at end of row.

Keeping the 2 front sts at each edge in Garter St, continue in pattern, increasing 8 sts (1 st before and 1 st after each marker) alternately on every 2nd and every 4th row until there are 275 (299-323) sts on needle, ending with a Wrong Side row. Break off yarn.

Removing all markers, slip the first 46 (49-52) sts on a stitch holder to be worked later for body; slip the next 57 (63-68) sts on another holder to be worked later for sleeve; slip the next 69 (75-83) sts on a holder for back. Attach yarn to next st, cast on 3 (4-4) sts, turn.

SLEEVE: Being careful to keep in pattern, work across the 3 (4-4) cast-on sts and next 57 (63-68) sts, cast on 3 (4-4) sts. Slip remaining 46 (49-52) sts on a holder.

For Large Size only: Next Row: Inc 1 st at beg of row.

For All Sizes: Work in pattern over the 63 (71-77) sts on needle, decreasing 1 st at both ends of every 8th row 10 (11-12) times in all.

Work even on 43 (49-53) sts until length from cast-on sts at underarm is 10½ (11½-12½) inches.

Work 4 rows in Garter St. Bind off. Slip sts for other sleeve on needle and work same as previous sleeve.

BODY: Slip sts from one front, back, and other front on needle. With Right Side facing, attach yarn to first st of left front, k 2, work in pattern across remaining sts of front, cast on 6 sts for underarm, work in pattern across sts of back, cast on 6 sts for underarm, work across right front, ending with k 2. Keeping the 2 front-edge sts in Garter St, work in pattern until length from underarm is 29½".

Work 4 rows of Garter St (allowing 1" for stretching).

NECKBAND: With Right Side facing, pick up and k 78 (82-86) sts evenly along neck edge.

Row 1: P 2, * k 2, p 2. Repeat from * across.

Row 2: K 2, * p 2, k 2. Repeat from * across.

Row 3: Work as for Row 1 to within last 5 sts, bind off next 2 sts, complete row.

Next Row: Cast on 2 sts over the 2 bound-off sts—buttonhole made. Work 2 rows of ribbing; then bind off in ribbing.

SCARF COLLAR: Cast on 36 sts.

Row 1: K across.

Row 2: K in front and back of first st, k across to within last 2 sts, k 2 tog.

Repeat Rows 1 and 2 until total length is 45 (46-47) inches. Bind off.

FINISHING: Block to measure 6 x 48 (49-50) inches. Sew scarf to top of neckband, leaving 2" free at each front edge.

WARMTH FOR THE "MODS"

Directions are for Small Size (8 to 10). Changes for Medium (12 to 14) and Large (16 to 18) are in parentheses.

MATERIALS REQUIRED:

Columbia-Minerva Nantuk Cascade Yarn (4 oz. skeins)—7 (8-8) skeins
#10½ and #13 Knitting Needles
1 Cable Needle

STITCH GAUGE: Stockinette St on #13 needles
5 sts = 2"   7 rows = 2"

CARDIGAN (Shown at Left)

KNITTING INSTRUCTIONS:

BACK: With #10½ needles cast on 42 (46-52) sts. K 1 and p 1 in ribbing for 4 rows, inc'ing 1 st on last row. Change to #13 needles. Starting with a p row, work in Stockinette St on the 43 (47-53) sts to 14½" from start, end on Wrong Side. Width across back is 17¼ (19-21) inches.

ARMHOLES: Bind off 2 (2-3) sts at beg of next 2 rows. Dec 1 st each side every other row 2 (3-4) times. Work on the 35 (37-39) sts until armholes measure 7 (7½-8) inches straight above underarm. Width across shoulders is 14 (14¾-15½) inches.

SHOULDERS: Bind off 5 sts at beg of next 2 rows then 6 (6-7) sts at beg of next 2 rows. Sl remaining 13 (15-15) sts to a holder for neck.

LEFT FRONT: With #10½ needles cast on 25 (29-31) sts.
Row 1 (Wrong Side): P 1, * k 1, p 1, repeat from * across.
Row 2: K 1, * p 1, k 1, repeat from * across.
    Repeat Rows 1 and 2 once, inc'ing 1 st at beg of last row *on Small and Large* only. Next row work 4 sts and sl them to a holder for buttonband, with #13 needle, k 1, p 6, k 1, p to end.
Row 2: K 14 (17-20), p 1, k 6, p 1.
Row 3: K 1, p 6, k 1, p to end.

WARMTH FOR THE "MODS"

Rows 4 and 5: Repeat Rows 2 and 3.

Row 6: K 14 (17-20), p 1, sl next 3 sts to cable needle and hold in back of work, k next 3 sts then k the 3 from cable needle for a cable twist, p 1.

Rows 7, 8 and 9: Repeat Rows 3, 4 and 3.

Repeat Rows 2 through 9 for pattern, working to same length as back to underarm, end on Wrong Side. Width across front not including buttonband is 9 (10-11¼) inches.

ARMHOLE: Bind off 2 (2-3) sts at side edge, work to end of row. Dec 1 st at same edge every other row 2 (3-4) times. Work on the 18 (20-21) sts until armhole measures 5 (5½-6) inches straight above underarm, end on Right Side.

NECK AND SHOULDER: Work 2 (4-4) sts and sl them to a holder for neck, work to end of row. Bind off 2 at neck twice then dec 1 st at same edge once. When armhole matches back armhole, bind off 5 sts at armhole once then 6 (6-7) at same edge once.

BUTTONBAND: With #10½ needles continue in ribbing on the 4 sts on holder to fit front to neck, when slightly stretched, end on Wrong Side. Sl sts to a holder. Sew band to front. Place markers for 4 buttons evenly spaced with first button 1" above lower edge. Fifth button is on neckband.

RIGHT FRONT: With #10½ needles cast on 25 (29-31) sts. Work ribbing same as on Left Front, inc'ing 1 st at end of 4th row *on Small and Large* only. Change to #13 needles and work on the 26 (29-32) sts as follows:

Row 1 (Wrong Side): P 14 (17-20), k 1, p 6, k 1, sl remaining 4 sts to a holder for buttonhole band.

Row 2: P 1, k 6, p 1, k to end.

Row 3: P 14 (17-20), k 1, p 6, k 1.

Rows 4 and 5: Repeat Rows 2 and 3.

Row 6: P 1, twist cable, p 1, k to end.

Rows 7, 8 and 9: Repeat Rows 3, 4 and 3.

Repeat Rows 2 through 9 for pattern, finishing to correspond to Left Front.

BUTTONHOLE BAND: Work same as buttonband with button-holes opposite markers: Starting at front edge, k 1, bind off next st, p last st. Next row cast on 1 st over buttonhole.

SLEEVES: With #10½ needles cast on 20 (22-24) sts. K 1 and p 1 in ribbing for 1½", inc'ing 1 st at beg of last row. Change to #13 needles. Starting with a p row, work in Stockinette St, inc'ing 1 st each side every 10th row 5 times. Work on the 31 (33-35) sts to 17", end on Wrong Side. Width across sleeve is 12½ (13¼-14) inches.

SLEEVE CAP: Bind off 2 (2-3) sts at beg of next 2 rows. Dec 1 st each side every other row until 17 (17-19) sts remain. *Large only,* dec 1 each side every 4th row once. *All sizes* bind off 2 sts at beg of next 4 rows. Bind off.

NECKBAND: Sew shoulder seams. With #10½ needle starting at Right Front work the 4 sts of buttonhole band then k the next 2 (4-4) from holder, pick up and k 14 along side, k the 13 (15-15) of back, pick up and k 14 on other side, k remaining sts from holders. Work in ribbing on the 53 (59-59) sts as follows:
Row 1 (Wrong Side): P 1, * k 1, p 1, repeat from * across.
Row 2: K 1, * p 1, k 1, repeat from * across.
   Work 5th buttonhole on next 2 rows. Work 2 more rows. Bind off in ribbing.

   Sew sleeves in place then sew underarm and sleeve seams. Work around buttonholes.

TURTLENECK PULLOVER (Shown at Right)

KNITTING INSTRUCTIONS:
BACK: With #10½ needles cast on 42 (46-52) sts. K 1 and p 1 in ribbing for 2", inc'ing 1 st on last row. Change to #13 needles. Work in Stockinette St on the 43 (47-53) sts to 15½" from start, end on Wrong Side. Width across back is 17¼ (19-21) inches.

RAGLAN ARMHOLES: Bind off 2 sts at beg of next 2 rows.
Dec Row: K 2, k 2 tog, k to last 4 sts, sl 1, k 1, psso, k 2.

Repeat dec row every 4th row 2 (2-1) times, then every other row until 13 (15-17) sts remain. Sl sts to a holder for neck.

FRONT: Work same as back until 19 (21-23) sts remain, end on Right Side.

NECK: P 5 and sl them to a holder, p center 9 (11-13) and sl them to 2nd holder for neck, p last 5 sts. Next row k 2, k 2 tog, k 1. P the 4 sts. K 2, k 2 tog. P 2 tog, p 1. K 2 tog and fasten off last st. Starting at neck work other side to correspond.

SLEEVES: With #10½ needles cast on 20 (22-24) sts. K 1 and p 1 in ribbing for 3", inc'ing 1 st on last row. Change to #13 needles. Work in Stockinette St on the 21 (23-25) sts to 4" from start, end on Wrong Side. Inc 1 st each side on next row then every 8th row 5 times more. Work on the 33 (35-37) sts to 16½" from start, end on Wrong Side. Width across sleeve is 13¼ (14-14¾) inches.

RAGLAN SLEEVE CAP: Bind off 2 sts at beg of next 2 rows.
Dec Row: K 2, k 2 tog, k to last 4 sts, sl 1, k 1, psso, k 2.
Repeat dec row every 4th row 3 times then every other row until 5 sts remain.
Sl sts to a holder.
Sew raglan seams, leaving right back seam open.

NECKBAND OR TURTLENECK: With #10½ needles on Right Side, starting at open raglan, pick up and k 44 (48-52) sts around neck, including holders. K 1 and p 1 in ribbing for 2" for neckband or 5" for turtleneck. Bind off loosely in ribbing.

Sew raglan seam, joining neckband, reversing seam for turtleneck. Sew underarm and sleeve seams.

THE PARK AVENUE

THE PARK AVENUE

Directions are for Size 10. Changes for Sizes 12, 14, 16 and 18 are in parentheses.

MATERIALS REQUIRED:

Columbia-Minerva Knitting Worsted or Nantuk 4-Ply Knitting Yarn (4 oz. skein)—5 (5-6-6-6) skeins
#8—24" Circular Needle
#10 Knitting Needles
Cable Needle
#0 Crochet Hook

STITCH GAUGE:

Stockinette St on #8 needles
9 sts = 2"   6 rows = 1"
Pattern on #10 needles
5 sts = 1"   6 rows = 1"

Note: Dress measures 34½ (34¾-35-35¼-35½) inches from hemline to back of neck.

KNITTING INSTRUCTIONS: With circular needle cast on 164 (172-180-188-198) sts. Working back and forth on circular needle, k 4 rows for Garter St border. Join and k around to 21" from start, dec'ing 2 sts on last row *on Size 18 only.* Hipline measures 36½ (38-40-42-44) inches.

BODICE: K across 82 (86-90-94-98) sts and leave on circular needle for front. With #10 straight needles work on the 82 (86-90-94-98) sts of back as follows:

Row 1 (Right Side): P 7 (9-9-11-11), [skip next st on left needle insert right-hand needle in front of next st and k it but do not drop from needle, then k the skipped st for a *right twist*, skip next st, insert right-hand needle in back of next st and k it but do not drop from left needle, then k in front of skipped st for a *left twist*] twice, p 4, sl next 3 sts to a cable needle and hold in back, k next 3 sts, then k the 3 sts from cable needle for a *cable twist*, p 4, [right twist, left twist] 6 (6-7-7-8) times, p 4, twist cable on next 6 sts, p 4, [right twist, left twist] twice, p 7 (9-9-11-11).

Row 2 and All Even Rows: K 7 (9-9-11-11), p 8, k 4, p 6, k 4, p 24 (24-28-28-32), k 4, p 6, k 4, p 8, k 7 (9-9-11-11).

Row 3: P 7 (9-9-11-11), [right twist, left twist] twice, p 4, k 6, p 4, [left twist, right twist] 6 (6-7-7-8) times, p 4, k 6, p 4, [right twist, left twist] twice, p 7 (9-9-11-11).

Row 5: P 7 (9-9-11-11), [right twist, left twist] twice, p 4, k 6, p 4, [right twist, left twist] 6 (6-7-7-8) times, p 4, k 6, p 4, [right twist, left twist] twice, p 7 (9-9-11-11).

Row 7: Repeat Row 3.

Row 8: Repeat Row 2.

Repeat these 8 rows for pattern, working to 3″ above Stockinette St, end on Wrong Side. Inc 1 each side on the next row, then every 6th row 1 (1-2-2-2) times more. Work on the 86 (90-96-100-104) sts to 8″ above Stockinette St, end on Wrong Side.

Width across back is 17¼ (18-19¼-20-20¾) inches.

ARMHOLES: Bind off 5 (5-6-6-6) sts at beg of next 2 rows. Dec 1 each side every other row 4 (5-6-7-8) times. Work on the 68 (70-72-74-76) sts to 3¾ (4-4¼-4½-4¾) inches above underarm. Width across shoulders is 13½ (14-14¼-14¾-15¼) inches.

OPENING: Work 34 (35-36-37-38) sts and sl them to a holder. Work on remaining sts until armhole measures 6¾ (7-7¼-7½-7¾) inches.

SHOULDER: Bind off 7 sts at armhole edge 1 (2-2-3-3) times then *on Sizes 10 (12-14) only* bind off 6 sts at same edge 2 (1-1) times. Sl remaining 15 (15-16-16-17) sts to a holder for neck. Starting at opening, work other side to correspond.

FRONT: Starting on Right Side and omitting opening, work same as back until armholes measure 5 (5¼-5½-5¾-6) inches straight above underarm. 68 (70-72-74-76) sts remain.

NECK AND SHOULDER: Work 24 (25-25-26-26) sts and sl them to a holder, work center 20 (20-22-22-24) sts and sl to 2nd holder for neck, work to end. Dec 1 st at neck every other row 5 times *and at the same time* when armhole matches back armhole bind off 7 sts at armhole edge 1 (2-2-3-3) times, then *on Sizes 10 (12-14) only* bind off 6 sts at same edge 2 (1-1) times. Work other side to correspond.

SLEEVES: With circular needle cast on 38 (40-42-44-46) sts. Working back and forth on circular needle k 1 and p 1 in ribbing for 1½". Change to #10 needles and work in pattern.

Row 1 (Right Side): P 4 (5-6-7-8), [right twist, left twist] twice, p 4, twist cable on next 6 sts, p 4, [right twist, left twist] twice, p 4 (5-6-7-8).

Row 2: K 4 (5-6-7-8), p 8, k 4, p 6, k 4, p 8, k 4 (5-6-7-8).

Row 3: P 4 (5-6-7-8), [right twist, left twist] twice, p 4, k 6, p 4, [right twist, left twist] twice, p 4 (5-6-7-8).

Working added sts in reverse Stockinette St and continuing in pattern, inc 1 st each side on next row, then every 6th row 9 times more. Work on the 58 (60-62-64-66) sts to 14½" or desired length to underarm. Width across sleeve is 11¾ (12-12¼-12½-12¾) inches.

SLEEVE CAP: Bind off 5 sts at beg of next 2 rows, then 2 sts at beg of next 2 rows. Dec 1 each side every other row until 32 sts remain. Bind off 2 at beg of next 6 rows. Bind off 20 sts.

NECKBAND: Sew shoulder seams. With circular needle, on Right Side starting at opening, pick up and k 72 (72-76-76-80) sts around neck, including holders. Working back and forth on circular needle k 4 rows. Bind off. Sew sleeves in place then sew underarm and sleeve seams. Join garter st edges at hemline. On Right Side crochet 1 row of sc on back opening making a buttonloop at neck. Cover buttonring with sc and draw sts tog at back.

PULLOVER IN STAINED-GLASS COLORS

PULLOVER IN STAINED-GLASS COLORS

Directions are for Small Size (10 to 12). Changes for Large (14·to 16) are in parentheses.

MATERIALS REQUIRED:

Columbia-Minerva Nantuk Dimension Yarn (1 oz. skein)
2 skeins of Color A (Dark Pink); 3 skeins of Color B (Light Pink); 1 skein of Color C (Royal Blue); 1 skein of Color D (Dark Green); 2 skeins of Color E (Gold); 2 skeins of Color F (Light Green); 2 skeins of Color G (Light Turquoise); 2 skeins of Color H (Blue); 2 skeins of Color J (Brown); 2 skeins of Black
#8 Knitting Needles
1 Set of Bobbins

STITCH GAUGE: Knitted—9 sts = 2"   7 rows = 1"
                  Blocked—17 sts = 4"   7 rows = 1"

Note: Use a bobbin for each change of color. When changing colors, always pick up next color from under dropped color to prevent a hole.

KNITTING INSTRUCTIONS:

BACK: With Black cast on 77 (87) sts. K 6 rows for Garter St border. Following Chart for back, work in Stockinette St for 90 rows, end on Wrong Side about 13" above border. Width across back is 17¼ (19½) inches. After blocking, it will measure 18 (20½) inches.

RAGLAN ARMHOLES: Bind off 2 (4) sts at beg of next 2 rows. Work 2 rows on the 73 (79) sts. Dec 1 st each side on next row, every 4th row 5 times more than every other row until 31 (33) sts remain. Sl sts to a holder.

FRONT: With Black cast on 77 (87) sts. K 6 rows for border. Follow Chart for front, shaping same as back.

SLEEVES: With Black cast on 61 (65) sts. K 6 rows for border. Follow Chart for sleeves in Stockinette St for 64 rows, end on Wrong Side about 9" above border. Width across sleeve is 13½ (14½) inches. After blocking, it will be 14¼ (15¼) inches.

KEY TO COLOR

A = Dark Pink
B = Light Pink
C = Royal Blue
D = Dark Green
E = Gold
F = Light Green
G = Light Turquoise
H = Blue
J = Brown

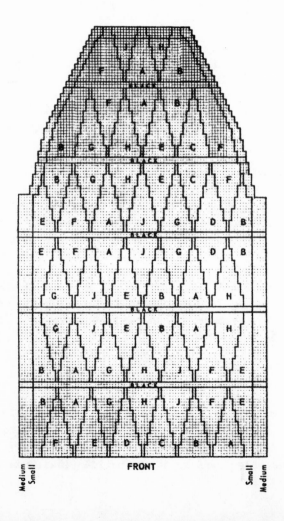

FRONT

Medium
Small

Small
Medium

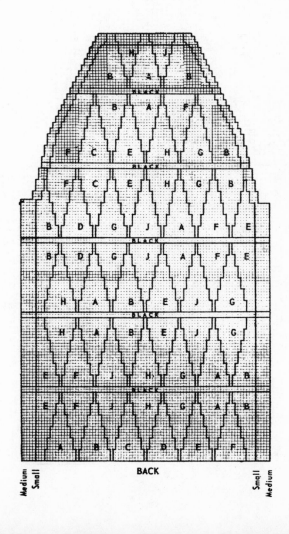

Medium Small   BACK   Small Medium

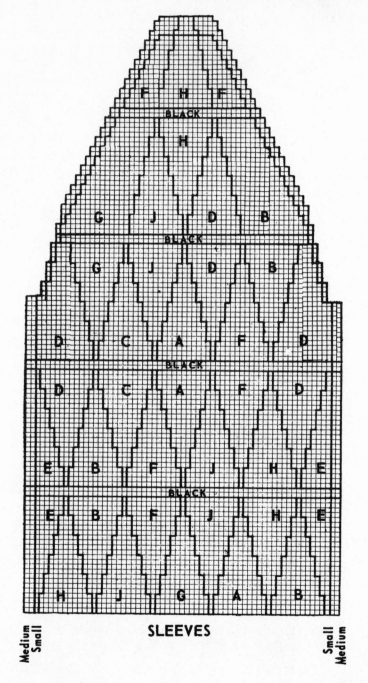

SLEEVES

RAGLAN SLEEVE CAP: Bind off 2 (3) sts at beg of next 2 rows. Work 2 rows on the 57 (59) sts. Dec 1 st each side on next row, every 4th row 3 (4) times more than every other row until 11 sts remain. Sl sts to a holder.

Steam pieces to measurements. Sew raglan seams, leaving right back open. Starting at open seam with Black k across sts of back, sleeve, front and second sleeve. K 5 more rows on the 84 (88) sts. Bind off. Sew raglan seam. Sew side and sleeve seams.

TWO-COLOR POCKET VEST

TWO-COLOR POCKET VEST

Directions are for Size 10. Changes for Sizes 12, 14, 16 and 18 are in parentheses.

MATERIALS REQUIRED:

Columbia-Minerva Featherweight Knitting Worsted (2 oz. skein)

3 (3-4-4-4) skeins of Color A
1 skein of Color B
#4 and #6 Knitting Needles
#2 Crochet Hook

STITCH GAUGE: Stockinette St on #6 needles
11 sts = 2"   13 rows = 2"

KNITTING INSTRUCTIONS:

BACK: With #4 needles and Color A cast on 92 (98-104-108-114) sts. K 1 and p 1 in ribbing for 10 rows inc'ing 2 (1-1-2-2) sts on last row. Change to #6 needles. Work in Stockinette St on the 94 (99-105-110-116) sts to 14½" from start. Width across back is 17¼ (18-19-20-21) inches.

ARMHOLES: Bind off 6 (6-7-7-8) sts at beg of next 2 rows. Dec 1 st each side every other row 3 (4-5-6-6) times. Work on the 76 (79-81-84-88) sts until armholes measure 6¾ (7-7¼-7½-7¾) inches straight above underarm. Width across shoulders is 13¾ (14¼-14-15¼-16) inches.

SHOULDERS: Bind off 8 sts at beg of next 2 (4-4-6-4) rows, then *on Sizes 10 (12-14-18) only* bind off 7 (7-7-9) sts at beg of next 4 (2-2-2) rows. Sl remaining 32 (33-35-36-38) sts to a holder for neck.

LEFT FRONT: With #4 needles and Color A cast on 51 (53-57-59-61) sts.
Row 1 (Right Side): K 1, * p 1, k 1, repeat from * across.
Row 2: P 1, * k 1, p 1, repeat from * across.

Repeat Rows 1 and 2 four times more. Change to #6 needles and work as follows:

Row 1 (Right Side): K to last 8 sts, p 1 and k 1 to end.

Row 2: [P 1 and k 1] 4 times, p to end.

Repeat last 2 rows to 6" from start, end on Wrong Side.

B Stripe:

Row 1: K 20 (20-22-23-24) A, join in a skein of B and k 9, join in a 2nd skein of A and work to end.

Note: When changing colors always pick up next color from under dropped color to prevent a hole.

Row 2: With matching colors [p 1 and k 1] 4 times, p to end.

Repeat last 2 rows to same length as back to underarm, end on Wrong Side. Width across front is 9¼ (9¾-10¼-10¾-11¼) inches.

ARMHOLE: Bind off 6 (6-7-7-8) sts at side edge for underarm. Dec 1 st at same edge every other row 3 (4-5-6-6) times. Work on the 42 (43-45-46-47) sts until armhole measures 3¼ (3½-3¾-4-4¼) inches straight above underarm, end at front edge.

NECK: Work first 14 (14-16-16-16) sts and sl them to a holder for neck, work to end. Dec 1 st at neck every other row 6 times. Work on the 22 (23-23-24-25) sts until armhole matches back armhole, end on Wrong Side.

SHOULDER: Bind off 8 sts at armhole edge 1 (2-2-3-2) times, then *on Sizes 10 (12-14-18) only* bind off 7 (7-7-9) sts at same edge 2 (1-1-1) times.

Place markers for 6 buttons on Left Front having the first one about ¾" above lower edge and the 6th one 2½" below neck. The 7th button will be on neckband.

RIGHT FRONT: With #4 needles and A cast on 51 (53-57-59-61) sts. Work 4 rows in ribbing as on Left Front.

Row 5: Starting at front edge, work 3 sts, bind off next 2 for buttonhole, work to end.

On next row cast on 2 sts over the buttonhole. Work 4 more rows in ribbing, end on Wrong Side. Change to #6 needles and work as follows:

Row 1 (Right Side): [K 1 and p 1] 4 times, k to end.

Row 2: P to last 8 sts, [k 1 and p 1] 4 times.

Repeat last 2 rows to same length as Left Front to B stripe, end on Wrong Side.

B Stripe:

Row 1: Work 22 (24-26-27-28) with A, join in a skein of B and k 9, join in a 2nd skein of A and k to end.

Working buttonholes opposite markers, finish to correspond to Left Front.

NECKBAND: Seam shoulders. On Right Side with #4 needles and A—starting at Right Front neck edge—k 1 and p 1 in ribbing on the 8 front band sts, pick up and k 63 (63-67-67-69) sts around neck to left front band including holders, work front band. Work on the 79 (79-83-83-85) sts:

Row 1 (Wrong Side): P 1, * k 1, p 1, repeat from * across.

Row 2: K 1, * p 1, k 1, repeat from * across. Repeat Row 1.

On next 2 rows work 7th buttonhole. Continue in ribbing for 3 more rows. Bind off in ribbing.

ARMHOLE RIBBING: On Right Side with #4 needles and A pick up and k 63 (65-67-69-71) sts. Work 3 rows in ribbing as on neckband. Bind off in ribbing.

POCKET: With #6 needles and B cast on 25 sts, k 1 row and p 1 row for 14 rows.

Row 15: K 11, bind off 3, k to end.

On next row cast on 3 sts over the bound-off sts. K 1 row, p 1 row and k 1 row. K next p row for turn. K 1 row and p 1 row for 4 rows. On next 2 rows work a buttonhole as before. Work 14 more rows. Bind off. Sew side seams. Fold pocket on turn and weave edges neatly. Sew at lower edge of B Stripe as illustrated. Work around buttonholes going through double thickness on pockets.

BUTTONS: Make 7 with B and 2 with A: Cover a buttonring with sc, turn to center and draw sts tog at back.

THE WOODSMAN SHIRT

THE WOODSMAN SHIRT

Directions are for Size 38. Changes for Sizes 40, 42 and 44 are in parentheses.

MATERIALS REQUIRED:

Columbia-Minerva Spectra (2 oz. pull skein)—9 (9-10-10) skeins of Color A

Columbia-Minerva Nantuk 4-Ply Knitting Yarn (4 oz. pull skein)—1 skein of Color B

or Columbia-Minerva Nantuk 4-Ply Knitting Yarn (4 oz. pull skein)—9 (9-10-10) skeins of Color A; one 4 oz. skein of Color B

#7 and #9 Knitting Needles

STITCH GAUGE: Stockinette St on #9 needles
9 sts = 2"   6 rows = 1"

SHIRT

KNITTING INSTRUCTIONS:

BACK: With #7 needles and Color A cast on 74 (78-82-86) sts. K 1 row and p 1 row for 7 rows. K next p row for turn, cast on 13 sts at end for turn and facing of slit. Change to #9 needles. K next row, cast on 13 sts at end. Work on the 100 (104-108-112) sts:

Row 1 (Wrong Side): P.

Row 2: K 6, with yarn at back sl 1 as if to p for turning st, k to last 7 sts, sl 1, k 6.

Repeat these 2 rows to 4½" above turn, end with a p row. Bind off 6 sts at beg of next 2 rows for slits. Work in Stockinette St on the 88 (92-96-100) sts to 14" above slits. Width across back is 19½ (20½-21½-22¼) inches.

ARMHOLES: Bind off 6 (6-7-7) sts at beg of next 2 rows. Dec 1 st each side every other row 3 (4-4-5) times. Work on the 70 (72-74-76) sts to 9 (9½-10-10½) inches straight above bound-off sts. Width across shoulders is 15½ (16-16½-17) inches.

SHOULDERS: Bind off 7 (7-7-8) sts at beg of next 4 (2-2-6) rows then *on Sizes 38, 40 and 42 only* bind off 8 sts at beg of next 2 (4-4) rows. Sl the 26 (26-28-28) sts to a holder for neck.

FRONT FACING: With #9 needles and Color B cast on 16 sts for facing. K 1 row and p 1 row for 9 rows. Next row p 8 and sl them to a safetypin for left facing, p remaining 8 sts and sl them to another safetypin for right facing. Break yarn.

FRONT: With #7 needles and Color A cast on 74 (78-82-86) sts. Work same as back to 4" above turn, end with a p row. Bind off 6 sts at beg of next 2 rows for slits. Work in Stockinette St on the 88 (92-96-100) sts to 11" above slits, end with a k row.

NECK: P 44 (46-48-50) sts and sl them to a holder for Right Front, p to end of row. With Color A k 41 (43-45-47) sts, join Color B and k 3 then starting at outer edge of facing, sl the 8 sts from safetypin to free #9 needle and k them onto same needle holding left front sts.
Note: When changing colors, always pick up color to be used from *under* color being dropped to prevent a hole.
Work on the 52 (54-56-58) sts:
Row 1: With Color B p 11. With Color A p to end.
Row 2: With matching colors, k to last 9 sts, with yarn at back sl 1 as if to p for turning st, k to end.
Repeat these 2 rows once then repeat Row 1 once more.

ARMHOLE: Bind off 7 sts at side edge, work to last 13 sts, yo, k 2 tog for eyelet, k 2, sl 1, k 2, k 2 tog, yo for eyelet on facing, k to end. Repeat eyelets every 12th row 3 times more *and at the same time* dec 1 st at armhole every other row 3 (4-4-5) times. After the 4th set of eyelets has been completed, p the 42 (43-45-46) sts. Inc 1 st at end of next row for front facing edge then every 4th row at same edge 3 (3-5-5) times more *and at the same time* when armhole matches back armhole, bind off 7 (7-7-8) sts at armhole edge 2 (1-1-3) times then *on Sizes 38, 40 and 42 only* bind off 8 sts at same edge 1 (2-2) times. P the 15 (15-17-17) B sts and sl them to a holder for collar, p the 9 (9-11-11) A sts and sl them to another holder for neck.

RIGHT FRONT: Starting at center of front facing, sl the 8 sts of facing to #9 needle. With B k the 8 sts of facing, sl the 44 (46-48-50) sts of Right Front to free needle and with B k 3, join A and k to end.
Row 1: With matching colors p the 52 (54-56-58) sts.

Row 2: With B k 8, sl 1, k 2. With A k to end.
Repeat these 2 rows once.

ARMHOLE: Bind off 7 sts at side edge, p to end. Finish to correspond to other side, working eyelets as follows:
On Right Side, k 4, yo, k 2 tog, k 2, sl 1, k 2, k 2 tog, yo, finish row.

SLEEVES: With #7 needles and B cast on 44 (46-48-50) sts. K 1 and p 1 in ribbing for 3½", inc'ing 9 sts across last row. Break off B. Change to #9 needles and A. Work in Stockinette St on the 53 (55-57-59) sts for 2", end with a p row. Inc 1 st each side on next row then every 8th row 9 times more. Work on the 73 (75-77-79) sts to 20" from start. Width across sleeve is 16¼ (16½-17-17½) inches.

SLEEVE CAP: Bind off 7 sts at beg of next 2 rows. Dec 1 st each side every other row until 43 sts remain. Bind off 2 sts at beg of next 12 rows. Bind off the 19 sts.

COLLAR: Sew shoulder seams. Starting at left front facing edge, sl the 15 (15-17-17) B sts to #9 needle. Join B and k 2, sl turning st, k 12 (12-14-14) sts then cast on 26 (26-28-28) sts for back of collar, starting at right front facing edge work across the 15 (15-17-17) B sts on holder.
Row 1: P the 56 (56-62-62) sts.
Row 2: K 2, sl 1, k 12 (12-15-15), inc 1 st in next st, * k 4, inc 1 st in next st, repeat from * 4 times more, work to end.
Row 3: P the 62 (62-68-68) sts.
Row 4: K 2, sl 1, k to last 3 sts, sl 1, k 2.
Repeat last 2 rows to 2¾" from cast-on sts, end with a p row. Next row bind off 5 sts, k to end. Bind off 5 sts at beg of next row, k to end for turn. K 1 row and p 1 row on the 52 (52-58-58) sts. Bind off.

LINING: On Right Side with #9 needles and A starting at Right Front k the 9 (9-11-11) sts of front, 26 (26-28-28) sts of back, 9 (9-11-11) sts of Left Front from holders.
Row 1: P the 44 (44-50-50) sts.

Row 2: K 9 (9-12-12), inc 1 in next st, * k 4, inc 1 in next st, repeat from * 4 times more, k to end.

P 1 row and k 1 row on the 50 (50-56-56) sts to 2½" from start. Bind off loosely.

Turn collar facing on turn and sew *only* adjoining edges at corners. Pin collar lining in place and sew to collar facing. Sew front facings and collar in place. Work around eyelets through double thickness. Sew sleeves in place. Sew hems and side slit facings. Starting above side slits, sew underarm and sleeve seams.

CARDIGAN

KNITTING INSTRUCTIONS:

BACK: With #7 needles and B cast on 74 (78-82-86) sts. K 1 row and p 1 row for 6 rows. Break off B. Join A and k 1 row. K next p row for turn, cast on 7 sts then join B and cast on 6 sts for facing of side slit. Change to #9 needles. Next row with B k 6, with A sl 1 as if to p for turning st, k to end, cast on 7 sts, join 2nd skein of B and cast on 6 sts for facing.

Note: When changing colors, always pick up color to be used from *under* color being dropped to prevent a hole. Work on the 100 (104-108-112) sts:

Row 1: With B p 6. With A p to last 6 sts. With B p 6.

Row 2: With B k 6. With A sl 1 as if to p, k to last 7 sts, sl 1. With B k 6.

Repeat these 2 rows to 4¼" above turn, end with a p row. Bind off 6 sts at beg of next 2 rows. Break off B. With A work in Stockinette St on the 88 (92-96-100) sts to 11" above slits, end with a p row. Width across back is 19½ (20½-21½-22½) inches.

RAGLAN ARMHOLES: Bind off 5 (6-6-7) sts at beg of next 2 rows.

Dec Row (Right Side): K 2, sl 1, k 1, psso, k to last 4 sts, k 2 tog, k 2.

Repeat dec every other row until 22 (22-24-24) sts remain. Sl sts to a holder for back of neck.

LEFT FRONT: With #7 needles and B cast on 38 (40-42-44) sts. K 1 row and p 1 row for 6 rows. Join A and k 1 row, cast on 4 sts at end then join 2nd skein of B and cast on 9 more sts at same edge for front edge and facing. Next row with B p 9. With A k to end for turn, cast on 7 sts. With B cast on 6 sts for facing. Change to #9 needles. Work on the 64 (66-68-70) sts:

Row 1: With B k 6. With A sl 1 for turn, k to last 9 sts. With B k 2, sl 1 for turn, k 6.

Row 2: With matching colors p.

Repeat these 2 rows to 4" above turn, end on Wrong Side.

Next Row: Bind off 6 sts at side edge for slit, work to end. Work on the 58 (60-62-64) sts:

Row 1 (Wrong Side): With B p 9, with A p to end.

Row 2: With A k to last 9 sts. With B k 2, sl turning st, k 6.

Repeat these 2 rows to 11" above slit, end with a p row. Width across front including facing is 13 (13½-13¾-14¼) inches.

RAGLAN ARMHOLE: Bind off 6 (7-6-7) sts at side edge, work to end of row. P 1 row.

Dec Row: K 2, sl 1, k 1, psso, work to end.

Repeat dec every other row 8 times more. P the 43 (44-47-48) sts. Next row k 2, sl 1, k 1, psso, work across, inc'ing 1 st in last st for facing inc. Continue to dec at raglan every other row 18 (19-20-21) times more *and at the same time* inc at facing every 4th row 5 (5-7-7) times more, end at facing edge. P the 15 (15-17-17) B sts and sl them to a holder for collar, p the 15 (15-17-17) A sts and sl them to 2nd holder for neck.

RIGHT FRONT: With #7 needles and B cast on 38 (40-42-44) sts. K 1 row and p 1 row for 6 rows. Join A and k 1 row, cast on 7 sts at end, join 2nd skein of B and cast on 6 sts for facing. Next row with B p 6. With A k to end for turn, cast on 4 sts then with B cast on 9 sts for front edge and facing. Work on the 64 (66-68-70) sts:

Row 1: With B k 6, sl 1 for turn, k 2. With A k to last 7 sts, sl 1 for turn. With B k 6.

Row 2: With matching colors p.

Finish to correspond to Left Front, dec'ing at raglan by working to last 4 sts, k 2 tog, k 2.

SLEEVES: With #7 needles and B cast on 44 (46-48-50) sts. K 1 and p 1 in ribbing for 3½", inc'ing 7 (7-7-9) sts across last row. Break off B. Change to #9 needles and A. Work in Stockinette St on the 51 (53-55-59) sts for 2", end with a p row. Inc 1 st each side on next row then every 8th row 9 times more. Work on the

71 (73-75-79) sts to 20" from start, end with a p row. Width across sleeve is 15¾ (16¼-16¾-17½) inches.

RAGLAN CAP: Bind off 6 (6-6-7) sts at beg of next 2 rows. Dec as on back raglan until 7 sts remain. P the 7 sts. Next row k 2, sl 1, k 2 tog, psso, k 2. P the 5 sts.
Next Row: K 1, sl 1, k 2 tog, psso, k 1. Sl the 3 sts to a holder.

Sew raglan sleeves to back and fronts.

COLLAR: Starting at facing of Left Front, sl the 15 (15-17-17) B sts to #9 needle. Join B and k 2, sl turning st, k 12 (12-14-14) sts, cast on 38 (38-40-40) sts for back of collar; starting at right front facing, work across the 15 (15-17-17) B sts on holder. P the 68 (68-74-74) sts.
Row 2: K 2, sl 1, k to last 3 sts, sl 1, k 2.
Repeat last 2 rows to 2¾" above cast-on sts, end with a p row. Next row bind off 5 sts, k to end. Bind off 5 sts at beg of next row, k to end for turn. K 1 row and p 1 row on the 58 (58-64-64) sts. Bind off.

LINING: On Right Side with #9 needles and A starting at Right Front k the 15 (15-17-17) sts of front, 3 sts of sleeve, 22 (22-24-24) sts of back, 3 sts of sleeve, 15 (15-17-17) sts of front. P 1 row and k 1 row on the 58 (58-64-64) sts to 2½" from start. Bind off loosely.
Turn collar facing on turn and sew *only* adjoining edges at corners. Pin collar lining in place and sew to facing. Sew front facings and collar in place. Sew hems and facings at lower edge of back and fronts. Starting above slits, sew underarm and sleeve seams.

LOOPS: Make 2. With #7 needles and B cast on 12 sts then bind off. Sew ends forming a loop. Sew loops inside of left front edge, first one 5" above lower edge and 2nd one 4" above.

TAILORED EASY-KNIT PULLOVERS

Directions are for Size 12. Changes for Sizes 14, 16 and 18 are in parentheses.

MATERIALS REQUIRED:
Columbia-Minerva Featherweight Knitting Worsted (2 oz. skein)—4 (4-5-5) skeins for each pullover
#5 and #7 Knitting Needles

STITCH GAUGE: Pattern Stitch on #7 needles
11 sts = 2"   7 rows = 1"

PATTERN STITCH: Multiple of 4 sts plus 2.
Row 1 (Right Side): K 2, * p 2, k 2, repeat from * to end.
Row 2: P 2, * k 2, p 2, repeat from * to end.
Repeat these 2 rows for pattern.
Note: Mark right side of each piece with colored thread.

SCOOP NECK PULLOVER (Shown at Left)

KNITTING INSTRUCTIONS:
BACK: With #5 needles cast on 98 (102-106-110) sts. Work in pattern for 1". Change to #7 needles and continue in pattern to 12½" from start.

ARMHOLES: Bind off 3 sts at beg of next 2 rows. Dec 1 st each side every other row 7 times. Work on the 78 (82-86-90) sts to 5¼ (5½-5¾-6) inches straight above underarm.

NECK: Work 22 (24-24-26) sts and sl them to a holder, work center 34 (34-38-38) sts and sl them to 2nd holder for neck, work to end of row. Bind off 2 sts at neck twice. Dec 1 st at neck every other row 1 (2-2-3) times. Work on the 17 (18-18-19) sts to 7¼ (7½-7¾-8) inches straight above underarm.

SHOULDER: Bind off 6 sts at armhole edge 2 (3-3-2) times then *on Sizes 12 and 18 only* bind off 5 (7) sts at same edge once.
Starting at neck, work other side to correspond.

TAILORED EASY-KNIT PULLOVERS

FRONT: With #5 needles cast on 98 (102-106-114) sts. Work in pattern for 1". Change to #7 needles and continue in pattern to same length as back to underarm.

ARMHOLES: Bind off 3 (3-3-4) sts at beg of next 2 rows. Dec 1 st each side every other row 7 (7-7-8) times. Work on the 78 (82-86-90) sts to 4 (4¼-4½-4¾) inches straight above underarm.

NECK: Work 24 (26-26-28) sts and sl them to a holder, work center 30 (30-34-34) sts and sl them to 2nd holder for neck, work to end of row. Bind off 2 (2-2-3) sts at neck twice. Dec 1 st at same edge every other row 3 (4-4-3) times. Work on the 17 (18-18-19) sts to match back armhole.

SHOULDER: Bind off 6 sts at armhole edge 2 (3-3-2) times then *on Sizes 12 and 18 only* bind off 5 (7) sts at same edge once. Starting at neck, work other side to correspond.

SLEEVES: With #5 needles cast on 42 (46-50-54) sts. Work in pattern for 1". Change to #7 needles. Working added sts in pattern, inc 1 st each side every 8th row 12 times. Work on the 66 (70-74-78) sts to 16" from start.

SLEEVE CAP: Bind off 3 sts at beg of next 2 rows. Dec 1 st each side every other row 13 times, then *every* row until 30 sts remain. Bind off 2 sts at beg of next 6 rows. Bind off 18 sts.

NECKBAND: With Right Sides tog, sew left shoulder seam. On Right Side starting at open shoulder with #5 needles, pick up and k 12 sts on Right Back, k across the 34 (34-38-38) sts on holder, pick up and k 12 sts on other side to shoulder then 18 sts on Left Front, k across the 30 (30-34-34) sts on holder, pick up and k 18 sts on other side.
Next Row (Wrong Side): k the 124 (124-132-132) sts for ridge. Work in pat for 2¼". Bind off loosely. Sew right shoulder seam, joining neckband. Fold neckband in half and sew to inside. Sew sleeves in place then sew underarm and sleeve seams.

PULLOVER WITH COLLAR (Shown at Right)

KNITTING INSTRUCTIONS:

BACK: With #5 needles cast on 98 (102-106-110) sts. Work same as back of scoop neck pullover until armholes measure 7¼ (7½-7¾-8) inches straight above underarm—78 (82-86-90) sts.

SHOULDERS: Bind off 8 (8-8-9) sts at beg of next 6 (4-2-6) rows then *on Sizes 14 and 16 only* bind off 9 sts at beg of next 2 (4) rows. Bind off remaining 30 (32-34-36) sts for neck.

FRONT: With #5 needles cast on 98 (102-106-114) sts. Work same as front of scoop neck pullover until armholes measure 5 (5¼-5½-5¾) inches—78 (82-86-90) sts.

NECK: Work 29 (30-31-32) sts and sl them to a holder, bind off center 20 (22-24-26) sts for neck, work to end of row. Dec 1 st at neck every other row 5 times. Work on the 24 (25-26-27) sts to match back armhole.

SHOULDER: Bind off 8 (8-8-9) sts at armhole edge 3 (2-1-3) times then *on Sizes 14 and 16 only* bind off 9 sts at same edge 1 (2) times. Starting at neck, work other side to correspond.

SLEEVES: With #5 needles cast on 58 (62-66-70) sts. Work in pattern for 1". Change to #7 needles. Working added sts in pattern, inc 1 st each side every 6th row 4 times. Work on the 66 (70-74-78) sts to 6½" from start.

SLEEVE CAP: Bind off 3 sts at beg of next 2 rows. Dec 1 st each side every other row 13 times, then *every* row until 30 sts remain. Bind off 2 sts at beg of next 6 rows. Bind off 18 sts.

COLLAR: With #5 needles cast on 94 (98-102-106) sts. Work in pattern for 1". Change to #7 needles and continue in pattern to 2" from start. Bind off loosely.

With Right Sides tog, sew shoulder seams. Sew sleeves in place then sew underarm and sleeve seams. If desired, crochet 1 row of sc around neck. Sew side edges of collar tog. Sew cast-on edge of collar in place easing in to fit neck.

CARDIGAN SET FOR BABY

Directions are for Size 6 months. Changes for Size 1 are in parentheses.

MATERIALS REQUIRED:
Columbia-Minerva Baby Nantuk (1 oz. skein)—5 skeins
#3 Knitting Needles
#1 Crochet Hook

STITCH GAUGE: Stockinette St—7 sts == 1″
10 rows = 1″

CARDIGAN

KNITTING INSTRUCTIONS:
YOKE: Starting at neck cast on 75 (79) sts.
Row 1: K 1, * p 1, k 1, repeat from * across. Repeat this row for Moss St. Work 2 rows more for a girl, 3 rows for a boy.

BUTTONHOLE: Work 2 sts, bind off next 2 sts, work to end of row. Next row cast on 2 sts over bound-off sts.

The buttonhole is repeated twice more, with 16 rows between buttonholes. Work 3 more Moss St rows for a girl, 2 rows for a boy.

Start raglan as follows:
Row 1 (Right Side): Work 7 Moss Sts for border, k 10 (11) for Left Front, * yo, k 1 for Seam St, yo *, k 5 for left sleeve, repeat from * to * once, k 27 (29) for back, repeat from * to * once, k 5 for right sleeve, repeat from * to * once, k 10 (11) for Right Front, work 7 Moss Sts for border.
Row 2: Work 7 Moss Sts, p to last 7 sts, work 7 Moss Sts.
Row 3: Work 7 Moss Sts, * k to Seam St, yo, k 1 for Seam St, yo, repeat from * 3 times, k to last 7 sts, work 7 Moss Sts.

Repeat Rows 2 and 3 until there are 243 (263) sts, end with Row 3. Divide sts as follows:

Work 38 (41) sts and sl them to a holder for Right Front, p next 49 (53) sts and sl them to a 2nd holder for right sleeve, p next 69 (75) sts and sl them to 3rd holder for back, p next 49 (53) sts for left sleeve, sl remaining 38 (41) sts to 4th holder for Left Front.

CARDIGAN SET FOR BABY

SLEEVE: Cast on 1 st, k the 50 (54) sts, cast on 1 st. P the 51 (55) sts. Continue in Stockinette St. Dec 1 st each side every 2" twice. Work on the 47 (51) sts to 5½ (6) inches from cast-on sts. Work 8 Moss St rows. Bind off in pattern. Sew sleeve seam. Work other sleeve the same.

BODY: Starting at left sleeve seam, work sts of Left Front. Next row work the 38 (41) sts of Left Front, pick up and k 2 sts at underarm, k the 69 (75) sts of back, pick up and k 2 sts at underarm, work the 38 (41) sts of Right Front. Keeping 7 Moss Sts at each front edge, work on the 149 (161) sts to 5½ (6) inches from underarm then work 8 Moss St rows. Bind off in pattern.

CAP

KNITTING INSTRUCTIONS: Cast on 77 (85) sts for front edge. Work in Moss St for 8 rows then work in Stockinette St for 4 (4¼) inches from start, end with a p row.

BACK OF CAP: K 50 (55), k 2 tog, turn.
Row 1: Sl 1, p 23 (25), p 2 tog, turn.
Row 2: Sl 1, k 23 (25), k 2 tog, turn.
Repeat these 2 rows until 25 (27) sts remain, end with a p row. Break yarn.

NECKBAND: With free needle starting at front edge, pick up and k 30 (32) sts on one side, k the 25 (27) sts on needle, pick up and k 30 (32) sts on other side. Work 4 Moss St rows on the 85 (91) sts.

EYELETS: Work 2 (5) sts, k 2 tog, yo, * work 4 sts, k 2 tog, yo, repeat from * 12 times more, work to end of row. Work 3 more Moss St rows. Bind off in pattern.

CORD: With double yarn crochet a 14" chain. Draw through eyelets; then sew a small pompon to each end.

BOOTEES

KNITTING INSTRUCTIONS: Starting at sole, cast on 35 (39) sts.
Row 1: P 17 (19), place marker on needle, p 1, place 2nd marker on needle, p to end.
Inc 4 sts as follows:
Row 1: Inc 1 st in first st, k to st before marker, inc 1 st in next st, sl marker, k 1, sl marker, inc 1 st in next st, k to last st, inc 1 st in last st.
Row 2: P.
Repeat Rows 1 and 2 twice more, then repeat Row 1. K the 51 (55) sts for turning ridge.

INSTEP:
Row 1: K to st before marker, inc 1 st in next st, k 1, inc 1 st in next st, k to end.
Row 2: P.
Repeat Rows 1 and 2 twice more—57 (61) sts.
Dec Row: K to 3 sts before marker, sl 1, k 2 tog, psso, k 1, k 3 tog, k to end of row.
Next Row: P. Repeat last 2 rows 3 times more—41 (45) sts remain. Work 2 Moss St rows.

EYELETS: Work 3 (5) sts, k 2 tog, yo, * k 1 st, k 2 tog, yo, repeat from * 10 times more, work to end of row. Work 5 more Moss St rows. Bind off in pattern.
Fold sole in half and sew flat center seam then sew back seam. On Right Side starting at back seam, crochet 1 row of sc on turning ridge.

CORD: With double yarn, crochet a 28″ chain. Draw through eyelets then sew a small pompon to each end.

AFGHANS FOR BABY
(One Knitted, One Crocheted)

MATERIALS REQUIRED:
Columbia-Minerva Nantuk Precious (1 oz. skein)—5 skeins White; 4 skeins Contrasting Color (Yellow, Pink, Blue, or Green) #10 Knitting Needles for Reversible Knitted Afghan #5 or G Crochet Hook for Crocheted Afghan

STITCH GAUGE:
Reversible Knitted Afghan—9 sts = 2"   7 rows = 1"
Crocheted Afghan—7 dc = 2"   1 shell pattern = 1½"

REVERSIBLE KNITTED AFGHAN Shown at Left

MOSS STITCH PATTERN:
Row 1: K 1, * p 1, k 1, repeat from * across.
Repeat this row for Moss St.

Note: When changing colors, twist yarns to prevent a hole.

KNITTING INSTRUCTIONS: With White cast on 131 sts. Work in Moss St for 10 rows. Continue to work first and last 7 sts in White in Moss St for border, joining a separate strand of White for end border, working butterfly pattern on center 117 sts as follows:
Row 1: With White p 3, * k 3, p 3, repeat from * across.
Row 2: K 3, * p 3, k 3, repeat from * across.
Rows 3 and 5: With CC repeat Row 1.
Rows 4 and 6: Repeat Row 2.
Row 7: With White p 3, * k 1, drop next st 5 rows down, k the dropped st under the 5 strands and sl onto left-hand needle and k this st again, k 1, p 3, repeat from * across.
Row 8: Repeat Row 2.
Repeat these 8 rows 24 times more. With White repeat Rows 1 and 2 then work 10 rows in Moss St on all sts. Bind off.

AFGHANS FOR BABY
(Knitted Style at Left, Crochet Style at Right)

CROCHETED AFGHAN (Shown at Right)

SHELL PATTERN: With White chain desired length. Work 1 dc in 4th chain from hook, * skip 2 sts, 1 sc in next st, skip 2 sts, in next st work 1 dc, ch 1, 1 dc, ch 1 and 1 dc—shell. Repeat from * across, ending skip 2 sts, 1 sc in next st then work 1 dc, ch 1 and 1 dc in last st—half shell. Drop White and draw CC through loop on hook.

Row 2: With CC 1 sc in first st, * 1 dc, ch 1 and 1 dc in next sc—shell, 1 sc in center dc of next shell, repeat from * across ending 1 sc in last st. Drop CC and draw White through loop on hook.

Row 3: With White work pattern as on Row 1, working sc in ch 1 space of shell and shell in sc.

Repeat Rows 2 and 3 for shell pattern.

CROCHETING INSTRUCTIONS: With White ch 106. Work in shell pattern until there are 29 White pattern rows from start. Break CC strand and fasten.

BORDER:

Row 1: With White crochet 1 row of sc around the four sides of afghan, working 4 sc to each 2 rows of pattern and 3 sc in each corner to keep work flat. Join with a sl st, ch 3.

Row 2: 1 dc in each st around, working 5 dc in center st of each corner.

Row 3: Same as Row 2.

Row 4: With CC crochet 1 sc in each st around, working 3 sc in each corner.

Row 5: With White repeat Row 2.

Row 6: With CC repeat Row 4. Break yarn and fasten.

RABBIT

RABBIT

MATERIALS REQUIRED:
Coats & Clark's "Red Heart" Orlon Sayelle, 4 Ply, Art. E. 266
(1 oz. "Tangle-Proof" Pull-Out Skeins)
3 skeins of No. 230 Yellow
2 Skeins of No. 900 Melon
3 yds. of White
¼ yd. each of Black and Red
#4 Knitting Needles
1½ yds. of Blue "Boiltex" Rickrack (Art. 29)
Scraps of White, Black, Blue, and Tangerine Felt
Cotton Batting or Other Material for Stuffing

STITCH GAUGE: 5 sts = 1"   9 rows = 1"

BODY FRONT: Starting at center bottom with Melon, cast on 23 sts.
Row 1: K across.
Next 2 Rows: K across, casting on 11 sts at end of each row for back legs. Work Garter St (k each row) for pattern.
Work even for 14 rows.
Following 2 Rows: Bind off 11 sts at beg of each row, k remaining sts.
Next 2 Rows: K 2 tog, k remaining sts.
Work even for 12 rows.
Next 2 Rows: K across, casting on 8 sts at end of each row for front legs.
Work even for 12 rows.
Following 2 Rows: Bind off 6 sts at beg of row, k remaining sts.
Next 2 Rows: K 2 tog, k remaining sts.
Following Row: Work even.
Repeat last 3 rows 5 times more. Bind off loosely knitting the sts.
BODY BACK: Work as for front.

BACK PAW (Make 2): Starting at top of paw with Yellow, cast on 9 sts (ankle edge). Work even for 4 rows.
Next Row (back of paw): K across, casting on 4 sts at end of row.
Work even for 3½", ending at top of paw.
Following Row: Bind off 4 sts, k remaining sts.

Work even for 4 rows. Bind off loosely knitting the sts.

HEAD (Make 2): Starting at neck with Yellow, cast on 13 sts.
Next Row: Work even.
Following Row: Inc 1 st in first st, k across to within last st, inc 1 st in last st.

Repeat last 2 rows until there are 29 sts on needle work even for 18 rows. **Following Rows:** K 2 tog, k across to within last 2 sts, k 2 tog. **Next 2 Rows:** Work even. Repeat last 3 rows 5 times more. Bind off loosely, knitting the sts.

EAR (Make 2): Starting at base with Yellow, cast on 13 sts.
Row 1: K across to within last st, sl last st as if to purl.

Repeat Row 1 until piece measures 3¾".
Dec Row: K 1, k 2 tog, k across to within last 3 sts, sl 1, k 1, psso, sl last st as if to purl.

Repeat Row 1 and Dec Row alternately 4 times more.
Next Row: Repeat Row 1.
Last Row: Sl 1, k 2 tog, psso. Break off.

FINISHING: Fold one back paw in half and sew together, leaving ankle edges open. Stuff paw. Complete other back paw in same way.

Sew entire bottom edge of front and back together, then sew top edges of back legs, leaving outer edges open.

Insert ankle edge of paws into legs and sew in place. Stuff legs and bottom.

Sew side seams of body, then sew together front legs, leaving outer edges open.

Fold one front paw in half and sew together, leaving ankle edges open. Stuff paw. Complete other paw in same way. Sew paws to front legs.

Stuff body and front legs. Sew remaining side seams of body and stuff.

Sew side seams of head, leaving neck edge open. Stuff head.

Sew head to body. Sew ears to top of head, folding inside edges back ¾" as shown.

PAW CUFF (Make 4): Starting at narrow edge with Melon, cast on 3 sts.

Repeat Row 1 of ear, until piece measures 4". Bind off.

Place the pieces around top of each paw and sew narrow edges together.

NECK CUFF: Starting at narrow edge with Melon, cast on 4 sts. Repeat Row 1 of ear, until piece measures 5½" long.

Place the 5½" piece around neck and sew narrow edges together.

FACE: Cut eyes of Tangerine and Blue felt and sew in place 1½" apart and 2" down from top of head. Cut nose of Black felt and sew in place between eyes and 3" down from top of head. Embroider mouth with Red just below nose. Cut 2 pieces of Black, each 4" long; fold in half and sew fold to top of each eye.

POMPON (Make 2): Wind White yarn 11 times around 2 fingers. Tie these strands at center. Cut loops at each end and trim. Sew 1 pompon to each side of mouth. Make 1 more pompon with Yellow yarn by winding the yarn 20 times around 2 fingers and completing as for White pompon. Sew to center of back at bottom.

APRON: Using White felt, cut a small apron and trim with rickrack, using rickrack for ties.

JIFFY HORSE

JIFFY HORSE

(10" tall)

MATERIALS REQUIRED:
Coats & Clark's "Red Heart" Knitting Worsted 4 ply "Tangle-Proof" Pull-Out Skeins
   2 ozs. of No. 793 Coral and a few yards of No. 1 White; and
Coats & Clark's O.N.T. "Speed-Cro-Sheen" Mercerized Cotton,
Art. C. 44
   1 Ball of No. 12 Black
   A few inches of Red Embroidery Floss.
   #5 Knitting Needles
   Scraps of Black, Yellow, and Blue Felt
   Cotton Batting for Stuffing

PATTERN STITCH: Entire toy is worked in Garter St (k each row).

STITCH GAUGE: 9 sts = 2"   10 rows = 1"

FIRST HALF: Starting at front of head with White, cast on 9 sts. Work 12 rows in Garter St, increasing 1 st (to increase one st, k in front and back loop of same st) at end of every 4th row 3 times for shaping top edge of head—12 sts on needle. Break off White.

Attach Coral and continue to work in Garter St, increasing 1 st at end of every 4th row for top of head until there are 16 sts on needle, ending at bottom edge. Slip these 16 sts onto a stitch holder. Break off.

FRONT LEG: Starting at front edge with Coral, cast on 8 sts.
Row 1: K across, increasing 1 st in last st for upper edge of leg.
Row 2: K across row.
Rows 3 through 20: Repeat last 2 rows 9 more times—18 sts on needle.
Row 21: K across.
Row 22: Cast on 4 sts for chest and neck, k across row.
Rows 23 through 26: Repeat last 2 rows twice more—30 sts on needle.
Row 27: K across. Slip the 16 sts from holder onto left-hand needle, k across these 16 sts—46 sts.

Row 28: K across to within last 2 sts, k 2 tog—1 st decreased at leg edge.

Row 29: K 2 tog, k across.

Repeat last 2 rows 3 more times—38 sts.

Work even for 16 rows, ending at head edge.

Next Row: Bind off 24 sts, k across.

Work even over 14 sts until total length from front edge of leg section is 5¾", ending at bottom edge.

BACK LEG: Cast on 6 sts for back leg and work even for 24 rows. Bind off.

SECOND HALF: Work as for first half.

JOINING: Sew pieces together, leaving an opening for stuffing. Stuff firmly. Sew opening.

MANE: (Loop Ring) (Make 7): Wind Black "Speed-Cro-Sheen" 30 times around a 1½" piece of cardboard. With a separate strand, tie loops together at one end; slip off cardboard. Starting 3" from front edge, tack rings, evenly spaced, along top of head and down back of neck.

Cut a piece of Yellow felt 1½" x 2¼", gather at center to form a bow; holding down some strands of first ring, tack bow to top of head.

Cut 2 pieces of Black felt for ears, 1¾" wide and 3¾" long, and trim end to a point. Fold base in half and sew firmly in place, 1¼" from back edge of head.

Cut 2 oval-shaped pieces of Blue felt, ⅝" x 1¼", for eyes. Cut 2 circles of Black felt, ⅝" in diameter, for pupils. Sew pupils inside one end of ovals. Sew eyes in place. With Red embroidery floss, work a lazy daisy stitch ½" long at each side of face for nostrils.

TAIL: Cut 12 strands of "Speed-Cro-Sheen" 12" long; draw thru sts at top of back corner of body, having strands even. Divide into 3 equal parts and braid to within 1½" of end. Cover end of braid with a small piece of Yellow felt; sew in place.

STRIPED AFGHANS (One Knitted, One Crocheted)
(Approximate size 42" x 62")

MATERIALS REQUIRED:
Columbia-Minerva Reverie Yarn (1 oz. ball)—11 balls of
Color A
   7 balls of Color B
   3 balls of Color C
   #10-29" Circular Needle for Knitted Afghan
   #H or I Crochet Hook for Crocheted Afghan

STITCH GAUGE:
Knitted Afghan—4 sts = 1"   one pattern = 5" across
Crocheted Afghan—7 dc = 2"   one pattern = 4¾" across

KNITTED AFGHAN (Shown at Right)

PATTERN STITCH FOR COLOR A and COLOR B STRIPES:
Row 1: K 2 tog, * k 9, yo, k 1, yo, k 9, sl 1, k 2 tog, psso, repeat
from * 7 times more, k 9, yo, k 1, yo, k 9, sl 1, k 1, psso.
Row 2: P.

PATTERN STITCH FOR COLOR C STRIPE:
Row 1: With Color C work same as Row 1 above.
Row 2: K.
Row 3: P.
Row 4: K.

KNITTING INSTRUCTIONS: With Color A cast on 199 sts. Work
in stripe pattern as follows: * 4 rows of Color A, 4 rows of Color
B, 4 rows of Color A, 4 rows of Color B, 4 rows of Color A and 4
rows of Color C, repeat from * 9 times more, ending 4 rows of
Color A, 4 rows of Color B, 4 rows of Color A, 4 rows of Color B
and 4 rows of Color A. Bind off. On Right Side with Color A work
1 row of sc on side edges.

FRINGE: Wind Color A over 4" cardboard. Cut yarn at one end
Fold and knot 2 strands in every other st at each end of afghan.

[141]

STRIPED AFGHANS
(Crochet Style at Left, Knitted Style at Right)

CROCHETED AFGHAN Shown at Left

CROCHETING INSTRUCTIONS: With Color A ch 152.

Row 1 (Right Side): 1 sc in 2nd ch from hook, 1 sc in next 6 chs, * 3 sc in next ch, 1 sc in each of next 7 chs, skip 2 chs, 1 sc in each of next 7 chs, repeat from * across, ending 3 sc in next ch, 1 sc in each of last 7 chs, ch 3, turn.

Note: Always work in back loop of sts.

Row 2: Ch 3 counts as first st. Skip next st, 1 dc in each of next 6 sts, * 3 dc in next st, 1 dc in each of next 7 sts, skip 2 sts, 1 dc in each of next 7 sts, repeat from * 7 times more, ending 3 dc in next st, 1 dc in each of next 7 sts, draw Color B through last loop on hook, drop Color A, turn.

Row 3: With Color B ch 1, * 1 sc in next 7 sts, 3 sc in next st, 1 sc in next 7 sts, skip 2 sts, repeat from * 7 times more, ending 1 sc in next 7 sts, 3 sc in next st, 1 sc in next 7 sts, ch 3, turn.

Row 4: Counting ch 3 as first st, skip next st, 1 dc in next 6 sts, * 3 dc in next st, 1 dc in next 7 sts, skip 2 sts, 1 dc in next 7 sts, repeat from * across, ending 3 dc in next st, 1 dc in next 7 sts, draw Color A through last loop on hook, drop Color B.

Repeat Rows 3 and 4 for pattern, working stripe pattern as follows: * two rows of Color A, two rows of Color B, two rows of Color A, two rows of Color B, two rows of Color A and two rows of Color C, repeat from * 8 times more, ending two rows of Color A, two rows of Color B, two rows of Color A, two rows of Color B and two rows of Color A. Break yarn and fasten.

BORDER: Attach Color A on Right Side at one corner. Work shell pattern at side edge as follows: * 5 dc at top of dc row, 1 sc at top of next dc row, repeat from * to corner, break yarn and fasten. Work border at other edge the same.

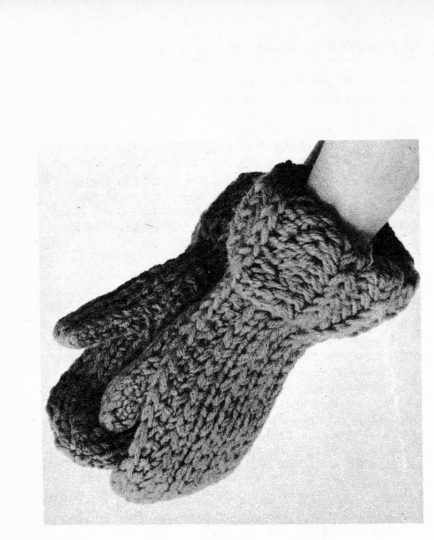

QUICK HUGE-CUFF MITTENS

QUICK HUGE-CUFF MITTENS

(Medium Size, Women's)

MATERIALS REQUIRED:

2 (2 oz.) Skeins of Columbia-Minerva Sayelle Nantuk Knitting Worsted

#11 Knitting Needles

1 "Hiawatha" Blunt-end Tapestry Needle

STITCH GAUGE: Slip St Pattern: 3 sts = 1"
For cuff: 1 pattern = 1½"

KNITTING INSTRUCTIONS:

Note: Mittens are worked with double strand of yarn throughout.

RIGHT MITTEN: Starting at cuff, cast on 20 sts.

Row 1: K 1, * yo, sl 1 (as if to purl), k 1, repeat from * across, ending k 2 instead of k 1.

Row 2: K 1, * yo, sl 1, k 2 tog, repeat from * across, ending k 1—29 sts.

Note: Always k tog the yo and sl st of previous row.

Repeat Row 2 until mitten measures 4" from start.

Next Row: K 1, * sl 1, k 2 tog, repeat from * across, ending sl 1.

Work in mitten pattern.

Row 1: Purl.

Row 2: * Sl 1, k 1, repeat from * across.

Rows 3 through 6: Repeat Rows 1 and 2 twice more.

Rows 7 and 8: P 10, sl remaining sts to a safety pin. Turn and k 4, sl the remaining 6 sts to another safety pin.

Work back and forth in Stockinette St on these 4 sts for 3", ending with a k row.

Next Row: P the 4 sts of thumb, p across the 10 sts from holder.

Work across all 20 sts in Sl St Pattern for 4", ending with a p row.

Dec Row: * K 2, k 2 tog, repeat from * across.

Next Row: P 15.

Dec Row: K 1, * k 2 tog, repeat from * across.

Next Row: P 8.

Cut yarn and draw thru remaining sts with tapestry needle.

LEFT MITTEN: Work same as right mitten through Row 6.

Row 7: P 4, sl remaining 16 sts to a safety pin.

Work back and forth in Stockinette St on these 4 sts for 3", ending with a k row.

Next Row: P 20 sts.

Finish remainder of mitten to correspond to right mitten.

FINISHING: With single strand of yarn, sew seam at side edge and side of thumb. Turn under 2" of cuff and sew lightly on Wrong Side at start of Sl St Pattern.

HOW TO CROCHET

BASIC CROCHET STITCHES: Crochet also is a very versatile needle art; articles produced range from the most delicate lingerie trimmings and highly styled outer garments through numerous household articles to the most intricate designs for altar laces.

There are several quite different types of crochet: the basic stitches, Irish crochet, afghan stitches, and filet. All are made with a hook.

Articles can be made heavy and warm (afghans and sweaters) or light and porous (laces), according to the size of hook and size of thread or yarn used.

Steel hooks are used for the finer threads, aluminum or plastic hooks for woolen yarns and for rug cotton.

STITCH GAUGE: The tightness or looseness of each stitch (and thus of the finished article) is determined by the size of hook used; and this is always chosen in relation to the size of thread or yarn to be used, modified somewhat by the tightness or the looseness desired. This tightness or looseness is called **Gauge,** and is influenced by one other element: **Tension,** which is the strain put upon the thread or yarn by the crocheter. Tension is a matter of nervous and muscular control of the fingers and is best regulated by always holding the work in the position which is most comfortable for *your* hands.

At the beginning of every set of instructions the proper **Stitch Gauge** for that piece of work is given, i.e., the number of stitches to the inch (a width measurement), and the number of rows or rounds to the inch (a length measurement). It is *necessary* that *you* get the *same* **Stitch Gauge** if your finished article is to be the size specified. Crochet a 3" square, using the Pattern Stitch, size of hook, thread or yarn specified in your instructions, press, then count the number of stitches to the inch and the number of rows to the inch. If you are crocheting *more* stitches to the inch or more rows to the inch, use a larger crochet hook; if *less* use a smaller crochet hook. As the work progresses some people automatically tighten or loosen the tension on their work. Check your **Stitch Gauge** frequently.

ABBREVIATIONS

Ch—Chain

Sc—Single Crochet

Sl St—Slip Stitch

Dc—Double Crochet

Inc—Increase

Dec—Decrease

St(s)—Stitches

Ch of Sc—Chain of Single Crochet

H dc—Half Double Crochet

D tr—Double Treble Crochet

Tr Tr—Treble Treble Crochet

Tog—Together

Yo—Yarn Over

R—Row

S—Same

Sk—Skip

Sp—Space

Tr—Treble Crochet

Rnd—Round

P—Picot

Beg—Beginning

Pr R—Previous Row or Rnd

Ch St—Chain Stitch

L Tr—Long Treble Crochet

* Repeat everything after asterisk [*] as many times as specified in instructions.

( ) Repeat everything within parentheses ( ) as many times as specified in instructions.

Abbreviations are usually listed at the beginning of every book of instructions. The presence of one or more asterisks [*] in the instructions indicates that the instructions following the symbol will be repeated a specified number of times, i.e., repeat from * 6 times (meaning 7 times in all), or repeat from * across row (or round). Occasionally, due to long and intricate directions, the instructions will read: repeat from * to * 6 times (in all). For many and varied repetitions, one [*] two [**] or three [***] asterisks are sometimes used.

Parentheses in the instructions indicate that the instructions within the parentheses are to be repeated a number of times, i.e., (ch 2, 3 dc in next sp) 4 times means to do everything within the parentheses 4 times in all.

TABLE OF STEEL HOOKS & THREAD SIZES

(Beginning with Smallest)

Thread	Steel Hook		Thread	Steel Hook
#150	#	15	#30	# 11 or 10
100		14	20	10, 9 or 8
80		13	10	7
70		13	Bedspread Cotton	5
60	12 or 13		Pearl Cotton	1
50	12 or 13		Straw Yarn	1 or 0
Tatting Cotton		12	Soft Chenille	0
40		11	Wired Chenille	00

Yarn	Hook	Yarn	Hook
Baby Yarn	Plastic #5	Knitting Worsted	Aluminum F
Angora	Plastic #5	Rug Cotton	Steel #5
Fingering Yarn	Plastic #6	Rug Wool	Aluminum G or H
Sport Yarn	Plastic #6	Rag Strips	Plastic G, H, J or K

BASIC STITCHES

CHAIN STITCH (ch)

The chain stitch is the basis of all crochet.

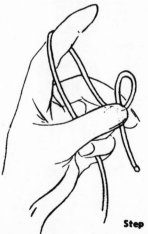

Step 1: To start a chain, place end of thread over and around outside of forefinger of Left Hand and over inside of other 3 fingers, leaving end dangle free for about 4". With the little finger grasp other thread securely where it falls on palm of hand. Hold this thread fairly taut, releasing it slightly each time as the thread is needed, and form loop between thumb and forefinger.

Step 1

Step 2: Take hook in Right Hand and insert hook thru loop and under thread between forefinger and middle finger. Twist hook until end of hook grasps the thread; now pull thread on hook and hook thru loop.

Step 2

Step 3: There is now one loop on hook; do not release thread between thumb and middle finger. Instead, insert the hook under thread again, grasp the thread with end of hook and pull the thread on hook, and hook thru loop (this is the first chain stitch).

Step 3

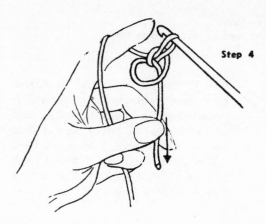

Step 4 **Step 4:** Now release loop between thumb and middle finger and pull end thread to tighten the first loop into a knot.

Step 5: Now hold work loosely between middle finger and thumb right under the hook, * twist hook on thread (this will be referred to as "thread over"), and pull thread thru loop on hook, repeat from * until chain is desired length.

Step 5

Note: In counting the stitches of a chain, every finished loop is counted, *but not the loop on the hook,* which is in fact part of whatever stitch is to be made next.

Foundation Chain

SINGLE CROCHET (sc)
Start in this instance with a foundation chain.

Step 1

Row 1: Insert hook in 2nd ch st from hook (not counting loop on hook), thread over hook and draw loop thru (2 loops now on hook), thread over hook and pull thru 2 loops on hook (Step 1 thru Step 5). * Insert hook in next ch st, (Step 6), thread over hook and draw loop thru, thread over

Step 2

Step 3

Step 4

Step 5

hook and draw loop thru 2 loops on hook, repeat from * across row (Illus. 1), ch 1, and turn (Illus. 2).

Row 2: 1 sc in each sc across row (Illus. 3). Ch 1, if turning to continue another row.

Step 6

Illus. 1

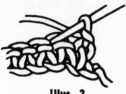

Illus. 2

Illus. 3

SLIP STITCH (sl st)

Insert hook in ch st or st, thread over hook and draw loop thru ch st or st and thru loop on hook. This is a flat st used for joining, strengthening an edge, retracing one's steps to a different position, or fastening off (Illus. 4).

Illus. 4

CHAIN OF SINGLE CROCHET (ch of sc)

Ch 2, 1 sc in 2nd ch st from hook (Step 1 thru Step 5), * insert hook under single top strand at LEFT edge of last sc made, thread over hook, pull thread thru (there are 2 loops on hook), thread over hook and thru the 2 loops on hook, repeat from * for desired length. This stitch is seldom used, although it provides a strong foundation chain with a well-finished edge (Illus. 5).

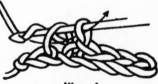

Illus. 5

DOUBLE CROCHET (dc)

Double crochet is twice as tall as single crochet; these 2 crochet stitches are the most popular and useful. Start with a foundation ch of any number of ch sts.

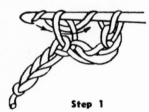

Step 1

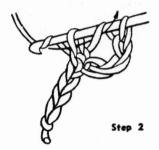

Step 2

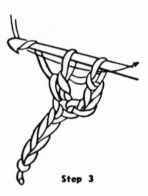

Step 3

Row 1: Thread over hook, insert hook in 4th ch st from hook, thread over hook and * draw loop thru ch st (Step 1), thread over hook and draw loop thru 2 loops on hook (Step 2), thread over hook and draw loop thru last 2 loops on hook (Step 3), thread over hook, insert hook in next ch st, repeat from * across row. Finish row with 1 dc in last ch st, ch 3 to turn (Illus. 6).

Row 2: Thread over hook, insert hook in next st, repeat from * of last row (Illus. 7).

Illus. 6

Illus. 7

HALF DOUBLE CRO-CHET (h dc)

Start with a foundation ch, thread over hook, insert hook in 3rd ch st from hook, * pull loop thru ch st, thread over hook and pull loop thru all 3 loops on hook, thread over, insert hook in next ch st, repeat from * across row (Illus. 8). At end of row, ch 2 to turn.

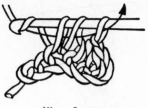

Illus. 8

Note: The h dc is taller than sc but not as tall as dc. The following 4 sts all increase in height.

Illus. 9

Step 1

Step 2

Step 3

TREBLE CROCHET (tr, tc, or tr c)

(Illus. 9) Start with a foundation ch, thread hook twice, insert hook in 6th ch st from hook and * draw the loop thru ch st (4 loops on hook), (thread over hook and draw loop thru 2 loops) 3 times, thread over hook twice, insert hook in next st, and repeat from * across row, ch 4 to turn.

[155]

DOUBLE TREBLE CROCHET (d tr)

Illus. 10

(Illus. 10) On a foundation ch, thread over hook 3 times, insert hook in 7th ch st from hook * and draw loop thru—5 loops on hook. (Thread over hook and draw loop thru 2 loops) 4 times, thread over hook 3 times, insert hook in next st, and repeat from * across row, ch 5 to turn.

TREBLE TREBLE CROCHET (tr tr)

Illus. 11

(Illus. 11) On a foundation ch, thread over hook 4 times, insert hook in 8th ch st from hook and * draw loop thru—6 loops on hook. (Thread over hook and draw loop thru 2 loops) 5 times, thread over hook 4 times, insert hook in next ch st, and repeat from * across row, ch 6 to turn.

LONG TREBLE CROCHET (l tr)

Illus. 12

(Illus. 12) This is a joining st seldom used except to bridge a wide distance. Thread over hook 6 times, insert hook in specified st or sp and draw loop thru—8 loops on hook. (Thread over hook and draw thru 2 loops) 7 times.

INCREASING (inc)

Increasing is usually done by making 2 sts in first st of Pr R, i.e., 2 sc in next sc, or 2 dc in next st. However, it is sometimes done at the beginning of a row by working first st of row in same place where turning ch started (this serves as 2 sts in first st, since turning ch is always regarded as first st of row).

DECREASING (dec)

Start with a foundation ch. **To Decrease sc:** Insert hook in 2nd ch st from hook and draw the loop thru, insert hook in next ch st and draw loop thru (3 loops on hook), thread over hook (Illus. 13) and draw loop thru all 3 loops on hook (Illus. 14).

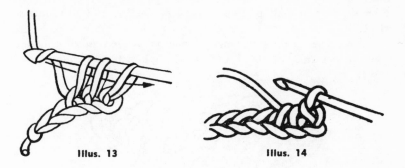

Illus. 13   **Illus. 14**

To Decrease dc: (Working, in this case, on a foundation ch, and after making 1 dc), thread over hook, (insert hook in next st and draw loop thru) 2 times, thread over hook and draw loop thru 2 loops on hook, thread over hook and draw loop thru last 3 loops on hook (Illus. 15 and Illus. 16).

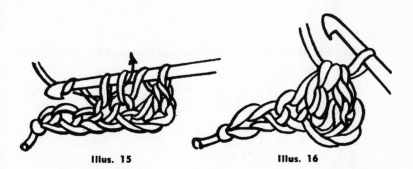

Illus. 15   **Illus. 16**

Note: These **10 Basic Stitches** (including **Increasing** and **Decreasing**) can be combined in various ways to form **Pattern Stitches** or can be used as they are in various combinations to form many useful and beautiful articles.

TRIANGLE
(Illus. 17)

Row 1: Ch 2, 1 sc in 2nd ch st from hook, ch 1, turn.
Row 2: 3 sc in sc of Pr R, ch 1, turn.
Row 3: 2 sc in first sc of Pr R, 1 sc in next sc, 2 sc in last sc, ch 1, turn.
Row 4: 2 sc in first sc, 1 sc in each of next 3 sc, 2 sc in last sc, ch 1.

Continue, making as many rows as desired in this manner (inc in first and last sts of each row, ch 1 to turn at beg of each row).

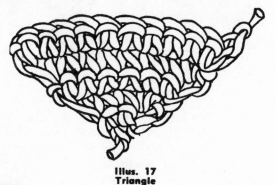

Illus. 17
Triangle

DIAMOND
Begin as for triangle, continue to desired width, then dec 1 st at beg and 1 st at end of each row (see dec of sc), ch 1 to turn until only 1 st remains.

RING
(Illus. 18) Ch 4 (Step 1) (or any given number), join to first ch st with a sl st (Step 2).

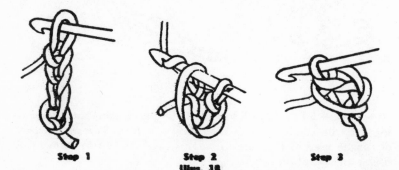

Step 1   **Step 2**   **Step 3**
Illus. 18

FLAT ROUND: Ch 4, join with sl st to form ring.

Rnd 1: 6 sc in ring. (Rounds can be joined or not as desired; however, joining makes an easily distinguishable seam line. If using joining, join with sl st to first sc, ch 1 to start next round. If working around and around, use a knitting marker, small safety pin, or bit of colored thread to mark beg of each round. It is an indispensable aid to counting.)

Rnd 2: 2 sc in each sc of Pr R (there are 12 sc on rnd, 6 sts have been increased).

Rnd 3: 2 sc in each sc of Pr R (there are 24 sc on rnd, 12 sts have been increased).

Rnd 4: 1 sc in each sc of Pr R (there are 24 sc, this is an even rnd, and there are no increases).

Rnd 5: (1 sc in next sc, 2 sc in next sc) 12 times, (there are 36 sc on Rnd, 12 sts have been increased).

Rnd 6: 1 sc in each sc of Pr R (36 sc, an Even Rnd).

Continue working in this manner, increasing in every 3rd, 4th, 5th st, or often enough to keep work flat, alternating Even Rnds with Increase Rnds.

CUPPED ROUND (For Calot): May be made in same manner, starting with 5 sc on Rnd 1, 10 sc on Rnd 2, 20 sc on Rnd 3, etc.

SIX-SIDED PIECE

Ch 4, join with sl st to form ring.

Rnd 1: 6 sc in ring.

Rnd 2: 2 sc in each sc of Pr R (12 sc on rnd).

Rnd 3: (1 sc in next sc, 2 sc in next sc) 6 times (18 sc on rnd).

Rnd 4: (1 sc in each of next 2 sc, 2 sc in next sc) 6 times (24 sc on rnd).

Rnd 5: Inc in every 4th st (30 sc on rnd).

Rnd 6: Inc in every 5th st (36 sc on rnd).

In this case increases always come over increases, and form corners. Continue in same manner, increasing 6 sts in each rnd, having 1 more st between the increases in each succeeding rnd.

SQUARE

Ch 4, join with sl st to form ring.

Rnd 1: Ch 1, working in back loop only of each st, 3 sc in each of the 4 ch sts of starting ring, do not join rnds, insert marker to denote beg and end of rnds.

Rnd 2: Working in back loop only of each sc, 1 sc in ch 1 of Pr R, 1 sc in next sc, 3 sc in next sc, (1 sc in each of next 2 sc, 3 sc in next sc) 3 times.

Rnd 3: Working in back loop only, (1 sc in each of next 4 sc, 3 sc in next sc) 4 times.

Continue working in this manner, having 2 more sc on each side in each succeeding rnd and always working 3 sc in center sc of corner of Pr R.

SQUARE worked from outside toward center

Start with chain of desired length, being careful to have it a multiple of 4 minus 1 (e.g.: $48 - 1 = 47$). Join to first ch st with sl st. Determine correct number of sc for each side of first row in following manner: add 1 to total number of ch sts, divide by 4, and subtract 2 (i.e.: $1 + 47 = 48 \div 4 = 12 - 2 = 10$), thus 10 sc for each of 4 sides.

Rnd 1: Ch 1, 1 sc in same ch st with sl st, 1 sc in each remaining ch st of one side (in this case 9 ch sts), sk 2 ch sts, 1 sc in each ch st of next side (in this case 10 ch sts), sk 2 ch sts 2 times, 1 sc in each ch st of last side (in this case 10 ch sts), sk last ch st, and begin next rnd by skipping first sc.

Continue working in this manner around and around, skipping first and last sc of Pr R *at each corner* and working 1 sc in all of the remaining sc of Pr R. At center, (decrease sc of 2 sides together) 2 times and fasten off. **Note:** Corners may be made in this manner if decreasing on square yoke.

CIRCLE worked from outside toward center

Start with ch of desired length, being careful to have it a multiple of 6 (e.g.: 48). Join to first ch with sl st. Determine correct number of sc for each side of first rnd in following manner: divide total by 6 and subtract 1 (i.e.: $48 \div 6 = 8 - 1 = 7$). Thus 7 sc for each of 6 sides.

Rnd 1: Ch 1, 1 sc in same ch st with sl st, 1 sc in each remaining ch st of one side (in this case 6 ch sts), sk 1 ch st, [1 sc in each ch st of next side (in this case 7 ch sts), sk 1 ch st] 5 times.

Continue, working in this manner around and around, decreasing 6 sts at *even* intervals in each rnd, (by skipping 1 sc for 6 times, being careful *not* to place dec directly over dec of Pr R). When 18 sc remain, dec (by skipping) every other sc for 2 rnds. At center, (dec sc tog) 2 times and fasten off. **Note:** Decreasing a curve in this manner is often used when working a double brim on a hat.

PICOT: (Illus. 19) (There are many variations of picot, of which the simplest and most often used is given. Ch 3, * 1 sl st in 3rd ch st from hook, ch 6, repeat from * for desired length. **Note:** Sometimes this is made in continuous ch as shown, but more often as a finish on the edge of doily or other crocheted articles, a ch 4 or 5 will give a longer picot.

Illus. 19 — Picot

POPULAR PATTERN STITCHES

Note: Make small sample of each pattern st in order to understand it. Number and multiple of foundation ch sts may vary. There are other pattern variations of single crochet; these given are the most popular.

RIBBED SINGLE CROCHET
(Illus. 20) Make ch desired length, turn.

Row 1: 1 sc in 2nd ch st from hook, 1 sc in each ch st to end of ch, ch 1, turn.
Row 2: (Always sk sp where turning ch started, unless you wish to increase.) Working in back loop only of sc of Pr R, 1 sc in each sc across row, 1 sc in turning ch, ch 1, turn. Repeat Row 2 until work is desired depth.

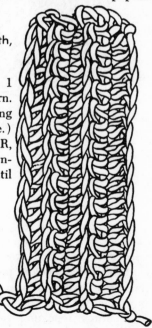

Illus. 20
Ribbed Single Crochet

DOUBLE SC

(Illus. 21) Make ch desired length, turn.

Row 1: Insert hook in 2nd ch st from hook and draw loop thru. *
Insert hook in next ch st, draw loop thru; thread over hook, draw
loop thru all 3 loops on hook. Insert hook in same ch st with last
loop and draw loop thru. Repeat from * across, end with ch 1,
fasten off, turn.

Row 2: Attach thread in first sc at right edge of *Right Side of
Work*, ch 1, * insert hook in *same* st (with last st) and draw loop
thru. Insert hook in next st and draw loop thru, thread over hook
and draw loop thru all 3 loops on hook, repeat from * across row,
crowding last Double-sc on by working in last st of Pr R and in
turning ch 1, ch 1, fasten off, turn. Repeat Row 2 until work is desired depth.

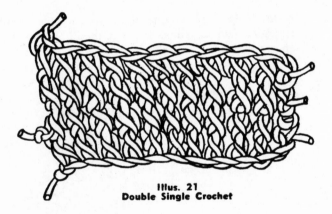

Illus. 21
Double Single Crochet

HIGH SC

(Illus. 22)

Make ch desired length, turn, thread over hook, insert hook in
3rd ch st from hook, draw loop thru same ch st and thread-over,
thread over hook and draw loop thru 2 loops on hook. * Thread
over hook, insert hook in next st and draw loop thru st and thread-
over, thread over hook and draw loop thru 2 loops on hook. Repeat
from * across row, end with last st in turning ch of Pr R, ch 1,
turn, continue repeating from * across next row.

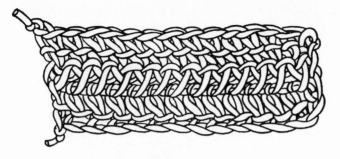

Illus. 22
High Single Crochet

HIGH SINGLE LOOP

(Illus. 23) Make ch desired length, turn.

Row 1: Insert hook in 4th ch st from hook, * draw loop thru, thread over hook and thru first loop, then thread over hook and draw loop thru 2 loops on hook, ch 1, sk 1 ch st. Insert hook in next ch st, repeat from * across, fasten off after last st, turn.

Row 2: Attach thread at right edge of *Right Side of Work*, ch 4, * insert hook between single strand and sc of Pr R, draw loop thru, thread over and thru first loop, thread over hook and draw loop thru 2 loops on hook, ch 1, repeat from * across; fasten off after last st, turn. Repeat Row 2 to desired depth.

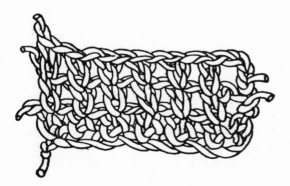

Illus. 23
High Single Loop

STAR ST

(Illus. 24) Make ch desired length, having an *uneven* number of sts, turn.

Illus. 24
Star Stitch

Row 1: Insert hook in 2nd ch st from hook and draw a loop thru, (insert hook in next ch st and draw up another loop) 3 times, thread over hook and draw loop thru all 5 loops on hook, * ch 1. Insert hook *between* single strand of ch 1 just made and the 5 loops which were taken off together (this is called the *eye* of a Star St), draw a loop thru. Insert hook in same ch st with last loop of previous Star St and draw a loop thru, (insert hook in next ch st and draw a loop thru) 2 times, thread over hook and draw loop thru all 5 loops on hook, ch 1, repeat from * across row, fasten off, turn.

Row 2: Attach thread at right edge of *Right Side of Work* in last ch st of foundation ch (not loop of Star St), ch 2. Insert hook in same ch st where thread was attached and draw loop thru. Then insert hook in back strand *only* of last loop of Star St and draw the loop thru, and then insert hook in eye of next Star St and draw loop thru. Insert hook in back strand *only* of last loop of next Star St and draw loop thru, thread over hook and draw loop thru all 5 loops on hook, ch 1. * Insert hook in eye of same Star St (just made) and draw loop thru, insert hook in back strand *only* of same st with last loop of previous Star St and draw loop thru; insert hook in eye of next Star St and draw loop through, insert hook in back strand *only* of last loop of next Star St and draw loop thru, thread over hook and draw loop thru all 5 loops on hook, ch 1. Repeat from * across, *crowding* last Star St in by working the 4th loop into the back strand *only* of the center and 5th loop in the eye of the center of last Star St of Pr R, fasten off. Repeat Row 2 to the desired depth.

KNOT STITCH

(Illus. 25) Make ch desired length (having multiple of 5 sts.)

Row 1: * Draw up a long loop (about ½" to ¾", according to size of thread or yarn), thread over hook (Step 1) and draw a short loop thru long loop, insert hook between long loop and single strand (to the left) (Step 2), thread over hook and draw loop thru, thread over hook (Step 3) and draw loop thru 2 loops on hook (Single Knot St made). Repeat from * once more (Double Knot St, Illus. 26, made), sk 4 ch sts of foundation ch, 1 sc in next ch st. Repeat from first * across row, end with 1 sc in last ch st, make 1 Double and 1 Single Knot St to turn.

Row 2: * 1 sc between first long loop and single strand of first Double Knot St of Pr R (to right of knot), 1 sc between next single strand and long loop of same Double Knot St (to left of same Knot), make Double Knot St and repeat from * across, turn as in Row 1. **Note:** An alternate way of making this st is sometimes used and the difference comes in Row 2: * 1 sc in sc at center of Double Knot St of Pr R, make Double Knot St and repeat from * across, turn same as in Row 1.

Illus. 25
Knot Stitch

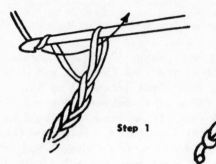

Step 1

Step 2

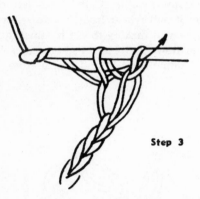

Step 3

LOOP STITCH

(Illus. 26) Usually worked on foundation of sc, with Wrong Side of work facing you.

Rnd 1: Insert hook in first sc, * draw up loop, wrap yarn around finger of left hand once, without dropping loop on finger, insert hook behind yarn and thru loop on finger (Step 1) and draw loop thru 1 loop on hook. Insert hook in front of loop on finger and back of yarn (Step 2) and draw yarn through remaining 2 loops on hook, drop long loop off finger. Insert hook in next sc and repeat from * around, j with sl st to first Loop St made.

Repeat Rnd 1 four times, fasten off.

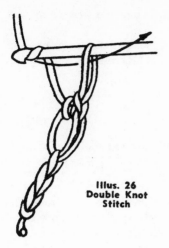

**Illus. 26
Double Knot
Stitch**

Step 1

Step 2

TWIN DC

(Illus. 27) Make ch desired length (having multiple of 2), turn, 1 dc in 4th ch st from hook.

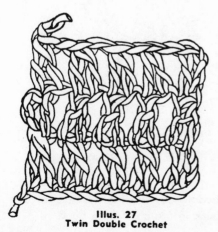

**Illus. 27
Twin Double Crochet**

Row 1: * Ch 1, thread over hook, insert hook in next ch st and draw loop thru, thread over hook and draw loop through 2 loops on hook. Thread over hook, insert hook in next ch st and draw loop thru, thread over hook and draw loop thru 2 loops on hook, thread over hook and draw loop thru all 3 loops on hook. Repeat from * across, ch 5, turn.

Note: In *any dc pattern* the turning ch 3 counts as *first dc* of next row.

Row 2: 1 dc in first dc of Pr R, * ch 1, make Twin-dc in ch 1 sp and in next Twin-dc of Pr R, repeat from * across, ch 3, turn. Repeat Row 2 to desired depth.

CROSSED DC

(Illus. 28) Make ch desired length (having multiple of 3 + 4), turn, 1 dc in 4th ch st from hook.

Row 1: * Ch 1, sk 2 ch sts, 1 dc in next ch st; working *around* dc just finished, make 1 dc in previous ch st (the second ch st skipped), repeat from * across, ch 3, turn.

Row 2: 1 dc in sp where ch 3 started, * ch 1, sk ch 1 sp and 1 dc of Pr R, 1 dc in next dc; working around last dc, make 1 dc back into skipped dc, repeat from * across, ch 3, turn. Repeat Row 2 to desired depth.

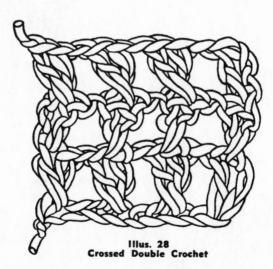

Illus. 28
Crossed Double Crochet

BUNDLE DC

(Illus. 29) Make ch desired length (having multiple of 3), turn, thread over hook, insert hook in 6th ch st from hook.

Row 1: * Draw loop thru (drawing it up to about ½" long), thread over hook, insert hook in same ch st and draw loop thru (slightly long, as before), thread over hook and draw a loop thru all 5 loops on hook, ch 2, sk 2 ch sts of foundation ch, thread over hook, insert hook in next ch st and repeat from * across, end with 1 dc in last ch st, fasten off, turn.

Row 2: Attach thread to right edge of Right Side of work in 2nd ch st before first Bundle-dc, ch 5, * thread over hook, insert hook *under main body* of Bundle-dc of Pr R from right to left and draw loop thru, thread over hook, insert hook again in same place and draw loop thru, then thread over hook and draw loop thru all 5 loops on hook, ch 2, repeat from *, end with 1 dc in end dc, fasten off, and turn. Repeat Row 2 to desired depth. **Note:** This st is sometimes made in the same manner but using a dc (single), in which case it is called a Post and is usually used as an overlay on a simple sc pattern so that the **Posts** form raised ridges.

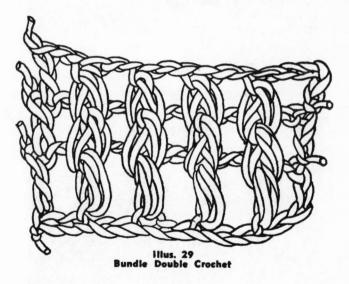

Illus. 29
Bundle Double Crochet

POPCORN

(Illus. 30) (This is the most popular overlay stitch, and is given here on a Ribbed-sc Pattern background.) Make ch desired length (having multiple of 5 + 1), turn.

Row 1: 1 sc in 2nd ch st from hook, 1 sc in each ch st across, ch 1, turn.

Row 2: (Sk sp where ch 1 started), working in back loop *only*, 1 sc in each sc of Pr R, ch 1, turn.

Row 3: Repeat Row 2.

Row 4: Working in back loop *only*, 1 sc in each of next 2 sc, 5 dc in front loop of 4th sc of Row 1, remove hook from loop of 5th dc, insert hook thru top of first dc and pull loop of 5th dc thru first dc, ch 1 to close the Popcorn, * sk 1 sc of Pr R, working in back loop only 1 sc in each of next 5 sc, sk 5 sc of Row 1, Popcorn (5 dc) in *front* loop only of next sc, repeat from * across, end with 1 sc in turning ch, ch 1, turn.

Row 5: Sk sp where ch 1 started, working in back loop *only*, 1 sc in each sc and in closing ch 1 of each Popcorn, end with 1 sc in turning ch 1, turn.

Row 6: Sk sp where ch 1 started, working in back loop *only*, 1 sc in each of first 5 sc, * Popcorn in 3rd st of 5 sc group of Row 3 which falls between Popcorns on Row 4, sk 1 sc of Pr R, working in back loop only 1 sc in each of next 5 sc, repeat from * across, end with 1 sc in turning ch, ch 1, turn.

Row 7: Repeat Row 5.

Row 8: Repeat Row 4.

Row 9. Repeat Row 5.

Row 10: Repeat Row 6.

Continue in this manner, alternating positions of Popcorns.

Note: Popcorns are sometimes made of tr, and various numbers of sts (e.g., 3 or 7).

Illus. 30 — Popcorn

CLUSTER
(Illus. 31)

Make ch desired length (having multiple of 4), holding back on hook last loop of ch st and of each dc, make 4 dc in 4th ch st from hook in following manner: (thread over hook, insert hook in ch st and draw loop through, thread over hook and draw loop through 2 loops *only*) 4 times, thread over hook and draw loop through all 5 loops on hook, * ch 3 (first ch st closed Cluster), sk 3 ch sts, holding back on hook last loop of last ch st and of each dc make a 5 dc Cluster in next ch st (noting that there are now 6 loops to be taken off together in top of Cluster), repeat from * across, fasten off. **Note:** The number of sts in a Cluster may vary, and they may be made of tr or dtr, and they are sometimes used as an overlay stitch to create a dotted effect.

Illus. 31 — Cluster

PUFF STITCH
(Illus. 32)

Make ch desired length (having multiple of 4), turn, thread over hook, insert hook in 4th ch st from hook and draw up a loop ½" high, (thread over hook, insert hook in same ch st and draw up loop ½" high) 3 times, thread over hook and draw loop thru all 9 loops on hook (Illus. 33), * ch 3 (first ch st closes Puff), sk 3 ch sts, thread over hook, insert hook in next ch st and draw up loop ½" high, (thread over hook, insert hook in same ch st and draw up loop ½" high) 3 times, thread over hook and pull loop thru all 9 loops on hook, repeat from * across, fasten off.

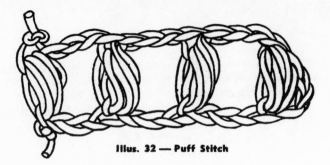

Illus. 32 — Puff Stitch

Illus. 33

5 DC SHELL

(Illus. 34) Make foundation ch of desired length (having multiple of 6 + 4), turn.

Row 1: 2 dc in 4th ch st from hook (half Shell), sk 2 ch st, 1 sc in next ch st, * sk 2 ch sts, 5 dc in next ch st (Shell), sk 2 ch sts, 1 sc in next ch st, repeat from * across, end with 3 dc in last ch st (half Shell), ch 1, turn.

Row 2: 1 sc in first dc of Pr R, * sk 2 dc, Shell (of 5 dc) in next sc, sk 2 dc, 1 sc in center dc of next Shell of Pr R, repeat from * across, end with 1 sc in top of half Shell, ch 3, turn.

Row 3: 2 dc in first sc of Pr R (half Shell), * 1 sc in center dc of next Shell, Shell in next sc, repeat from * across, end with half Shell (of 3 dc) in last sc, ch 1, turn. Repeat Rows 2 and 3 alternately to desired depth. **Note:** This same type of Shell is made with tr or with a different number of dc (e.g., 3 or 7).

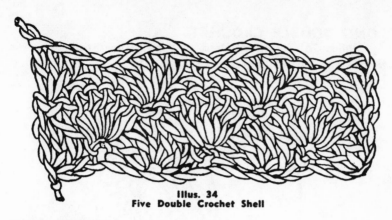

Illus. 34
Five Double Crochet Shell

RICE STITCH
(Illus. 35)

Make ch of desired length, turn, holding back on hook last loop of ch and of each tr make 2 tr in 5th ch st from hook in the following manner: * thread over hook twice, ** insert hook in 5th ch st and draw loop thru, thread over hook and draw loop thru 2 loops on hook, thread over hook and draw loop thru next 2 loops on hook, thread over hook twice, insert hook in same ch st and draw loop thru, thread over hook and draw loop thru 2 loops on hook, thread over hook and draw loop thru next 2 loops on hook, thread over and draw loop thru all 3 loops on hook, ch 1 to close (Single Rice St made), ch 4, repeat from * once more, sk 4 ch sts of foundation ch, 1 sc in next ch st (Double Rice St made), thread over hook twice, sk 4 ch sts, repeat from ** across ch. **Note:** This stitch is not usually used as an allover Pattern; when it is used, make 1 Double and 1 Single Rice St to turn at end of each row.

Illus. 35 — Rice Stitch

LONG DOUBLE CROCHET

(Illus. 36) Sometimes used on edge of an article to give a fringed effect if fine thread is used.

Illus. 36
Long Double Crochet

Make ch desired length, insert hook in 6th ch st from hook, *
pull up a *long* loop and a *long* thread over, hold loop and thread
securely with thumb and forefinger where they come out of st,
thread over hook, work off 2 loops, thread over, work off remaining 2 loops, insert hook in next ch st and repeat from *.

DESIGNS FOR CROCHETING

AFGHANS FOR BABY

STRIPED AFGHANS

PONCHOS PLUS

Illustrations and instructions for the above designs can be found in the knitting section on pages 131, 141 and 49, respectively.

THE PRISCILLA AFGHAN
(Approximately 54" x 72")

MATERIALS REQUIRED:
16 ozs. each of 4 shaded colors in Lion. Brand Knitting Worsted
#00 Crochet Hook

PLAN: This afghan is started at center with 11 squares, each square attached to one another in a diamond-shape fashion. The Ripple Pattern is then worked onto the point of each square, working downwards.

CROCHETING INSTRUCTIONS:

SQUARE FOR CENTER STRIP:
Row 1: With 1st color ch 6, join with a sl st to form a ring, ch 3, dc 3 into ring * ch 2, dc 4 into ring *. Repeat between stars 2 more times, ch 2, join with sl st to top of ch 3 at beg of row. Sl st across each st of row below, sl st into corner sp.
Row 2: Ch 3, turn, * dc in each of next 4 sts, dc 1, ch 2, dc 1 into corner sp *, repeat between stars twice, dc 1 in each of next 4 sts, dc 1 into sp, ch 2, join with a sl st to ch 3 at beg of row. Sl st across each st of row below, sl st into corner sp. Change to 2nd color.

Row 3: Ch 3, turn, * dc in each of next 6 sts, dc 1, ch 2, dc 1 into corner sp *, repeat between stars twice, dc 1, in each of next 6 sts, dc 1 into corner sp, ch 2, join with a sl st to ch 3 at beg of row. Sl st across each st of row below, sl st into corner sp, ch 3, turn.

Row 4: * Dc 1 in each of next 8 sts, dc 1, ch 2, dc 1 into corner sp *, repeat from * to * twice, dc 1 in each of next 8 sts, dc 1 into corner sp, ch 2, join with a sl st to ch 3 at beg of row. Make 10 more squares same way, join each square in diamond fashion.

RIPPLE PATTERN: With 3rd color, join yarn at corner ch sp.

Row 1: Ch 3, sk next st, * dc 1 in each of next 9 sts, picking up the back thread only, dc 1, ch 2, dc 1 into point sp formed by square, dc 1 in each of next 9 sts, picking up the back thread only, sk 2 sts *, repeat between stars across the next 10 squares, ending row with dc into ch sp of last square, ch 3 turn.

Row 2: Sk 1 dc on last row, * dc 1 into each of next 9 sts, picking up the back thread only, dc 1, ch 2, dc 1, into point sp, dc 1 in each of next 9 sts, picking up the back thread only, sk 2 sts *, repeat from * to * across row.

Change to 4th color, work 2 rows same way as Row 2 of Ripple Pattern.

Note: Follow this Pattern, shading the colors as directed in the color chart. When work measures 36" from center, end off. Join 3rd color to 2nd half of center square and follow instructions in above manner.

BORDER: With first color, join at any corner, sc 1 into corner st, ch 4, sk 2 rows, sc into next st, repeat all along side edge to next corner. Ch 4, sk 4 sts sc 1 into space between 4th and 5th st, ch 4, sk 4 sts, sc into space between 8th and 9th st, ch 4, sk 2 sts, sc 1 into point, ch 4, sk 2 sts, sc into sp between 2nd and 3rd st, ch 4, sc 1 into sp between 6th and 7th st, ch 4, sc 1 into center sp.

Repeat across each point.

Repeat in above manner all around.

Join 2nd color. * Ch 4, interlace as follows, sl hook from the chains just made, insert hook under ch of Pr R and pull loop thru the chain *. Repeat between stars all around.

Note: This is a crocheted afghan. However, instructions for those who desire to knit are as follows:

THE PRISCILLA AFGHAN

KNITTING INSTRUCTIONS:

With #10 14″ knitting needles and 4th color, cast on 231 sts.

Row 1: Knit all sts.

Row 2: * K 2 tog, k 8, k 1, p 1, k 1 into next st (point increase), k 8, k 2 tog *. Repeat between stars across row.

Repeat Rows 1 and 2 once more.

Change colors every 4th row throughout the entire afghan for 72″ in length.

BORDER: Work same border pattern as on crochet afghan.

COLOR CHART

ROSE AND RED COMBINATION:

First Color—Pink	Third Color—Cardinal
Second Color—Ash Rose	Fourth Color—Garnet

BROWN AND GREEN COMBINATION:

First Color—Emerald Green	Third Color—Brick
Second Color—Tile	Fourth Color—Wood Brown

GRANNY'S HEIRLOOM AFGHAN

GRANNY'S HEIRLOOM AFGHAN

MATERIALS REQUIRED:

Coats & Clark's "Red Heart" Knitting Worsted, 4 Ply, Art. E. 234 (4-oz. "Tangle-Proof" Pull-Out Skeins)

8 skeins of No. 12 Black and 7 skeins of No. 970 Greens

"G" Crochet Hook

Afghan = 48" x 72"   Motifs = 6" square

CROCHETING INSTRUCTIONS:

MOTIF (Make 96): Starting at center with Greens, ch 5. Join with sl st to form ring.

Rnd 1: Ch 3, 2 dc in ring, (ch 2, 3 dc in ring) 3 times; ch 2. Join with sl st to top of ch-3.

Rnd 2: Sl st in next 2 dc and in next sp, ch 3, in same sp make 2 dc, ch 2—corner sp—and 3 dc; (ch 1, in next sp make 3 dc, ch 2—corner sp—and 3 dc) 3 times; ch 1. Join as before. Break off and fasten.

Rnd 3: Attach Black to any corner sp, ch 3; in same sp make 2 dc, ch 2, and 3 dc, (ch 1, 3 dc in next ch-1 sp, ch 1; in next corner sp make 3 dc, ch 2, and 3 dc) 3 times; ch 1, 3 dc in last ch-1 sp, ch 1. Join. Break off and fasten.

Rnd 4: Attach Greens to any corner sp, ch 3; in same sp make 2 dc, ch 3, and 3 dc; ch 1, (in each ch-1 sp make 3 dc, ch 1 to next corner; in next corner sp make 3 dc, ch 2, and 3 dc; ch 1) 3 times; make 3 dc, ch 1, in each of the remaining ch-1 sps. Join. Break off and fasten.

Rnd 5: With Black repeat Rnd 4.

JOINING: With Black sew 8 x 12 Motifs neatly together.

BORDER:

Rnd 1 (Right Side): With Black sc closely around, making 3 sc in each corner. Join to first sc. Turn.

Rnd 2 (Wrong Side): Sl st in each sc around. Join. Break off and fasten. Block to measurements.

SCALLOPED TOILET SEAT COVER AND BATHROOM RUG

SCALLOPED TOILET SEAT COVER AND
BATHROOM RUG

MATERIALS REQUIRED:
American Thread Company "Aunt Lydia's" Heavy Rug Yarn
3 Skeins Dk. Rose
1 Skein each Lt. Rose and Old Rose
#13 Wooden Crochet Hook or Aluminum Hook Size K

SCALLOPED TOILET-SEAT COVER:

Rnd 1: With Lt. Rose ch 4, join to form ring, ch 1, 12 sc in ring, join.

Rnd 2: Ch 1, working in back loop of st, 2 sc in each sc, join.

Rnd 3: Ch 1, sc in same sp, working thru back loop of st and the loop in back of st, * ch 2, sk 2 sc, sc in next sc, repeat from * all around, ch 2, join.

Rnd 4: Ch 1, * 1 sc, 5 dc, 1 sc in next loop, ch 1, repeat from * all around, join.

Rnd 5: * Ch 4, sc in ch-1 sp between 2 sc, repeat from * all around, join.

Rnd 6: * 1 sc, 7 dc, 1 sc in next loop, ch 1, repeat from * all aound, join.

Rnd 7: * Ch 3, sc in loop in back of center dc of next dc group, ch 3, sc in next ch-1 space, repeat from * all around, ch 3, join, cut yarn.

Rnd 8: Attach Old Rose in any loop and work same as 4th round.

Rnd 9: Same as 5th round.

Rnd 10: Same as 4th round.

Rnd 11: Same as 5th round, cut yarn.

Rnd 12: Attach Dk. Rose in any loop and work same as 6th round.

Rnd 13: Repeat 5th round.

Rnd 14: Same as 12th round.

Rnd 15: Ch 4, sc in next ch-1 sp, repeat from * 9 times, cut yarn.

Rnd 16: Attach Dk. Rose in 1st ch-4 loop, 1 sc, 7 dc, 1 sc in same loop, 1 sc, 7 dc, 1 sc in each of the next 9 loops, sl st in ch-1 space with sc of Pr R.

Rnd 17: * Ch 3, sc in center dc of next dc group, ch 3, sc in next ch-1 space, repeat from * all around, ch 3, join.

Rnd 18: * 1 sc, 7 dc, 1 sc in next loop, ch 1, repeat from * all around, join.

Rnd 19: Same as 5th round.

Rnd 20: Same as 18th round.

Rnd 21: Same as 17th round.

Rnd 22: Same as 4th round.

Rnd 23: Same as 5th round.

Rnd 24: Work 5 sc in each loop all around, join.

Rnd 25: Ch 1, 1 sc in each sc, join.

Rnd 26: Ch 1, sc in same space, * ch 1, sk 1 sc, sc in next sc, repeat from * all around, ch 1, join, cut yarn.

CORD: Crochet a chain long enough to go all around seat cover and lace thru beading.

SCALLOPED BATHROOM RUG

(Approximately 24" in diameter)

MATERIALS REQUIRED:
American Thread Company "Aunt Lydia's" Heavy Rug Yarn
2 Skeins each Lt. Rose and Old Rose
4 Skeins Dk. Rose
#13 Wooden Crochet Hook or Aluminum Hook Size K

Rnd 1: With Lt. Rose ch 4, join to form ring, ch 1, 12 sc in ring, join.

Rnd 2: Working in back loops of each st, 2 sc in each sc, join.

Rnd 3: Ch 1, 1 sc in each sc, join.

Rnd 4: Ch 1, working through back loop of st and the loop in back of st, sc in same space, ch 3, * skip 2 sc, sc in next sc, ch 3, repeat from * all around, ch 1, join.

Rnd 5: * Ch 1, 1 sc, 5 dc, 1 sc in next loop, repeat from * all around, ch 1, join in 1st sc.

Rnd 6: Ch 4, sc in ch-1 space between scallops, repeat from beg all around, join.

Rnd 7: * 1 sc, 7 dc, 1 sc in next loop, ch 1, repeat from * all around, join.

Rnd 8: * Ch 3, sc in loop in back of center dc of next dc group, ch 3, sc in ch-1 space, repeat from * all around, join.

Rnd 9: * 1 sc, 5 dc, 1 sc in next loop, ch 1, repeat from * all around, join.

Rnd 10: Same as Rnd 6, cut Lt. Rose.

Rnd 11: Attach Old Rose and work same as Rnd 5.

Rnd 12: Same as Rnd 6.

Rnd 13: Same as Rnd 7.

Rnd 14: Same as Rnd 8.

Rnd 15: * 1 sc, 4 dc, 1 sc in next loop, ch 1, repeat from * all around, join.

Rnd 16: Same as Rnd 6.

Rnd 17: Same as Rnd 15.

Rnd 18: Same as Rnd 6, cut Old Rose.

Rnd 19: Attach Dk. Rose and work same as Rnd 15.

Rnd 20: Same as Rnd 6.

Rnd 21: Same as Rnd 9.

Next 6 Rounds: Repeat the last 2 rounds 3 times, cut yarn.

BATHROOM SET

BATHROOM SET

(Rug: 26" x 36")

MATERIALS REQUIRED:
Coats & Clark's O.N.T. Rug Yarn, Art. C. 205
16 skeins for Rug
4 skeins for Seat Cover of No. 44 Rose
"J" Crochet Hook

STITCH GAUGE: 5 sts = 2"

CROCHETING INSTRUCTIONS:

RUG: Starting at narrow end, make a chain 25" long, having 11 ch to 4".

Row 1: Sc in 2nd ch from hook and in each ch across until row measures 24". Cut off remaining chain. Ch 4, turn.

Row 2: Sk first sc, *working in back loop only throughout*, tr in each sc across. Ch 1, turn.

Row 3: Insert hook in back loop of first tr and in free loop of first sc on preceding row, and complete 1 sc; * make 1 sc thru back loop of next tr and free loop of next sc. Repeat from * across, ending with sc in top of turning chain and free loop of last sc. Ch 1, turn.

Row 4: Sc in each sc across. Ch 1, turn.

Row 5: Repeat Row 4. Ch 4, turn.

Repeat Rows 2 through 5 for Pattern. Work in Pattern until length is about 34", ending with Row 3. Break off and fasten.

BORDER:

Rnd 1: Attach yarn to any corner, 2 sc in same place, sc closely around, making 3 sc in each of next 3 corners and ending with sc in same corner as first 2 sc. Join with sl st to first sc.

Rnds 2 and 3: Ch 1, 2 sc in joining, sc in each sc around, making 3 sc in center sc of 3-sc group at each corner, ending with sc in same place as first sc. Join as before. Break off at end of Rnd 3.

SEAT COVER: Starting at back edge, ch 17 to measure 7".
Row 1: Sc in 2nd ch from hook and in each ch across—16 sc. Ch 1, turn.

Rows 2 and 3: Repeat 2 and 3 of Rug.

Row 4: 2 sc in first sc, sc in each sc across, 2 sc in last sc—*1 sc increased at each end.* Ch 1, turn.

Row 5: Sc in each sc across. Ch 4, turn. Repeat Rows 2 thru 5 of seat cover for pattern. Work in pattern until there are 26 sts on row. Omitting the increases on Row 4, continue in Pattern until total length is about 9", ending with Row 3. There should be 8 ribs completed.

Next Row: Draw up a loop in each of next 2 sc, and draw thru all loops on hook-1 sc decreased; sc in each sc across to within last 2 sc, dec 1 sc over last 2 sc. Ch 1, turn. Continue in Pattern, decreasing 1 st at each end on every Row 4 of Pattern until 20 sts remain on row, ending with Row 4.

Row 5: Decreasing 1 st at each end, sc across—18 sc. Ch 4, turn. Work Rows 2 and 3 of Pattern.

Next Two Rows: Decreasing 2 sc at each end, sc across. (To *dec 2 sc,* draw up a loop in each of next 3 sc, and draw thru all loops on hook. Work Rows 2 and 3 over remaining 10 sts. Break off and fasten.

BORDER:

Rnd 1: With Right Side facing, attach yarn to first ch of starting chain, 3 sc in same place, sc in each of next 14 ch, 3 sc in corner ch; working along end of sc rows, sc over end sc of next 2 rows. Repeat from * across, sc in each sc across last row; work across end of rows to correspond with opposite side. Join with sl st to first sc.

Rnds 2 and 3: Ch 1, sc in joining and in each sc around, making 3 sc in center sc of each 3-sc group. Join.

Next 4 Rnds: Ch 1, sc in joining and in each sc around. Join.

Rnd 8: Ch 1, sc in joining, * ch 3, skip 3 sc, sc in next sc. Repeat from * around, ending with ch 3. Join to first sc. Break off and fasten.

Make a chain 54" long and draw thru loops.

SUNFLOWER

MATERIALS REQUIRED:
Coats & Clark's O.N.T. "Speed-Cro-Sheen" Mercerized Cotton:

For Sunflower: 1 Ball of No. 10-A Canary Yellow; 18 yards each of No. 12 Black and No. 48 Hunter's Green

For Pansy: 1 Ball each of No. 10-A Canary Yellow and No. 12-A Blue Sparkle; 15 yards of No. 48 Hunter's Green

For Dahlia: 1 Ball of No. 126 Spanish Red; 15 yards each of No. 131 Fudge Brown and No. 48 Hunter's Green

#1 and #0 (zero) Milwards Steel Crochet Hooks

A Piece of Felt to Be Used as Backing for Each Pot Holder

3 Bone Rings

SUNFLOWER POT HOLDER

CROCHETING INSTRUCTIONS:
FLOWER: Starting at center with Black, ch 5. Join with sl st to form ring.

Rnd 1: Ch 1, 11 sc in ring. Do not join.

Rnd 2: Ch 1, 4 sc in next sc, drop loop from hook, insert hook from front to back in first sc of 4-sc group and draw dropped loop through, ch 1 tightly—**pc st made;** make 1 pc st in each sc around —11 pc sts.

Rnd 3: * Sc in top of next pc st, pc st in the ch-1 sp between this and next pc st. Repeat from * around. Join to first sc. Break off and fasten.

PETALS: Attach Yellow to joining of last rnd.

Rnd 1: Ch 1, sc in same place, (ch 13, sl st in 2nd ch from hook and in each of next 10 ch, ch 1, sk next pc st, sc in next sc) 10 times; ch 13, sl st in 2nd ch from hook and in next 10 ch, ch 1. Join to first sc.

Rnd 2: * Skip next ch, picking up the free loop of the ch, dc in each of next 8 ch, h dc in next ch, sc in next ch, 3 sc in next ch; working along opposite side of same ch and using the same loop used previously for the sl st, sc in next ch, h dc in next ch, dc in each of next 8 ch, sk remaining ch, sl st in next sc. Repeat from * around—11 petals.

SUNFLOWER

Rnd 3: Ch 1, holding petals forward, * sc in center st at base of next petal, ch 13, sl st in 2nd ch from hook and in each of next 10 ch, ch 1. Repeat from * around. Join to first sc.
Rnd 4: Repeat Rnd 2 of Petals. Break off and fasten.

STEM: With Green, ch 2.
Row 1: 2 sc in 2nd ch from hook. Ch 1, turn.
Row 2: 2 sc in first sc, sc in next sc. Ch 1, turn.
Next 9 Rows: Sc in next 3 sc. Ch 1, turn. Break off and fasten.

LEAF (Make 2): With Green, ch 18, sc in 2nd ch from hook, h dc in next ch, dc in next ch, 2 tr in each of next 2 ch, tr in each of next 6 ch, 2 dc in next ch, dc in each of next 2 ch, h dc in next ch, sc in next ch, 3 sc in last ch; working along opposite side of starting ch, h dc in each of next 3 ch, 2 dc in each of next 2 ch, 2 tr in next ch, tr in each of next 7 ch, dc in next ch, h dc in next ch, sc in next ch. Ch 1, turn, sl st in each st around. Break off and fasten. Sew one leaf to each side of stem and sew to flower as shown.

RING: With Yellow, sc closely around ring.

FINISHING: Cut felt slightly smaller than the outline of pot holder and sew in place. Sew ring to back of flower.

PANSY

PANSY

PANSY POT HOLDER

CROCHETING INSTRUCTIONS:

FLOWER——FIRST 3 PETALS: Starting at center with Yellow, ch 5. Join with sl st to form ring.

Rnd 1: Ch 1, 12 sc in ring. Do not join.

Rnd 2: (In next sc make sc, h dc and dc; 3 tr in each of next 2 sc; in next sc make dc, h dc, and sc) 3 times. Join to first sc—3 petals. Break off and fasten.

Rnd 3: Attach Blue to joining, ch 1, (sc in next sc, h dc in next h dc, 2 dc in next dc, 2 tr in each of next 6 tr, 2 dc in next dc, h dc in next h dc, sc in next sc) 3 times—60 sts.

Rnd 4: (Sc in next sc, in next st make h dc and dc, 2 tr in each of next 16 sts, in next st make dc and h dc, sc in next sc) 3 times.

Rnd 5: Picking up front loop only throughout, sc in each st around. Join to first sc.

FOURTH PETAL:

Row 1: Ch 1, picking up the *back loop only of each st of next-to-last rnd,* skip first st, sc in next st, (ch 3, skip next 3 sts, sc in next st) 5 times—5 loops. Break off and fasten.

Row 2: Attach Yellow to first sc of last row, ch 5, in each of next 4 loops make (d tr, *ch 3, sl st in top of d tr just made*—picot made) 6 times; skip next loop, sl st in last sc. Break off and fasten.

FIFTH PETAL:

Row 1: Skip first 20 sts on third petal, picking up *back loop only of each st of Rnd 4,* attach Blue in next st, sc in same place, (ch 3, skip next 3 tr, sc in next st) 4 times. Break off and fasten.

Row 2: Attach Yellow to first sc of last row, in first loop make h dc, picot, (dc, picot) twice, and (tr, picot) twice; in each of next 2 loops make (d tr, picot) 8 times; holding the first 6 d tr of fourth petal forward, join with sl st to next d tr on fourth petal. Break off and fasten.

LEAF (Make 2): With Green ch 13, sc in 2nd ch from hook, 2 h dc in next ch, 2 dc in next ch, 2 tr in next ch, d tr in next 4 ch, 2 d tr in each of next 3 ch, 7 tr in last ch; working along opposite side of starting ch, make 2 tr in each of next 2 ch, d tr in each of next 5 ch, tr in next ch, dc in next ch, h dc in next ch, sc in next ch. Ch 1, turn, sl st in each st around. Break off and fasten.

FINISHING: Sew leaves to flower as shown.
  Work ring and finish as for Sunflower.

DAHLIA

DAHLIA

DAHLIA POT HOLDER

CROCHETING INSTRUCTIONS:

FLOWER: Starting at center with Brown, ch 4. Join with sl st to form ring. Ch 1, 6 sc in ring. Do not join.

Rnd 1: In each sc around make (sc, ch 5) twice—12 sc.

Rnd 3: Sc in first sc, ch 1, holding loops forward, * sc in next sc, ch 1. Repeat from * around—12 sc.

Rnd 4: In each sc around make (sc, ch 7) twice.

Rnd 5: Repeat 3rd rnd. Join to first sc—24 sc. Break off and fasten.

PETALS:

Rnd 1: Attach Red to joining, * in next ch-1 sp make h dc, dc, 3 tr, dc and h dc; sc in next ch-1 sp. Repeat from * around—12 petals. *Hereafter do not join.*

Rnd 2: Ch 4, holding petals forward, * sc in base of the center tr of next petal, ch 4. Repeat from * around.

Rnd 3: In each loop around, make sc, h dc, dc, tr, 3 d tr, tr, dc, h dc, and sc—13 petals.

Rnd 4: Ch 2, * sc in base of the center d tr of next petal, ch 5. Repeat from * around.

Rnd 5: In each ch-5 loop around make sc, ch 2, dc, tr, 5 d tr, tr, dc, ch 2, and sc. Join to first sc. Break off and fasten.

STEM: With Green, ch 20. H dc in 3rd ch from hook, h dc in next ch, * 2 h dc in next ch, h dc in each of next 3 ch. Repeat from * across. Break off and fasten.

LEAF (Make 2): Make 2 leaves same as for Sunflower.

JOINING: Sew one leaf to each side of stem and sew to flower as shown.

RING: With Red, sc closely around ring. Finish as for Sunflower.

PRINCE THE PONY

PRINCE THE PONY

(Approx. 10" tall)

MATERIALS REQUIRED:
Coats & Clark's "Red Heart" Super Fingering (3-Ply "Tangle-Proof" Pull-Out Skeins)
3 Skeins of No. 1 White and a small amount of No. 12 Black
"G" Plastic Crochet Hook
10 Pipe Cleaners
Dacron Batting for Stuffing
Few Yards of Pink Yarn for Embroidering Nose and Mouth

STITCH GAUGE: With double strand of yarn:
4 sts = 1"   4 rnds = 1"

CROCHETING INSTRUCTIONS: Entire pony is crocheted with double strands of yarn.

BODY: Starting at front with double strand of White, ch 2.
Rnd 1: 8 sc in 2nd ch from hook. Do not join rnds, but mark beg of rnds for accurate shaping.
Rnd 2: 2 sc in each sc around (16 sc).
Rnd 3: * Sc in next sc, 2 sc in next sc. Repeat from * around (24 sc).
Rnd 4: * 2 sc in next sc, sc in next 2 sc. Repeat from * around (32 sc).
Rnds 5 and 6: Continue to inc 8 sc evenly on each rnd.
Work even on 48 sc until 22 rnds have been completed from beg.
Shape Back:
Rnd 23: * Draw up a loop in each of the next 2 sc, yo and draw thru all 3 loops on hook (1 sc decreased), sc in next 4 sc. Repeat from * around (8 sc decreased).
Rnd 24: * Sc in next 3 sc, dec 1 sc. Repeat from * around.
Stuffing body firmly before opening is closed, continue to dec 8 sc at even intervals on each rnd until 8 sc remain.

TAIL BASE: Pinch last rnd tog; working thru double thickness, sc in each sc (4 sc). Ch 1, turn. Dec 1 sc at each edge on next row. Ch 1, turn, dec 1 sc. Break off and fasten.

NECK: Starting at top, work same as body for 2 rnds (16 sc).
Rnd 3: * 2 sc in next sc, sc in next 3 sc. Repeat from * around (20 sc).
Rnds 4 through 9: Work even.
Shape Front of Neck:
Rnd 10: H dc in next 2 sc, dec in next 6 sc, h dc in next 2 sc, sc in remaining 10 sc.
Rnd 11: H dc in next 4 sts, dc in next 2 sts, h dc in next 4 sts, sc in 10 sc.
Rnd 12: H dc in next 3 sts, 2 dc in next 4 sts, h dc in next 3 sts, sc in next st, sl st in next st. Break off and fasten.

Stuff neck firmly and sew to front of body with long part of neck covering center front, and short part stretched over back.

HEAD: Starting at nose, work same as neck until 7 rnds have been completed (20 sc).
Shape Forehead and Jaw:
Rnd 8: * 2 sc in next sc, sc in next 3 sc. Repeat from * around (25 sc).
Rnd 9: * Sc in next 4 sc, 2 sc in next sc. Repeat from * around (30 sc).
Rnds 10 through 15: Work even.
Shape Back of Head:
Rnd 17: * Dec 1 sc, sc in next 3 sc. Repeat from * around (24 sc).

Inserting stuffing before opening is closed, dec 8 sc evenly on next 2 rnds, then dec around until opening is closed. Break off and fasten.

Sew head to top of neck, with first dec rnd of head just behind back of neck.

EARS: With double strand of White, ch 10. Dc in 4th ch from hook, dc in next 2 ch, h dc in next 3 ch, 3 sc in last ch for tip of ear; working along opposite side of ch, h dc in next 3 ch, dc in next 3 ch, ch 3, sl st in base of turning chain. Break off and fasten.

Draw a pipe cleaner through top of head and sew ears to ends of pipe cleaner. Cupping ears forward, sew base of ears to head.

FRONT LEG (Make 2): Starting at top with double strand of White, ch 11.

Rnd 1: Sc in 2nd ch from hook, h dc in next 2 ch, dc in next 3 ch, h dc in next 2 ch, sc in next 2 ch, ch 10 for inner side of leg, join with sl st in first sc, taking care not to twist sts, to form a circle.

Rnd 2: Dec 1 sc over next 2 h dc, dec 1 sc over next 2 dc, sc in next dc, dec 2 sc over next 4 sts, sc in each remaining st around (16 sts).

Rnds 3, 4 and 5: Work even.

Rnd 6: Dec 1 sc around (8 sc).

Rnds 7 through 15: Work even.

Rnd 16: 2 sc in each sc around (16 sc).

Rnd 17: Work even.

Rnd 18: Repeat Rnd 6. Break off and fasten.

HOOF: Hold leg against body and mark back edge of left-front or right-front leg.

Rnd 1: Attach double strand of Black at marker, sl st in base of marked st (in row before last), sc in next sc, 2 sc in next 4 sc, sc in next sc, sl st in next sc.

Rnd 2: Sc in each st around (12 sc). Join 2 pipe cleaners by twisting the ends around one another for 1½", then fold back twisted ends to keep them from pulling apart. Insert length of pipe cleaners through leg with about 2" extending through hoof. Wrap this end around finger to form a circle to fit hoof.

Rnd 3: Working over circle of pipe cleaner, sc in each sc around.

Stuff leg and hoof firmly, then dec around until opening is closed. Stuffing curved top of leg, sew leg to front of body.

Make other front leg to correspond, reversing position of hoof.

HIND LEG (Make 2):

Rnd 1: Work same as front legs for 1 rnd.

Rnd 2: Sc in each sc, h dc in each h dc, dc in each dc, and sc in each ch around.

Rnd 3: Sc in next 2 sts, dec 1 st, sc in next 2 sts, dec 1 st, sc in each remaining st around (18 sc).

Rnds 4 and 5: Work even.

Rnd 6: Repeat Rnd 3 (16 sc).

Rnd 7: * Make 3 decs, sc in next 2 sc. Repeat from * once more (10 sc).

Rnds 8, 9, and 10: Work even. Hold leg against body and mark back edge.

Rnd 11: Sc in each st to marker, h dc in next st, 2 dc in next st, h dc in next st for hock, sc in each remaining st around (11 sts).

Rnd 12: Sc in each st to next h dc, make 2 decs, complete rnd (9 sc).

Rnds 13 through 17: Work even, decreasing 1 sc on Rnd 17 (8 sc).

Starting with Rnd 18, complete to correspond to front leg and hoof.

Make other hind leg to correspond, reversing position of hock and hoof.

Stuff legs and sew to body.

FINISHING: With Black, embroider eyes. Wrap White yarn around a 2" cardboard until 6" of cardboard are covered closely. With sewing thread, sew strands tog along one edge, fastening each one securely to the next ones. Remove cardboard, clip loops. Sew in place from top of head to shoulders for mane.

Knot several 3" strands at center and sew back of feet above hooves for fetlocks.

Cut about 30 strands of White 12" long. Fold each strand in half and sew folded end to tail base, forming tail.

Turn head to one side and sew lower edge of neck in place to hold head in position.

Run strands of White through body to hold inner sides of legs together, so pony will stand firmly.

With Pink yarn, embroider nostrils and mouth.

BULLDOG

BULLDOG

MATERIALS REQUIRED:

Coats & Clark's "Red Heart" Knitting Worsted, 4 Ply, Art. E. 232 (1-oz. "Tangle Proof" Pull-Out Skeins)

3 Skeins each of No. 588 Amethyst and No. 330 Sandstone, and 1 Skein of No. 12 Black

"G" Aluminum Crochet Hook

A few yards of Pink Pearl Cotton

½ yd. of Narrow Red Ribbon

12" of Eyelet Embroidery

Small Pieces of Black and Red Felt for Facial Features

Cotton Batting for Stuffing

STITCH GAUGE: 5 sc = 1″   5 rnds = 1″

CROCHETING INSTRUCTIONS:

HEAD: Starting at nose with Sandstone, ch 2.

Row 1: 6 sc in 2nd ch from hook. *Do not join rnds, but mark last sc on each rnd to insure proper shaping.*

Rnd 2: 2 sc in each sc around.

Rnd 3: * Sc in next sc, 2 sc in next sc (an increase made). Repeat from * around (18 sc).

Rnd 4: Inc 6 sc evenly on rnd.

Repeat Rnd 4 until there are 66 sc on rnd.

Mark Rnds 14 and 16 for approximate placement of ears in finishing.

Work even until 24 rnds in all have been made.

Next Rnd: Dec 8 sc evenly on next rnd (to dec 1 sc, pull up a loop in each of 2 sc, and draw thru the 3 loops on hook).

Stuffing head firmly as work progresses, dec 8 sc evenly on each rnd until all sc have been worked off. Break off.

EAR (Make 2): Starting at center with Black, ch 8.

Row 1: Sc in 2nd ch from hook and in each ch across. Ch 1, turn. *Work in rnds.*

Rnd 1: Sc in each sc across, 2 sc in side of last sc made, 2 sc in end sc of Row 1; working across opposite side of starting chain, sc in each ch across, 2 sc in side of each of next 2 sc.

Rnds 2 and 3: Sc in each sc around, increasing 2 sc at each end of each rnd. Sl st in next sc. Break off and fasten.

Gather one end slightly and sew to head over Rnds 14 and 16 4″ apart.

FACE: Following diagram, cut eyes and nose from Black felt and tongue from Red felt. Sew to face. With Black worsted make long stitches for mouth and across face as shown.

BODY: Starting at chest with Amethyst, ch 9.

Rnd 1: 2 sc in 2nd ch from hook, sc in each ch across, 3 sc in last ch; working across opposite side of starting chain, sc in each ch, sc in same ch as first 2 sc were made.

Rnd 2: Sc in each sc, increasing 3 sc evenly across each rounded end (24 sc).

Next 6 Rnds: Inc 3 sc evenly across each rounded end (60 sc on last rnd).

Work even until 15 rnds in all have been made. Fold body in line with starting chain; mark the center sc at each rounded end.

Rnd 16: Sc in each sc to within first marked sc, dec 1 sc, sc in next 28 sc, dec 1 sc.

Continue decreasing 1 sc over each dec until there are 14 sc between each decreased sc.

Next Rnd: Work even on the 30 sc. Break off.

HINDQUARTERS: Attach Sandstone and work even for 9 rnds. Stuff body firmly. Dec 6 sc evenly on each rnd until all sc's are worked off. Break off. Sew head to body.

FRONT LEG (Make 2): Starting at foot with Sandstone, work as for head until 4 rnds have been made (24 sc).

Work even for 2 rnds.

Rnd 7: (Dec 1 sc over next 2 sc) 6 times—toe shaping.

Work even on 18 sc for 4 rnds. Break off.

Attach Amethyst and work 6 rnds. Break off. Stuff leg.

With 3 strands of Pink Pearl Cotton, embroider toes by making 4 long stitches over the 4 rnds before toe shaping. Sew legs in place 1" apart, tucking the inner half of last 3 rnds under so that legs will be straight.

BACK LEG (Make 2): Using Sandstone only, work as for front leg until 14 rnds in all have been made. Break off; stuff and sew in place ¼" apart.

TAIL: With Sandstone, ch 2.

Rnd 1: 6 sc in 2nd ch from hook.

Rnd 2: Inc 3 sc evenly.

Work even on 9 sc for 4 rnds. Break off; stuff and sew in place.

COLLAR: Make a small hem on narrow edges of eyelet embroidery. Gather to fit neck and tack in place. Make a bow from ribbon and sew to front.

OWL

OWL

MATERIALS REQUIRED:

Coats & Clark's "Red Heart" Knitting Worsted, 4 Ply Art. E. 232 (1-oz. "Tangle-Proof" Pull-Out Skeins)

2 Skeins of No. 418 Lt. Natural and 1 Skein of No. 330 Sandstone; and Art. E. 245 (⅓-oz. "Tangle-Proof" Pull-Out Skeins)

1 Skein of No. 1 White

A few yards of No. 12 Black and No. 356 Taupe

A few yards of No. 81 Dk. Brown Pearl Cotton

#7 Milwards Steel Crochet Hook for Pearl Cotton Only

"G" Crochet Hook

#18 Milwards Tapestry Needle

Scraps of White, Orange, Yellow, and Black Felt for soles of feet

Cotton Batting for Stuffing

STITCH GAUGE: 5 sc = 1"   5 rnds = 1"

CROCHETING INSTRUCTIONS:

HEAD: Starting at center top with Lt. Natural, ch 2.

Rnd 1: Make 6 sc in 2nd ch from hook.

Rnd 2: 2 sc in each sc around.

Rnd 3: * Sc in next sc, 2 sc in next sc (and inc).

Repeat from * around.

Rnd 4: Sc in each sc around, increasing 6 sc evenly spaced but do not have an inc directly over a previous inc.

Repeat Rnd 4 until there are 36 sc on rnd.

Mark Rnd 7 of head for approximate placement of ears in finishing.

Next Rnd: Sc in each sc around, increasing 3 sc evenly spaced.

Repeat last rnd until there are 57 sc on rnd.

Work even until piece measures 5" from start.

Next Rnd: Sc in each sc around, decreasing 11 sc around (To dec 1 sc draw up a loop in each of next 2 sc, and draw thru all loops on hook).

Repeat last rnd until 24 sc remain, stuffing piece firmly while working.

Next Rnd: Dec 12 sc around.

Following Rnd: Dec 6 sc around. Break off, leaving a 6" strand.

Thread into a needle and draw up sts tightly.

BODY: Starting at neck with Lt. Natural, ch 18. Join with sl st to form a ring.

Rnd 1: Sc in each sc around.

Rnd 2: Sc in each sc, increasing 4 sc evenly spaced.

Repeat Rnd 2 until there are 50 sc on rnd.

Break off and attach Taupe (center back).

Next Rnd: With Taupe sc in next 12 sc, inc 1 sc in next sc (right-hand side), sc in next 24 sc, inc 1 sc in next sc (left-hand side), sc in next 12 sc.

Next 2 Rnds: Sc in each sc around. Break off and attach Sandstone. With Sandstone work 11 rnds even.

Next Rnd: Sc in each sc, decreasing 2 sc at each side.

Repeat last rnd until 44 sc remain. Work 1 rnd even, ending at center back.

RIGHT LEG:

Rnd 1: Sc in next 22 sc, ch 2, sk next 22 sc.

Rnd 2: Sc in next 22 sc and in next 2 ch.

Rnd 3: Sc in each sc around, decreasing 2 sc at inner leg.

Rnd 4: Sc in each sc, decreasing 4 sc around.

Rnd 5: Repeat Rnd 4, ending with a sl st in last sc.

Break off and fasten.

LEFT LEG: Attach yarn to first skipped sc on last rnd of body, sc in each sc around and in the opposite side of each ch of the ch-2. Continue to work same as for right leg.

LOWER LEG (Make 2): Starting at upper edge with White, ch 9 very loosely. Join with sl st to form a ring.

Rnd 1: Sc in each ch around.

Rnds 2 through 5: Sc in each sc around.

Before making 2nd lower leg, finish first lower leg piece by working directions for a foot.

FOOT:

Rnd 1: Make 3 toes as follows: (sc *in next sc,* ch 4, sc in 2nd ch from hook and in next 2 ch, so in *same sc* as first sc of toe) 3 times; sc in remaining 6 sc.

Rnd 2: Sc in next sc (working in opposite side of starting chain of toe, sc in next 3 ch, 3 sc in next sc, sc in next 4 sc) 3 times; sc in each remaining sc, sl st in first sc. Break off and fasten.

RIGHT WING: Starting at lower edge with Sandstone, ch 5.

Row 1: Make 2 sc in 2nd ch from hook (inner edge), sc in next 3 ch. Ch 1, turn.

Rows 2, 3 and 4: Increasing 1 sc at beg of row, sc in each sc across. Ch 1, turn. Break off at the end of Row 4. Attach Taupe.

Rows 5, 6 and 7: With Taupe, sc in each sc across. Ch 1, turn. Break off at the end of Row 7. Attach Lt. Natural.

Row 8: With Lt. Natural, sc in each sc across, increasing 1 sc in last sc. Ch 1, turn.

Row 9: Increasing 1 sc at both ends, sc in each sc across. Ch 1, turn.

Row 10: Repeat Row 8—(12 sc).

Rows 11 through 15: Sc in each sc across. Ch 1, turn.

Rows 16 and 17: Sc in each sc across, decreasing 1 sc at end of row. Ch 1, turn.

Row 18: Decreasing 1 sc at beg of row, sc in each sc across. Ch 1, turn.

Row 19: Repeat Row 16. Do not ch 1. Turn.

Row 20: Sl st in first 2 sc, sc in next 5 sc, sl st in next sc. Break off and fasten.

FINISHING: Stuff beak firmly and sew in place on head. Stuff body and legs firmly. Sew neck edge of body to head. Trace outline of both feet onto Yellow felt and cut out. Sew to bottom of feet to form soles. Stuff lower legs firmly and sew to last rnd of legs. Sew wings in place.

FACE: From White felt, cut 2 discs, 2¾" in diameter. Slash edges ⅜" deep, closely around to form a fringe. Cut 2 Orange felt discs ¾" in diameter and 2 Black discs ½" in diameter. Place 1 Black disc over 1 Orange and both over the center of 1 White disc and sew in place for each eye with the centers 2" apart on the face and in line with the top of the beak.

LEFT WING: Starting at lower edge with Sandstone, ch 5.
Row 1: Make 2 sc in 2nd ch from hook, sc in next 2 ch, 2 sc in next ch. Ch 1, turn.
Starting with Row 2, work same as for Right Wing.

WING EDGES: With Taupe and front of wings facing, sc closely around the entire edge of each wing.

EAR (Make 2): Leaving a 6" strand of Black and starting at center, ch 3.
Row 1: Make 2 sc in 2nd ch from hook, 3 sc in next ch and,

working along opposite side of starting chain, make 2 sc in next ch, sl st in first sc, turn.

Row 2: Sc in next 3 sc, 3 sc in next sc for tip of ear, sc in next 3 sc, sl st in next st. Break off and fasten.

Thread the 6″ strand into the tapestry needle and make two ½″ loops at tip of ear. Sew ears in place on Rnd 7 of head.

BEAK: Starting at tip with Pearl Cotton, ch 2.
Rnd 1: Make 3 sc in 2nd ch from hook.
Rnd 2: Increasing 1 sc in first sc, sc in each sc around.

Repeat Rnd 2 until there are 9 sc. Break off, leaving a 6″ strand for sewing.

PINWHEEL DOILY

PINWHEEL DOILY

(Approx. 15″ in diameter)

MATERIALS REQUIRED:
2 Balls of American Thread "Puritan" Mercerized White Crochet Cotton
#7 Steel Crochet Hook

CROCHETING INSTRUCTIONS:

Rnd 1: Ch 5, join to form a ring, ch 4, dc in ring, ch 1, dc in ring, repeat from * 7 times, ch 1, join in 3rd st of ch.

Rnd 2: Ch 3 (counts as 1st dc), dc in same space, * ch 3, 2 dc in next dc, repeat from * all around, ch 3, join in 3rd st of ch.

Rnd 3: Sl st to center of first loop, * ch 7, sc in next loop, repeat from * all around, ch 7, join in last sl st.

Rnd 4: Sl st to 2nd st of first loop, ch 3, 4 dc in same loop, * ch 2, 5 dc in next loop, repeat from * all around, ch 2, join in 3rd st of ch.

Rnd 5: Ch 3, 1 dc in each of the next 2 dc, * ch 2, 4 dc in next loop, 1 dc in each of the next 3 dc, repeat from * all around, ending last repeat with 4 dc in last loop, join in 3rd st of ch.

Rnd 6: Ch 5, skip next 2 dc, 4 dc in next loop, 1 dc in each of the next 5 dc, * ch 2, 4 dc in next loop, 1 dc in each of the next 5 dc, repeat from * all around, ending last repeat with 1 dc in each of the next 4 dc, join in 3rd st of ch.

Rnd 7: Ch 3, 3 dc in 1st loop, 1 dc in each of the next 7 dc, * ch 2, 4 dc in next loop, 1 dc in each of the next 7 dc, repeat from * all around, ch 2, join in 3rd st of ch.

Rnd 8: Ch 3, 1 dc in each of the next 8 dc, * ch 2, 4 dc in next loop, 1 dc in each of the next 9 dc, repeat from * all around, ending with 4 dc in last loop, join in 3rd st of ch.

Rnd 9: Ch 3, 1 dc in each of the next 6 dc, * ch 2, skip next dc, dc in next dc, ch 2, sk next loop, 1 dc in each of the next 11 dc, repeat from * all around, ending to correspond, join.

Rnd 10: Ch 3, 1 dc in each of the next 4 dc, * ch 2, sk next 2 dc, dc in next loop, ch 2, dc in next loop, ch 2, 1 dc in each of the next 9 dc, repeat from * all around, ending to correspond, join.

Rnd 11: Ch 3, 1 dc in each of the next 2 dc, * ch 2, sk next 2 dc, dc in next loop, ch 2, dc in next loop, ch 2, dc in next loop, ch 2, 1 dc in each of the next 7 dc, repeat from * all around, ending to correspond, join.

Rnd 12: Ch 5, sk next dc, dc in next dc, * ch 2, dc in next loop, repeat from * 3 times, ch 2, 1 dc in each of the next 5 dc, ch 2, sk next dc, dc in next dc, repeat from 1st * all around, ending to correspond, join.

Rnd 13: Ch 5, dc in next mesh, * ch 2, dc in next mesh, repeat from * 4 times, ch 2, 1 dc in each of the next 3 dc, ch 2, sk next dc, dc in next dc, ch 2, dc in next loop, repeat from 1st * all around, ending to correspond, join.

Rnd 14: Sl st into mesh, ch 5, dc in next mesh, * ch 2, dc in next mesh, repeat from * 4 times, ** ch 2, dc in next dc, ch 2, sk next dc, dc in next dc, * ch 2, dc in next loop, repeat from * 7 times, repeat from ** all around, ending to correspond, join.

Rnd 15: Sl st into mesh, ch 3, 2 dc in same mesh, * ch 2, sk next mesh, 3 dc in next mesh, repeat from * all around, ch 2, join.

Rnd 16: Sl st to next mesh, ch 4, 2 tr in same mesh, * ch 5, sc in next mesh, ch 5, 3 tr in next mesh, repeat from * all around, ending to correspond, join.

Rnd 17: Ch 1, sc in same sp, 1 sc in each of the next 2 tr, * ch 9, 1 sc in each of the next 3 tr, repeat from * all around, ch 9, join in 1st sc.

Rnd 18: Sl st in next sc, sc in same sp, * ch 5, 3 tr in next loop, ch 5, sc in center sc of next sc group, repeat from * all around, ending to correspond, join.

Rnd 19: Sl st to 1st tr of next tr group, sc in same sp, 1 sc in each of the next 2 tr, * ch 11, sk next 2 loops, 1 sc in each of the next 3 tr, repeat from * all around, ch 11, join in 1st sc.

Rnd 20: Sl st to next sc, sc in same sp, ch 7, 3 tr in next loop, * ch 7, sc in center sc of next sc group, ch 7, 3 tr in next loop, repeat from * all around, ending with ch 3, tr in 1st sc (this brings thread in position for next round).

Rnd 21: Ch 3, dc in next loop, * ch 7, sc in center tr of next tr group, ch 7, keeping last loop of each st on hook, 1 dc in each of the next 2 loops, thread over and work off all loops at one time, repeat from * all around, ending to correspond, join in 1st dc.

Rnd 22: Sl st into loop, ch 3, 6 dc in same loop, then work 7 dc in each remaining loop, join in 3rd st of ch.

Rnd 23: Ch 3, dc in next dc, * ch 4, sk next 3 dc, 1 dc in each of the next 4 dc, repeat from * all around, join.

Rnd 24: Sl st to mesh, ch 4 (counts as first tr), 5 tr in same loop, * ch 3, 2 tr, ch 3, 2 tr in next mesh, ch 3, 6 tr in next mesh, repeat from * all around, ending to correspond, join.

Rnd 25: Ch 1, sc in same sp, 1 sc in each of the next 5 tr, * ch 4, sk next loop, 2 tr, ch 3, 2 tr in next loop, ch 4, sk next loop,

1 sc in each of the next 6 tr, repeat from * all around, ending to correspond, join.

Rnd 26: * 1 sc in each of the next 5 sc, ch 6, sk next loop, 6 tr in next loop, ch 6, sk next loop and 1 sc, repeat from * all around, join in 1st sc.

Rnd 27: * 1 sc in each of the next 4 sc, ch 6, sk next loop, 1 tr in each of the next 6 tr, with ch 1 between each tr, ch 6, sk next loop and 1 sc, repeat from * all around, join in first sc.

Rnd 28: ** 1 sc in each of the next 3 sc, ch 6, 2 tr in next tr, * ch 1, 2 tr in next tr, repeat from * 4 times, ch 6, sk next loop and 1 sc, repeat from ** all around, join in 1st sc.

Rnd 29: ** Sc in next sc, ch 5, sc in next tr, * ch 5, sl st in 3rd st of ch for picot, ch 2, sc in next ch—1 sp, repeat from * 4 times, ch 5, sl st in 3rd st from hook for picot, ch 2, sk next tr, sc in next tr, ch 5, sk next loop and 1 sc, repeat from ** all around, join in first sc, cut thread.

PICOT CENTER DOILY

PICOT CENTER DOILY

(Approx. 12" in diameter)

MATERIALS REQUIRED:

1 Ball of American Thread Company "Puritan" Mercerized White Crochet Cotton
#7 Steel Crochet Hook

CROCHETING INSTRUCTIONS:

Rnd 1: * Ch 5, sl st in first st of ch (picot), repeat from * 7 times, join in first picot.

Rnd 2: Ch 1, sc in same picot, ch 11, sc in same picot, ch 11, sc in same picot, ** sc in next picot, * ch 11, sc in same picot, repeat from * once, repeat from ** 6 times, join in first sc.

Rnd 3: Sl st to center st of loop, ch 3 (ch 3 counts as 1 dc), 4 dc in same sp, * 5 dc in center st of next loop, repeat from * all around, join in 3rd st of ch.

Rnd 4: Sl st to center dc, ch 3, 2 dc in same sp, ch 3, sk 1 dc, sc between next 2 dc, * ch 3, 3 dc in center st of next dc group, ch 3, sk 1 dc, sc between next 2 dc, repeat from * all around, ch 3, join.

Rnd 5: Sl st to next dc, ch 3, 4 dc in same sp, * ch 3, 5 dc in center st of next dc group, repeat from * all around, ch 3, join.

Rnd 6: Sl st to center dc, ch 3, 2 dc in same sp, * ch 3, sc in next loop, ch 3, 3 dc in center dc of next dc group, repeat from * all around, ending to correspond, join.

Rnd 7: Sl st to next dc, ch 3, 6 dc in same sp, * ch 3, 7 dc in center dc of next dc group, repeat from * all around, ch 3, join.

Rnd 8: Ch 3, dc in same sp, 1 dc in each of the next 5 dc, 2 dc in next dc, sc in next loop, * 2 dc in next dc, 1 dc in each of the next 5 dc, 2 dc in next dc, sc in next loop, repeat from * all around, join.

Rnd 9: * Ch 4, 2 dc in first st of ch (cluster st), repeat from * 3 times, sc between 2nd and 3rd cluster sts, cluster st, dc in between 1st and 2nd cluster sts, cluster st, skip next 7 dc, sc in next dc, sk next sc, sc in next dc, repeat from first * all around, ending to correspond, join, cut thread.

Rnd 10: Attach thread at top between 3rd and 4th cluster sts, ch 6, tr in same sp, * ch 2 tr in same sp, repeat from * twice, * * ch 2, thread over hook 3 times, insert in sc between 2nd and 3rd cluster sts and work off 2 loops 3 times, thread over hook 3 times, insert in base of sc between 2nd and 3rd cluster sts of next cluster-st group, work off all loops 2 at a time, ch 2, 5 tr with ch 2 between each tr between next 2 cluster sts, repeat from * * all around, ending to correspond, join.

Rnd 11: Sl st in next ch 2 loop, ch 3, 2 dc in same loop, * ch 2, 3 dc in next loop, repeat from * twice, * * ch 2, sc in sc between next two ch-2 loops, * ch 2, 3 dc in next ch 2 loop between tr, repeat from * 3 times, repeat from * * ending to correspond, join in 3rd st of ch.

Rnd 12: Sl st to next ch 2 loop, ch 3, 2 dc in same loop, ch 3, 3 dc in next loop, ch 3, 3 dc in next loop, * * ch 3, sc in next sc, * ch 3, 3 dc in next ch-2 loop between dc group, repeat from * * twice, repeat from * * all around, ending to correspond, join.

Rnd 13: Sl st to next ch 3 loop, ch 3, 2 dc in same loop, ch 4, 3 dc in next loop, * * ch 4, sc in next loop, ch 3, sc in next loop, * ch 4, 3 dc in next ch-3 loop between dc group, repeat from * once, repeat from * *, ending to correspond, join.

Rnd 14: Sl st to next ch 4 loop, ch 3, 2 dc in same loop, * ch 5, sc in next loop, ch 4, sk ch-3 loop, sc in next loop, ch 5, 3 dc in next loop, repeat from * all around, ending to correspond, join.

Rnd 15: Sl st to center dc, ch 3, 2 dc in same space, ch 3, 3 dc in same sp, * 5 sc in next loop, 4 sc in next loop, 5 sc in next loop, sk 1 dc, 3 dc, ch 3, 3 dc in next dc, repeat from * all around, ending to correspond, join, cut thread.

HOW TO DO FILET CROCHET

FILET LACE IS PICTURE LACE. It is formed by rows of squares. Some of the squares are open; these are called *spaces* and usually constitute the background. Some of the squares are filled in and are called *blocks;* these usually form the design. Any picture or decorative motif that can be reduced to a pattern of light and dark squares can be executed in filet. The piece may be any shape—square, oblong, round, oval, or many-sided. Edges can be straight, scalloped, or curved. The lace may be worked in one piece. It can consist of a central panel with a border worked around it, or it may be made of several panels joined together. A decorative openwork stitch of *lacets* and *bars* is used occasionally for contrast, either as a border or as part of the background.

Here we give you all the information necessary to copy any filet pattern or execute your own designs.

STITCH GAUGE: The tightness or looseness of each stitch (and thus of the finished article) is determined by the size of hook used, and is always chosen in relation to the size of thread or yarn to be used, modified somewhat by the tightness or the looseness desired. This tightness or looseness is called **Gauge,** and is influenced by one other element: **Tension,** which is the strain put upon the thread by the crocheter. Tension is a matter of nervous and muscular control of the fingers and is best regulated by always holding the work in the position which is most comfortable for *your* hands.

At the beginning of every set of instructions the proper **Stitch Gauge** for that piece of work is given, i.e., the number of stitches to the inch (a width measurement), and the number of rows or rounds to the inch (a length measurement). It is *necessary* that *you* get the *same* **Stitch Gauge** if your finished article is to be the size specified. Crochet a 3" square, using the Pattern Stitch, size of hook and thread specified in your instructions, press, then count the number of stitches to the inch and the number of rows to the inch. If you are crocheting *more* stitches to the inch or more rows to the inch, use a larger crochet hook; if *less* use a smaller crochet hook. As the work progresses some people automatically tighten or loosen the tension on their work. Check your **Stitch Gauge** frequently.

MATERIALS: Any thread—cotton, linen, nylon, silk, metallic, etc.—can be used for making filet lace. Cotton thread is the easiest to obtain, the least expensive, and comes in standard weights. The following chart gives the sizes (weights) of cotton thread, the hook usually used for each size, the gauge (how many squares to the inch) for each combination and the approximate number of yards required to make 100 squares, based on the assumption that one-third of the squares will be filled in to form blocks.

TABLE OF STEEL HOOK & THREAD SIZES

Note: The higher the number of thread, the finer the thread.
The higher the number of hook, the finer the hook.

Thread Size (Cotton Thread)	Steel Hook Recommended	Gauge Squares per inch	Average yardage for 100 squares
No. 70	No. 14	7 squares = 1"	6 yds.
No. 60	No. 13	6½ squares = 1"	6½ yds.
No. 50	No. 12	6 squares = 1"	7 yds.
No. 40	No. 11	5½ squares = 1"	8 yds.
No. 30	No. 10	5 squares = 1"	9 yds.
No. 20	No. 9	4½ squares = 1"	10 yds.
No. 10	No. 8	4 squares = 1"	11 yds.

OTHER THREADS: Select a hook that is fine enough to give the lace a firm texture, large enough to catch the thread easily without splitting it. Once a hook has been selected, make a sample piece of filet 10 squares wide, 10 rows deep. (Make 3½ rows of blocks, remaining rows of spaces.) Count the number of squares per inch to obtain the gauge. If stitch gauge is correct, unravel the sample and measure the thread that was used to estimate yardage. If 10 squares measure more or less than 10 rows, you will have to *correct your tension.*

CORRECTING TENSION: If work is wider than it is longer: work the ch sts between dc sts slightly tighter, work the dc sts slightly longer; keep first loop on hook tight, thread over hook, insert hook in st, thread over hook and thru 2 loops (these are the loops to loosen before pulling hook thru to make the dc longer, *not* the next 2 loops). **Note:** Sometimes tension can automatically be corrected by changing the crochet hooks as described under **Stitch Gauge.**

Charts: The chart, or design, shows the squares to be made and which squares are to be filled in. Since it is easier to decrease the number of squares than to increase, start at the wider edge, if possible, or on a straight edge if there is one. Once you have decided where to start, make a foundation chain that will be long enough to accommodate the squares for the first row. The first row will start at the right-hand edge of the chart and end at the left-hand edge. The next row will start at the left-hand edge and end at the right-hand edge. Mark off each row as it is completed. Some patterns are the same on both sides; in that case only half of each row may be given and the work is done from the edge to center, then back to edge, on every row. To make your own chart, buy a large piece of graph paper, preferably 10 squares per inch. Fill in the squares that are to form the design and outline the shape of the edges.

ABBREVIATIONS

Ch—Chain
Ch St—Chain Stitch
Sc—Single Crochet
Dc—Double Crochet
Tr—Treble Crochet
D Tr—Double Treble
Sl St—Slip Stitch
Beg—Beginning
Sp—Space

Sps—Spaces
Bl—Block
Bls—Blocks
St—Stitch
Sts—Stitches
Sk—Skip
Pr R—Previous Row
Rnd—Round

*—The presence of one or more asterisks [*] in the instructions indicates that the instructions following the symbol will be repeated a number of times, i.e.: repeat from * 6 times (meaning 6 times in all), or repeat from * across row. Occasionally, due to long and intricate directions, the instructions will read: repeat from * to * 6 times (in all). For many and varied repetitions, one [*], two [**] or three [***] asterisks are sometimes used.

Block—Solid parts of design are blocks and are indicated on chart by squares with solid circles.

Space—Open parts of design are spaces and are indicated on chart by empty squares.

Double Space—After the dc that forms the bar, ch 5, sk 5 sts of Pr R or (2 blocks or 2 spaces as diagram specified), make dc that forms next bar.

CHAIN STITCH: The chain stitch is the basis of all filet crochet.

FILET CROCHET

FOUNDATION CHAIN: To determine number of sts on chain count the number of squares in Row 1, multiply the number of squares by 3 (3 ch sts for each square); if Row 1 starts with a space add 5 ch sts for turning, if Row 1 starts with a block add 3 ch sts; this is the number of ch sts required on foundation chain. **Example:** For a row of 10 squares that starts with a space: 10 squares x 3 ch sts = 30 ch sts plus 5 ch sts for turning = 35 ch sts on foundation chain. **Note:** A *long* foundation chain can be made without counting the stitches; make the chain half again as long as necessary, work Row 1, then cut off excess chain 2 sts beyond last dc.

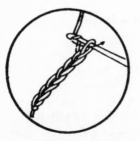

Note: In counting the stitches of a chain, every finished loop is counted, *but not the loop on the hook*, which is in fact part of whatever stitch is to be made next.

Foundation Chain

SPACES OVER SPACES

Row 1: Make 1 dc in 8th ch st from hook, this makes the first sp (Steps 1, 2, 3 and 4), * ch 2, sk the next 2 ch sts of foundation chain, make 1 dc in next ch st (which is the 3rd ch st from last dc made), repeat from * across foundation chain.

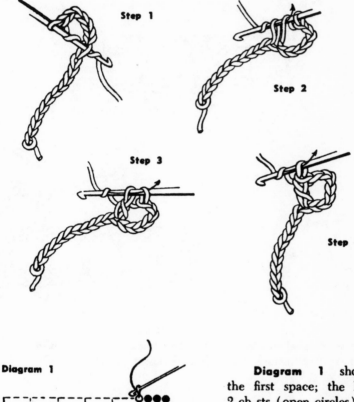

Step 1

Step 2

Step 3

Step 4

Diagram 1

Diagram 1 shows the first space; the last 2 ch sts (open circles) of Foundation Chain and the first ch st of turning ch 5 (solid circles) form the bottom. The next 2 ch sts of turning ch 5 finish forming the side. The last 2 sts form the rest of the top of first space. The solid line is the dc in 8th ch st from hook that forms other side of first space. The dotted lines indicate where other spaces are to be made.

Row 2: Ch 5 (Illus. 1) to turn, turn; make 1 dc into the second dc from end of Row 1 (Illus. 2) in the following manner: thread over hook, insert hook into the top of second dc so that the 2 top loops

of the dc are on hook, thread over hook and complete the dc, *
ch 2, sk the next 2 ch sts, make 1 dc in next dc, repeat from *

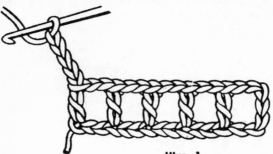

Illus. 1

Illus. 2

across row; when last dc has been completed, ch 2; make 1 dc in
3rd ch st of turning ch 5 at beg of Row 1 (Illus. 3).

Illus. 3

Diagram 2

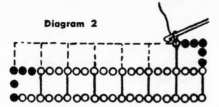

Diagram 2 shows the work turned, the turning ch 5 (solid circles) and the dc made into the second dc from end of Row 1, the last dashed dc is the last dc that will be made on Row 2 into the 3rd ch st of turning ch 5 at the beg of Row 1.
Row 3: Ch 5 to turn, 1 dc in second dc from end of Pr R, * ch 2, 1 dc in next dc, repeat from * across row, end with 1 dc in last dc of row, ch 2, 1 dc in 3rd ch st of turning ch 5 of Pr R.

Repeat Row 3 as many times as desired.

ALTERNATE BLOCKS & SPACES

(Starting and Ending with a Block): Make a foundation ch desired length. (See **Foundation Chain**.)
Row 1: 1 dc in 4th ch st from hook, 1 dc in each of the next 2 ch sts of foundation ch (this is first block), * ch 2, sk the next 2 ch sts, 1 dc in next ch st (this completes a space), 1 dc in each of next 3 ch sts (these 3 dc and dc of space complete the next block), repeat from * across chain, complete last space, 1 dc in each of last 3 ch sts (these 3 dc and dc of last space make the last block).

Diagram 3

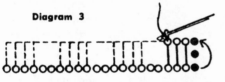

Diagram 3 shows the first block. The first solid vertical line is the dc in 4th ch st from hook, the remaining 2 lines are the dc in each of the next 2 ch sts.

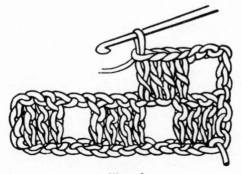

Illus. 4

The dashed lines indicate where other spaces and blocks are to be made.

Row 2: Ch 5 to turn, sk last 3 dc of Pr R, 1 dc in next dc, * 1 dc in each of next 2 ch sts, 1 dc in next dc, (Illus. 4), ch 2, sk next 2 dc, 1 dc in next dc, repeat from * across row, end with ch 2, sk 2 dc, 1 dc in 3rd ch st of turning ch.

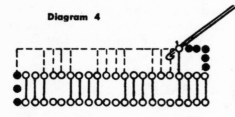

Diagram 4

Diagram 4 shows the work turned, the first space of Row 2, the 5 solid circles are the turning ch 5. At beg of Row 2 the first solid vertical line is the first dc made. Dashed lines indicate where other blocks and spaces are to be made.

Row 3: Ch 3 to turn, 1 dc in each of the next 2 ch sts, * 1 dc in next dc, ch 2, sk 2 dc, 1 dc in next dc, 1 dc in each of the next 2 ch sts, repeat from * across row, end with ch 2, 1 dc in last dc, 1 dc in each of the last 3 ch sts of turning ch 5 at beg of Row 2.

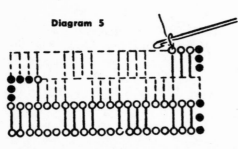

Diagram 5

Diagram 5 shows work turned, first block of Row 3; the 3 solid circles are turning ch 3 at beg of Row 3 (side of block), the next 2 vertical solid lines are the first 2 dc in ch-2 sp (center of block), the 3rd vertical solid line is the dc in next dc (other side of block). Dotted lines indicate where other spaces and blocks are to be made.

Repeat Rows 2 and 3 alternately as many times as desired.

SPACES OVER BLOCKS: Make a foundation ch desired length.
Row 1: 1 dc in 4th ch st from hook, 1 dc in each ch st across chain.

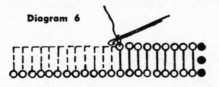

Diagram 6

Diagram 6 shows the first dc in 4th ch st; the solid lines are the dc sts in each ch st, the dotted vertical lines indicate where other dc sts are to be made.

Row 2: Ch 5, turn, sk last 3 dc of Pr R, 1 dc in next dc, * ch 2, sk next 2 dc, 1 dc in next dc, repeat from * across row to within the last 2 dc, end with ch 2, sk the last 2 dc, 1 dc in 3rd ch st of turning ch 3.

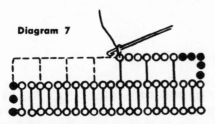

Diagram 7

Diagram 7 shows work turned, the first dc in 4th ch st, and all the dc sts made in Row 1. On Row 2, the 5 solid circles at the beg of Row 2 are the turning ch 5 at beg of Row 2, the 3 spaces are the first 3 spaces made. The dotted lines indicate where other spaces are to be made.

Row 3: Ch 3 to turn, 1 dc in each of next 2 ch sts, * 1 dc in next dc, 1 dc in each of the next 2 ch sts, repeat from * across Row, end with 2 dc in end sp, 1 dc in 3rd ch st of turning ch 5 at beg of Pr R.

Repeat Rows 2 and 3 alternately for as many times as desired.

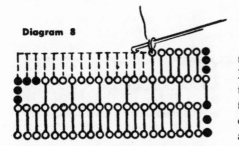

Diagram 8

Diagram 8 shows turning ch 3 at beg of Row 3 (solid circles) and the first two blocks on this row. Dotted lines indicate where other dc sts are to be made.

BLOCKS OVER SPACES: Make a foundation ch desired length.
Row 1: Repeat Row 1 of SPACES OVER SPACES.
Row 2: Repeat Row 3 of SPACES OVER BLOCKS.
Row 3: Repeat Row 2 of SPACES OVER BLOCKS.

Repeat above Rows 2 and 3 alternately as many times as desired.

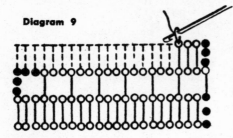

Diagram 9

Diagram 9 shows the work turned, first space completed at the beg of Row 3. Dotted lines indicate where other dc sts are to be made.

INCREASING SPACES & BLOCKS

INCREASING SPACES AT THE BEG OF A ROW THAT STARTS WITH A SPACE: At end of last row when last dc of that row has been completed, always ch 2 for first space to be added, ch 3 for each additional space, ch 8 for last space.

Next Row: 1 dc in 8th ch st from hook, * ch 2, sk 2 ch sts, 1 dc in next ch st, repeat from * until first dc of Pr R is reached, end with ch 2, 1 dc in first dc of Pr R, work across Pr R as indicated on chart.

Diagram 10 shows 5 ch sts added for 2 spaces, the 8 solid circles are the ch 8 for last space.

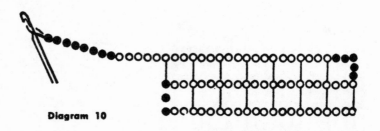

Diagram 10

Diagram 11 shows work turned; the first solid vertical line is the dc in 8th ch st which makes the first space of next row; the last solid vertical line is the dc in first dc of Pr R. Dotted lines indicate where other spaces are to be made.

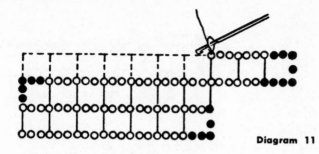

Diagram 11

INCREASING AT THE END OF A ROW WHEN THE NEXT ROW STARTS WITH A SPACE: Method #1 is the simplest but not the neatest. Method #2 is simple, but will require slip-stitching back to the starting point sometimes. Method #3 is the most difficult as it requires careful attention to that part of the Pr d tr st that the next d tr st is to be made in, but when the last space is completed you will always be in the proper starting position for next row.

METHOD #1: When the last dc of the row that has spaces added has been completed, disengage hook from loop, leaving loop free (to be picked up again later). Attach another thread in same place where last dc was made. To attach thread, insert hook from top thru st, grasp end of thread between forefinger and work, thread over hook, pull a short loop thru, hold on to end of thread until first ch st is made, ch 3 for each additional space to be added, break thread 2" beyond last ch st. Replace free loop on hook, ch 2, working in added chain, sk first 2 ch sts of added chain, 1 dc in next ch st, * ch 2, sk next 2 ch sts, 1 dc in next ch st, ch 2, repeat from * across, ch 5 to turn if beg of next row is a space.

Diagram 12 shows added chain (9 open circles) at top of Pr R; hook has been replaced in dropped loop.

Diagram 12

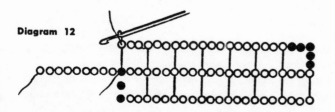

Diagram 13

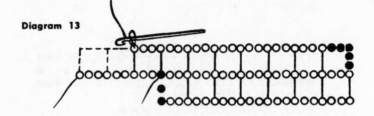

Diagram 13 shows the first space made on added chain. Dotted lines indicate where other spaces are to be made.

METHOD #2: Complete last dc of row that has spaces added, ch 5, 1 dc in s pl last dc was made (3rd ch st of turning ch of Pr R), this is first upside-down added space (Illus. 5), * ch 5, turn, 1 dc in 3rd ch st of last ch 5 turn, this is next right-side-up space (Illus. 6), turn, ch 5, 1 dc in 3rd ch st of last ch 5, this is next upside-down added space, repeat from * for as many spaces as are required. **Note:** If the last added space is made right-side-up you will automatically be at the proper starting point for the next row. If the last added space is made upside down, turn, work 1 sl st in each of the last 3 ch sts of the last ch 5 to arrive at proper starting point of next row.

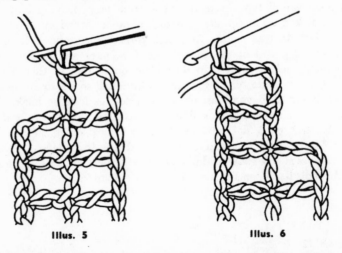

Illus. 5　　　　　　　　**Illus. 6**

Diagram 14 shows 3 added spaces, the first 5 solid circles are the ch 5 of first upside-down space, the first solid line with arrow (indicating direction) is the dc made in 3rd ch st of turning ch of Pr R, the next 5 open circles are the ch 5 of next right-side-

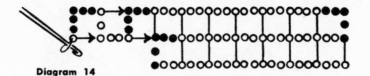

Diagram 14

up space, the end 5 solid circles are the last ch of next upside-down space, the last dc has been made.

Diagram 15 shows work turned and 1 sl st (tiny triangles on Diag.) in each of the last 3 ch sts of last ch 5.

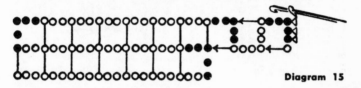

Diagram 15

METHOD #3: Complete last dc of row that has spaces added, ch 2, make 1 d tr in same place last dc was made in following manner: Thread over hook 3 times, insert hook in ch 3 of turning ch of Pr R (Illus. 7), pull up a loop (5 loops on hook), thread over hook and thru the first 2 loops, thread over hook and thru next 2 loops, *note the position of these 2 loops* over working thread (Illus. 8), it is into these 2 *loops* that the next d tr will be made, (thread over hook and thru 2 loops) 2 times (Illus. 9), * ch 2, 1 d tr into that part of last d tr where the *second set* of loops were taken off (Illus. 10), repeat from * for as many spaces as required.

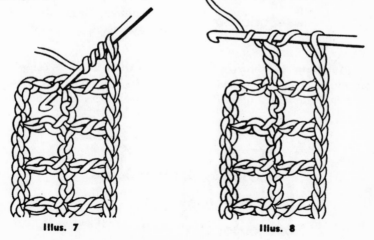

Illus. 7   Illus. 8

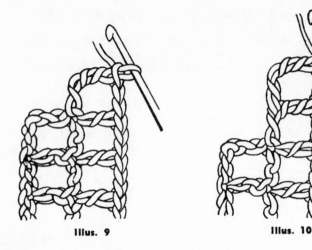

Illus. 9   Illus. 10

INCREASING BLOCKS AT THE BEG OF A ROW: At end of last row when last dc of that row has been completed always ch 3 for each additional block, ch 3 to turn, on next row work 1 dc in 4th ch st from hook, 1 dc in each ch st across.

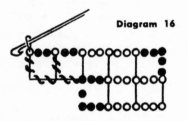

Diagram 16

Diagram 16 shows 2 added spaces, the 2 solid circles are the turning ch 2, the 4 short heavy wavy lines are each 2 loops that are taken off while working 1 d tr, ch to turn as required, turn work, and continue across next row.

Diagram 17 shows work turned with first block completed on added chain, the 3 solid circles are the turning ch 3. Dashed lines indicate where other dc sts for 2 more blocks are to be made.

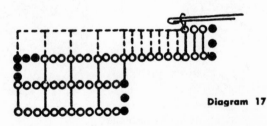

Diagram 17

INCREASING BLOCKS AT THE END OF A ROW:

METHOD #1: When the last dc of the row that has blocks added has been completed, disengage hook, leaving loop free. Attach another thread in same place last dc was made, ch 3 for each additional block, break thread 2" away from last ch st. Pick up free loop and work 1 dc in each ch st across added chain.

Diagram 18 shows added chain with first block completed, dashed lines indicate where other dc sts are to be made for 2 more blocks.

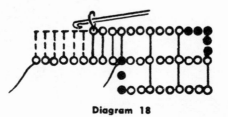

Diagram 18

METHOD #2: Complete the last dc of row, which has blocks added, in the following manner: Thread over hook, insert hook in 3rd ch st of turning ch, thread over hook and pull a loop thru, thread over hook and thru the first loop (this is the *foundation ch st for next dc*), thread over hook and thru next loop on hook (Illus. 11), thread over hook and work off the remaining 3 loops on hook 2 at a time, make next dc in foundation ch st in following manner: * thread over hook, insert hook into the foundation ch st of last dc (this ch st emerges from base of last dc) (Illus. 12), thread over hook (Illus. 13), pull loop thru, ch 2 thru this loop, work off remaining 3 loops on hook 2 at a time, repeat from * for as many dc sts as are necessary. **Note:** On last dc *ch 1* thru first loop. Illus. 14 shows 1 block added.

METHOD #3: Complete *the last dc* of the row, which has blocks added, in the following manner: Thread over hook, insert hook in 3rd ch st of turning ch, thread over hook, pull a loop thru, * ch 1 thru this loop (this is the foundation ch st for next dc), work remaining 3 loops off 2 at a time. Next dc: thread over hook, insert hook in foundation ch 1 of Pr dc, pull a loop thru, repeat from * for as many dc sts as necessary.

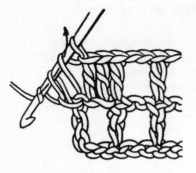

Illus. 11

Illus. 12

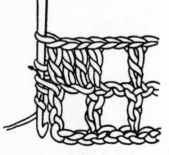

Illus. 13

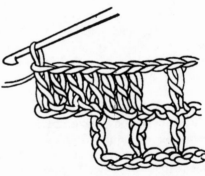

Illus. 14

DECREASING SPACES & BLOCKS

DECREASING SPACES OR BLOCKS AT THE END OF A ROW:
Work last block or space as indicated on chart, disregard remaining blocks or spaces on Pr R, make a turning ch as required, turn work and continue across row just finished as indicated.

DECREASING SPACES OR BLOCKS AT THE BEG OF A ROW:

METHOD #1: When last row is completed ch 1, turn, sl st in every st of each square to be eliminated, always sl st into the dc that forms the side of last square over which the first square of next row is to be made, ch as required for turning, work across new row as indicated on chart.

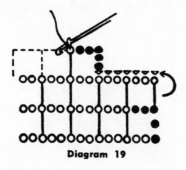

Diagram 19 shows the work turned, 1 sl st (tiny triangles) in each ch st and in each of the first 3 dc to decrease 2 spaces. The 5 solid circles on top row are the turning ch 5, the first dc has been made on this row.

Diagram 19

METHOD #2 FOR DECREASING 1 SPACE AT END OF ROW & AT THE BEG OF NEXT ROW: When making the first dc of last space (which is *directly underneath beg of next row*), leave the last 2 loops on hook, thread over hook 3 times (Illus. 15), insert hook in last dc of this row, draw up a loop, thread over hook and thru 2 loops at a time until 3 loops remain on hook, thread over

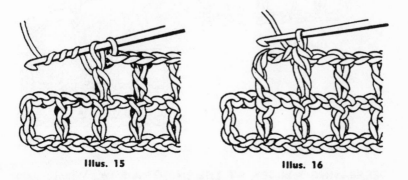

Illus. 15   Illus. 16

hook and thru last 3 loops on hook. You are now at the top of the first dc of last sp (Illus. 16) and ready to ch as required for turning for next row.

DECREASING 2 OR MORE SPACES AT END OF A ROW: When making the first dc of the space which is *directly underneath* beg of next row, leave the last 2 loops on hook (Illus. 15), * thread over hook 3 times, insert hook in next dc, draw up a loop, thread over hook and thru 2 loops on hook, repeat from * to end of row (Illus. 17, 18, and 19), ** thread over hook and thru 2 loops on hook, repeat from ** until 3 loops remain, thread over hook and thru all 3 loops. You are now at the top of the first dc underneath beg of next row (Illus. 20), ready to ch as required for turning for next row.

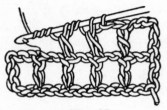

Illus. 17

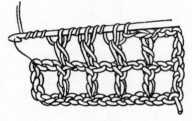

Illus. 18

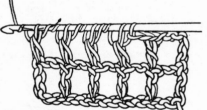

Illus. 19

Illus. 20

DECREASING 1 BLOCK AT THE END OF A ROW: When making the last dc of the sp or blk (which is directly underneath beg of next row), leave the last loop of this dc and each dc to be decreased on hook, thread over hook 2 times before inserting hook in 3rd ch st of turning ch (Illus. 21), draw up a loop, * thread over hook and thru 2 loops at a time, repeat from * until all remaining loops on hook are worked off, last loop on hook will be at top of first dc of sp or bl *directly underneath* beg of next row (Illus. 22). You are now ready to ch as required for turning for next row. **Note:** Combination of bls and sps can be decreased by combining the 2 methods as required.

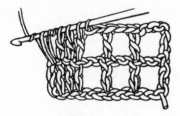

Illus. 21

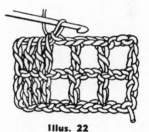

Illus. 22

JOINING SCALLOPS OR SEPARATE SECTIONS

The connecting chs (open circles on diagram) must be made on the last row of each section. It is always important to anticipate the next row and to make the foundation chain on which any extra sps or bls are to be worked.

Diagram 20 shows 3 groups of scallops, each group consists of 5 rows, on the 2nd and 3rd Scallops the solid lines represent the 4 rows already worked with an added ch 3 for an extra sp on next row, Row 5 is finished on first scallop and 8 ch sts have been added (for 3 spaces between on next row), the end dc has been made at the beg of 5th row on 2nd scallop. Dashed lines represent sps to be made.

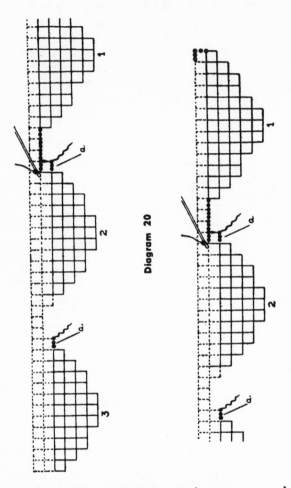

Diagram 20

TO FINISH SEPARATE SECTIONS: Work one section, decreasing where necessary. Attach thread where next section is to be worked, skipping any squares of last row between the 2 sections, finish next section in same manner. **Ex.**—Hold Diagram 20 upside down, the dashed section would be finished, the *scallops* would each be worked separately.

BARS & LACETS

Bars and lacets are used to fill in background, they are decorative, faster to work and are more interesting to work than all spaces.

BAR: When last sp or bl is completed ch 5, skip the dc between the next 2 sps, make 1 dc in the next dc. **Note:** Over bls, 5 dc are skipped.

When bars are used alone, make bars over 1 row, on next row alternate the bls so that the ch 5 is over the dc of Pr R, the dc of bar is made in the 3rd ch st of ch 5 of Pr R, the beg and end of every other row usually starts and ends with a bl or sp when the background is an even shape such as a square or rectangle.

LACET: Complete last dc before lacet, * ch 3, 1 sc in next dc, ch 3, 1 dc in next dc, repeat from * for as many as desired. When bars and lacets are used for a background, they are worked in alternate rows (1 row of lacets, 1 row of bars). Since sps and bls cannot be made over a lacet, they will have to be started over the bars. Illus. 23 shows several rows of single lacet and bar which forms a line thru center.

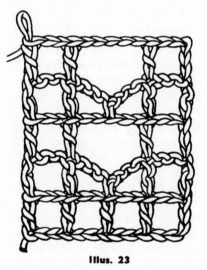

Illus. 23

BAR OVER LACET: When first dc over lacet is completed, * ch 5, sk the sc of lacet, make 1 dc in next dc, repeat from * across a row of lacets.
Note: When making your own design, sketch in the lacets and bars, then add sps or bls wherever necessary to fill in wherever lacets or bars cannot be made.

TURNING A CORNER WITH SPACES: If you are working an edging and want to change the directions so that the piece will fit around a corner, decrease 1 sp at inner edge on every row (Diag.

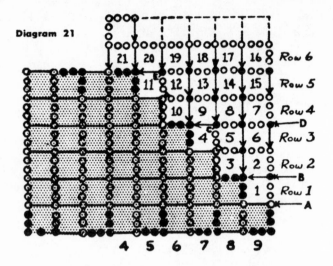

Diagram 21

21). The shaded part of Diag. 21 is the original direction of edging; note the decreased edge on this Piece. **Note:** You must end at *inner* corner of last sp (A on Diag. 21), ch 2, 1 dc in 3rd ch st of turning ch at beg of Row 8 on Diag. 21. This completes #1 sp and you are now at B on Diag.: ch 5, 1 dc in same place as last dc (this completes #2 sp), ch 2, sl st in top of end dc of Row 7 (tiny triangle on Diag.—#3 sp), ch 2, 1 dc in 3rd ch st of turning ch at beg of Row 6 (#4 sp). You are at C on Diag.: ch 2, turn, 1 dc in next dc of Row 2 (#5 sp), ch 2, 1 dc in 3rd ch st of turning ch at beg of Row 2 (#6 sp). You are at D on Diag.: ch 5, turn, 1 dc in next dc of Row 3 (#7 sp), ch 2, 1 dc in dc at C on Diag. (#8 sp), ch 2, 1 dc in 3rd ch st of turning ch at beg of Row 6 (#9 sp), ch 2, 1 sl st in dc at end of Row 5 (#10 sp), ch 2, 1 dc in 3rd ch st of turning ch at beg of Row 4 (#11 sp). You are at E on Diag.: ch 2, turn, 1 dc in next dc of Row 4 (#12 sp), (ch 2, 1 dc in next dc) 2 times (#13 & #14 sps), ch 2, 1 dc in 3rd ch st of turning ch at beg of Row 4 (#15 sp), ch 5, turn, * 1 dc in next dc, ch 2, repeat from * across Row 6 on Diag. There are now an equal number of spaces on each side of corner; continue edging in same manner as before.

On Diag. 21, arrows indicate the direction of each dc.

TURNING A CORNER WITH BLOCKS: Decrease 1 bl on inner edge on every row. The shaded part of Diag. 22 is the original direction of edging. Note the decreased edge on this piece. You must end at A; arrows indicate direction in which each group of dc sts are to be made.

The 2 center dc sts of #2 bl are made *into* the *first* and *second* part of the last dc of #1 bl. The 2 center dc sts of #3 bl are made *into* the turning ch at beg of Row 8, sl st into top of last dc at end of Row 7, work 3 dc in end bl of Row 6 for #4 bl, turn, work #5 and #6 bls across Pr R, ch 3, turn. Work Row 4 same as Row 2, work #11 bl in same manner as #4, turn and work across Pr R, on next row, continue edging same as before.

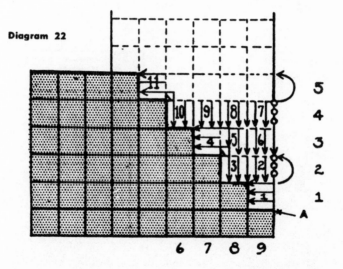

Diagram 22

WORKING AROUND A CORNER: A filet edging can be worked around a square or rectangle as shown in Diag. 23. Work the first rnd around all 4 sides, join with sl st as required to finish rnd. On next row ch 3 or 5 as required for first sp or bl. On Diag. 23, after completing the last sp before corner you are at A, ch 5, 1 dc in same place as last dc, on 3rd rnd: 1 Block, 1 Space at corner, 1 Block have all been worked into the corner ch 5 of Pr R, on 4th rnd: 3 spaces have been worked into the corner ch 5 of Pr R; continue in this manner for as many rnds as desired. **Note:** Solid circles are the corner ch 5 on each rnd.

FINISHING: Wherever possible, conceal ends by working over them with edging. Where this is not possible, thread each loose end in a sewing needle and run it thru work until it has been securely hidden, reverse direction of needle and make a knotted st or take a backstitch to keep ends from pulling loose. When sewing sections of lace together, use sewing thread, which is not as hard as crochet cotton and easier to manage. Join pieces together on Wrong Side, sewing each st to corresponding st on other piece, catching the back loop of each st on each piece. Make a knotted st about every ½″ to keep thread from slipping.

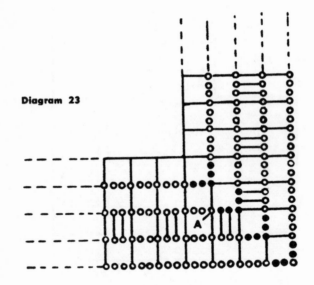

Diagram 23

EDGINGS: Filet lace is usually finished with an edging. The edging makes a firm edge for the lace besides covering turning chs and loose ends.

SC EDGING (Illus. 24): The classic edging for filet lace is 1 row of sc, work 3 sc in each sp, 1 sc in each dc of a bl, 7 sc in each corner sp. A deeper edging can be made with additional rows of sc. On each additional row, make 1 sc in each sc; on corner sc, make 3 sc in 4th sc of each corner sp.

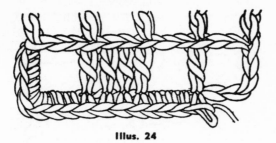

Illus. 24

PICOT EDGING: Make * 2 sc in next sp, ch 3, 1 sc in last sc made (picot made), 2 sc in s sp, repeat from * over sps; in each corner sp, make 2 sc, picot, 2 sc, picot, 2 sc. At a bl, ** make 1 sc in each of the first 2 dc, picot, 1 sc in each of last 2 dc, repeat from ** over bls.

PICOT SCALLOPED EDGING (Illus. 25): 1 sc in next dc, * ch 3, sk next dc, 1 dc in next sp, ch 3, 1 sc in dc just made (picot made), 1 dc in s pl as last dc, ch 3, sk next dc, 1 sc in next dc, repeat from * over sps. At a bl, 1 sc in first dc, * ch 3, sk next dc, 1 dc in next dc, ch 3, 1 sc in dc just made (picot), 1 dc in s pl as last dc, ch 3, sk next dc, 1 sc in next dc, repeat from * over bls.

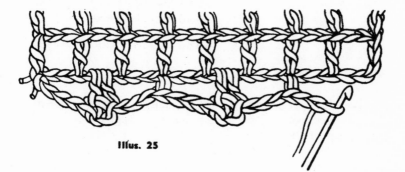

Illus. 25

CHAIN LOOP EDGING (Illus. 26): * Ch 3, sk 2 sts, 1 sc in next st, repeat from * for one row; on next row, ** ch 3, 1 sc in ch 3 loop of Pr R, repeat from ** over Pr R.

Illus. 26

WASHING: Cotton thread may shrink slightly in washing. Use lukewarm water for sudsing and rinsing. Bleach may be used for removing stains. Follow directions for use of bleach as given on label, rinse thoroughly afterwards. Starch lace lightly, pin to shape on a padded surface with rust-proof pins, cover with dry cloth and press until thoroughly dry.

TO MOUNT LACE FOR FRAMING: After lace is completed, wash and press. Remove backing and glass from frame. Cut a piece of cardboard and a piece of thin wadding same size as glass. Cut a piece of dark fabric for background 1" larger all around. Fabric may be velvet, velveteen, linen, or similar material. Mark outline of glass on Right Side of fabric and sew lace within this outline. Cover cardboard with wadding and fabric, fastening edges of fabric over cardboard with thread or staples. Replace glass, insert the cardboard with lace against glass, replace backing.

TRIANGULAR SHAPES

The chart for a corner motif to match Insertion and Edging has a stepped edge: Start at the longest straight edge, and decrease 1 sp at the beg and end of every row until 1 sp is left.

The chart for the Diamond Insertion with alphabet or design has a straight edge on all 4 sides. This is done in the following manner:

Row 1: Ch 7, 1 tr in 7th ch st from hook, ch 7 to turn.

Row 2: 1 dc in tr, ch 2, sk 2 ch sts, 1 dc in next ch st, ch 2, 1 tr in s pl as last dc, ch 7 to turn.

Row 3: 1 dc in tr, (ch 2, 1 dc in next dc) 2 times, ch 2, sk 2 ch sts of turning ch 7 of Pr R, 1 dc in next ch st, ch 2, 1 tr in s pl as last dc, ch 7, turn.

Continue working in this manner at beg and ends of each row following chart after finishing the 11th Row, ch 3 to turn, 1 dc in first dc from end of Pr R, follow chart to last bl. After the dc that completes the last bl is made, make 1 tr into 3rd ch st of turning ch of Pr R, ch 3, turn, 1 dc in 2nd dc from end of Pr R. Follow chart, decreasing in this manner at beg and end of each row above center of Diamond. If a larger Diamond is desired simply add more rows below center, then decrease the same number of rows above center. **Note:** With a stitch gauge of 6 sps = 1", 6 rows = 1", the finished Diamond would be approximately 3" square.

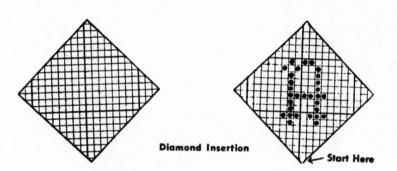

Diamond Insertion

← Start Here

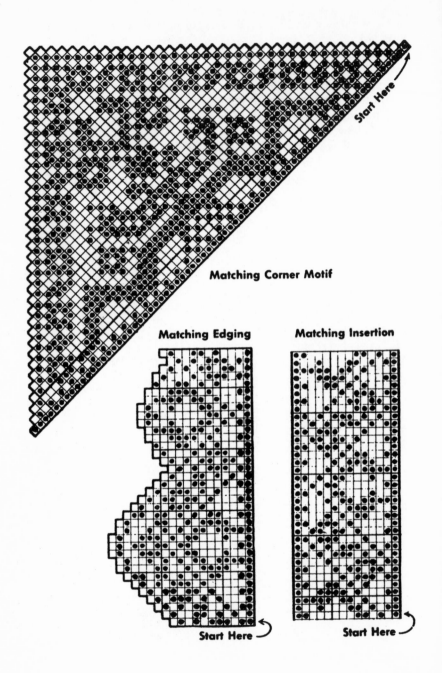

Matching Corner Motif

Matching Edging

Matching Insertion

Start Here

Start Here

Start Here

FILET ALPHABET

The Diamond Insertion with a letter or design may be used on bed linens, table linens, runners, etc.

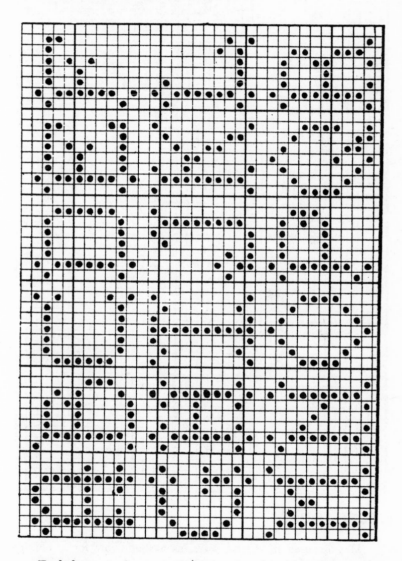

Each letter is the same height and width. The letter desired should be marked into the empty Diamond Insertion in same manner as letter "A." Work all squares of letter in bls, remainder of Insertion in open spaces.

LACET SQUARE

May be used in several ways, as a single row for an edging with single squares or more single rows used as an insertion, as an all-over pattern for runners, place mats, square doilies, etc.

FILET CROCHET VANITY SET

For a single row, make 1 square, then repeat the square for desired length.

For more than 1 row, repeat Row 1 as many times as desired, then repeat Row 2 across each Row 1, etc. The corners will automatically form a design.

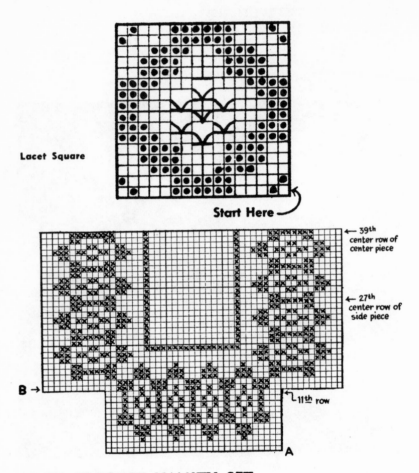

Lacet Square

Start Here

B →

A

39th center row of center piece

27th center row of side piece

11th row

FILET CROCHET VANITY SET

(Side pieces: 10½″ square. Centerpiece: 10½″ x 15″.)

MATERIALS REQUIRED:
    J. & P. Coats "Big Ball" Best Six-Cord Mercerized Crochet, Art. A. 104, Size 30
    4 Balls of No. 1 White, No. 61 Ecru, or No. 42 Cream; or Clark's "Big Ball" Mercerized Crochet, Art. B. 34, Size 30
    3 Balls of No. 1 White, No. 61 Ecru, or No. 42 Cream
    #10 Milwards Steel Crochet Hook

STITCH GAUGE: 5 sps = 1″   5 rows = 1″

CROCHETING INSTRUCTIONS:

CENTERPIECE: Starting at narrow edge, ch 98 to measure 7".

Row 1: Starting at A on chart, dc in 8th ch from hook *starting sp made;* * ch 2, sk 2 ch, dc in next ch *another sp made.* Repeat from * across—making 31 sps on row. Ch 5, turn.

Row 2: Skip first dc, dc in next dc—starting sp over sp made; * ch 2, dc in next dc. Repeat from * across, ending with dc in last dc, ch 2, sk 2 ch of last sp, dc in next ch. Ch 5, turn.

Row 3: Make 6 sps, 2 dc in next sp, dc in next dc—*bl over sp made;* (make sps, 1 bl) 3 times, and 6 sps. Ch 5, turn.

Row 4: Make 5 sps and 1 bl, dc in next dc—*bl over bl made;* make another bl, (3 sps, 3 bls) 3 times, and 5 sps. Ch 5, turn.

Row 5: Make 5 sps, (3 bls, 3 sps) 3 times, 3 bls, 5 sps. Ch 5, turn.

Row 6: Make 2 sps, 3 bls, ch 2, sk 2 dc in next dc—*sp over bl made;* make 2 more sps, (3 bls, 3 sps) 3 times, 3 bls, 2 sps. Ch 5, turn.

Rows 7 thru 11: Follow chart. Ch 37, turn at end of Row 11.

Row 12: Dc in 8th ch from hook, continue to follow chart across ending with 2 sps following last 3 bls. Drop loop from hook, attach a separate strand of thread to same ch as last dc, ch 33. Break off. Pick up dropped loop, make 11 sps across chain. Ch 5, turn.

Starting with Row 13, follow chart until Row 39 has been completed. Turn chart. Omitting last row made on chart (center row), follow chart back to B. Break off.

Next Row: Turn work, skip first 11 sps, attach thread to next dc, ch 5, dc in next dc, follow chart across. Continue to follow chart to end.

SIDE PIECE (make 2): Work as for centerpiece until Row 27 has been completed. Turn chart, and complete work as for centerpiece.

EDGING:

Rnd 1: Attach thread to any corner sp on centerpiece, 7 sc in same sp, * 3 sc in each sp to next corner sp, 7 sc in corner sp. Repeat from * around. Join with sl st to first sc.

Rnd 2: Ch 1, sc in each sc to center sc of corner group, in center sc make sc, ch 5 and sc,—*corner picot made;* sc in next 5 sc, * ch 5, sc in next 5 sc—*another picot made.* Repeat from * around, being sure to make a corner picot in center sc of each corner group. Join to first sc. Break off and fasten.

Work around side pieces the same way.

Starch lightly and press.

HOW TO MAKE
HAIRPIN LACE

HAIRPIN LACE: Hairpin lace has really never left the needlework scene for very long. Currently, it is enjoying another revival. Combinations of the new threads, textured yarns and ribbons produce new and interesting effects on a *hairpin staple*.

Once mastered, yards and yards of lace can be turned out in a short time. It is simply crocheting around a wire bent like a hairpin. The basic stitches are crocheting stitches—a chain stitch and single crochet.

Fine threads, such as tatting thread, produce beautiful handkerchief edgings with delicate, fragile appearances that crochet alone cannot duplicate. On edgings, the lace is usually combined with 1 or more rows of crochet. Other threads are suitable for edgings on tablecloths, place mats, runners, cases, etc.

The different types of wool yarns used on different width staples can be used to make strips which are joined with 1 row of crochet for afghans, baby blankets, stoles, capes, etc.

Braiding, edgings, and bandings can be made of cotton or metallic threads, wool yarns, cordé, etc. The width of the staple and thickness of thread used will determine the length of loops produced.

ABBREVIATIONS

Ch—Chain
Sc—Single Crochet
Sl St—Slip Stitch
Pr R—Previous Row or Round
Incl—Inclusive
Tr—Treble
Sp—Space

* Repeat everything after asterisk [*] for as many times as specified in instructions.
( ) Do what is in parentheses the number of times indicated.

CHAIN STITCH (ch)

The chain stitch is the basis of all crochet.

Step 1: To start a chain, place end of thread over and around outside of forefinger of left hand and over inside of other 3 fingers, leaving end dangle free for about 4". With the little finger grasp other thread securely where it falls on palm of hand. Hold this thread fairly taut, releasing it slightly each time as the thread is needed, and form loop between thumb and forefinger.

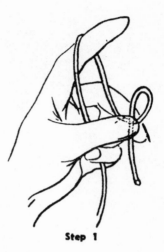

Step 1

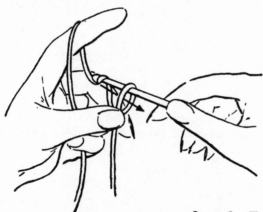

Step 2

Step 2: Take hook in right hand and insert hook thru loop and under thread between forefinger and middle finger. Twist hook until end of hook grasps the thread. Now pull thread on hook and hook thru loop.

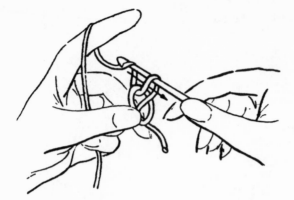

Step 3

Step 3: There is now one loop on hook; do not release thread between thumb and middle finger. Insert the hook under thread again, grasp the thread with end of hook and pull the thread on hook, and hook thru loop (this is the first chain stitch).

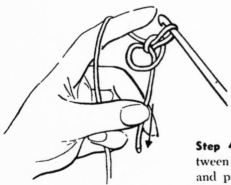

Step 4: Now release loop between thumb and middle finger and pull end thread to tighten the first loop into a knot.

Step 4

Step 5

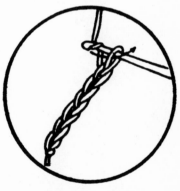

Step 5: Now hold work loosely between middle finger and thumb right under the hook, * twist hook on thread (this will be referred to as "thread over"), and pull thread thru loop on hook, repeat from * until chain is desired length.

Note: In counting the stitches of a chain, every finished loop is counted, *but not the loop on the hook*, which is in fact part of whatever stitch is to be made next.

Foundation Chain

SLIP STITCH (sl st)

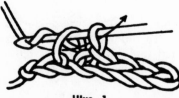

Illus. 1

Insert hook in ch st or st, thread over hook and draw loop thru ch st or st and thru loop on hook. This is a flat st used for joining, strengthening an edge, retracing one's steps to a different position, or fastening off (Illus. 1).

SINGLE CROCHET (sc)

Start in this instance with a foundation chain.

Step 1

Step 2

Step 3

Step 4

Step 5

Row 1: Insert hook in 2nd ch st from hook (not counting loop on hook), thread over hook and draw loop thru (2 loops now on hook), thread over hook and pull thru 2 loops on hook (Step 1 thru Step 5). * Insert hook in next ch st (Step 6), thread over hook and draw loop thru, thread over hook and draw loop thru 2 loops on hook, re-

Step 6

peat from * across row (Illus. 2), ch 1 and turn (Illus. 3).

Row 2: 1 sc in each sc across row (Illus. 4). Ch 1, if turning to continue another row.

Illus. 2

Illus. 3   **Illus. 4**

INSTRUCTIONS

Hairpin Lace is worked on a round wire, bent evenly in half with a circular bend (like hairpin). This is called a hairpin staple or loom or a crochet fork (Illus. 5). The size of the staple (½″,

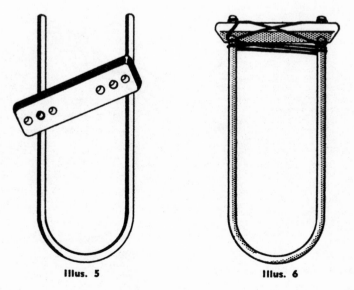

Illus. 5   **Illus. 6**

¾", 1", etc.) denotes the width between prongs. Different sizes are used for thread, yarn or ribbon. The size of crochet hook used is always specified in instructions. The staples usually come in one set of 3 different sizes with a plastic block that has holes to fit all sizes. The prongs of a staple are inserted into matching holes on block to keep prongs stationary while working and can be slipped off easily when work is to be removed. To prevent the block from sliding up or down on prongs, twist an elastic band around block at top of prongs (Illus. 6).

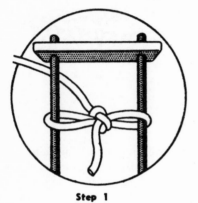

Step 1

Fasten block securely in place at top of prongs. Wrap end of yarn around both prongs of staple about ¾ of the way down from block, tie thread together securely in center between prongs of staple with a knot (Step 1), (pull end thread to center knot).

Step 2

With end of thread dangling down in rounded end of staple and working thread behind left prong, place working thread over left forefinger, hold left prong of staple between left thumb and ring finger. Using right hand, insert hook from bottom up between the 2 threads of left loop, working thread over hook and thru left loop (Step 2), thread over hook (Step 3), and thru loop on hook (Step 4).

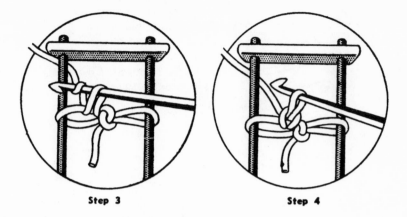

Step 3 **Step 4**

Remove hook to leave loop free (Step 5). With yarn still on left forefinger, turn right prong forward to left for ½ turn. Thread is now around front of right prong and behind both prongs (Step 6). Insert hook back into free loop, pull working thread to tighten loop on hook (Step 7); insert hook from bottom up into left loop, thread over hook (Step 8) and thru left loop. There are now 2 loops on hook (Step 9); thread over hook and thru both loops on hook (Step 10).

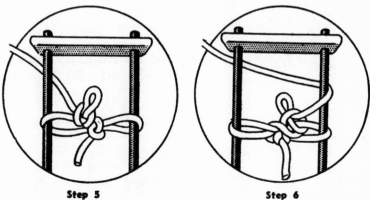

Step 5 **Step 6**

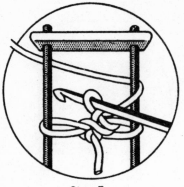

Step 7

Step 8

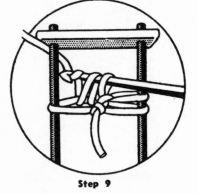

Step 9

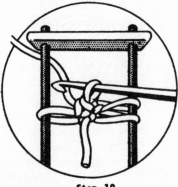

Step 10

* Remove hook, leaving loop free, turn staple to left for ½ turn, insert hook back into free loop, tighten loop on hook, insert hook from bottom up into top-left loop, thread over hook and thru the left loop, thread over hook and thru this left loop, thread over hook and thru both loops on hook (Step 11), repeat from * for length desired (Illus. 7).

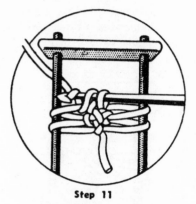

Step 11

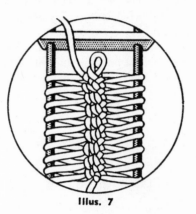

Illus. 7

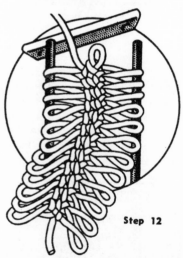

Step 12

Crowd loops down on staple while working. When staple has been filled with loops remove block, slide work off, insert prongs back into last 3 pairs of loops made, being careful to replace these loops so that the twist of each loop lays in the proper position (Step 12).

Instructions usually specify a certain number of loops or a length measurement. When measuring length, lay lace down on flat surface, measure thru center of lace, *do not stretch.*

There are several variations of this basic stitch which make a decorative wider band thru the center of the lace.

METHOD #1: Tie loop on staple in same manner as basic stitch, work 2 sc over the top thread of first left loop, * turn staple, work 2 sc over the top thread of next left loop, repeat from * for length desired.

METHOD #2: Tie loop on staple in same manner as basic stitch, insert hook into left loop, ch 1, turn staple, work 1 sc over top thread of left loop, work 1 sc over bottom thread of same left loop, * ch 1, turn staple, 1 sc in ch 1 of Pr R, 1 sc over top thread of next left loop, 1 sc over bottom thread of same left loop, repeat from * for length desired.

STRAIGHT EDGING: Make hairpin lace desired length, using #30 crochet cotton, #9 steel crochet hook and a ¾" wide staple. To crochet a heading to sew lace to article, attach thread in last loop, work 1 sl st in each loop across, being careful to keep the twist of each loop. For an insertion or banding, work a heading along other side of lace in same manner.

Straight Edging

POINTED EDGING: * 1 sl st in each of next 6 loops, 1 sl st in next 5 loops (this is inner point), 1 sl st in each of next 6 loops [ch 1, 1 sl st in next loop] 5 times (this is outer point, 3rd loop is exact point), repeat from * for desired number of points. For an insertion or banding, work other side in same manner, reversing the points, work inner point thru the other half of all outer point loops, and outer point thru the other half of same loops in inner point with ch 1 between.

Pointed Edging

ROUND EDGING: Work 1 sl st thru each 2 loops for length of lace; if necessary (for a larger circle) work a ch 1 between every 2 or 3 loops.

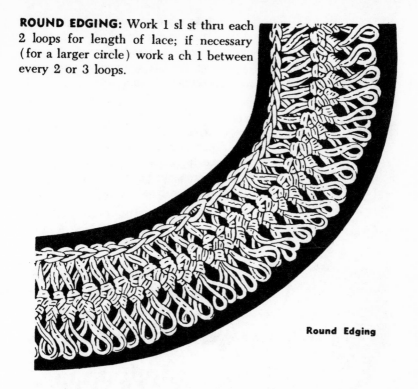

Round Edging

WAVY EDGING: * 1 sl st in each of next 4 loops, 1 sl st in next 4 loops at one time, 1 sl st in each of next 4 loops, ch 1, 1 sl st in next loop 4 times, repeat from * for desired length. For an insertion or banding, reverse the shaping, working 1 sl st, ch 1 over other half of loops that were taken off together and taking the other part of the 4 loops (with ch 1 between) off at one time.

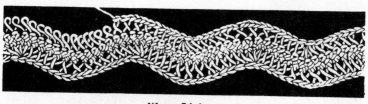

Wavy Edging

CORNERS: On an *inner corner*, insert hook thru 5 or 6 loops, thread over hook and thru all loops on hook.

On an *outside corner*, ch 1 between each of the other half of each inner-corner loop.

Note: The number of loops to be taken off together—to form an inner corner or point—will vary with the thickness and length of loops. On outer corners or points, work thru the other half of the same loops that form inner corner or point, working ch 1 between each loop.

If the loop seems too thin for the center, try using 2 strands of thread together as one. A strip of metallic lace makes a sparkling edging for a round neckline: shape 1 edge by working 1 sl st in 2 loops, ch 1, 1 sl st thru next 2 loops, etc., being careful to keep the twist in loops when inserting hook.

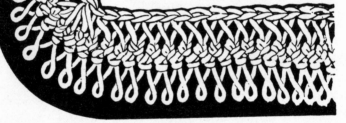

Corner

HOW TO MAKE HAIRPIN LACE STRIP

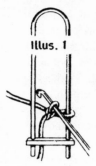

Illus. 1

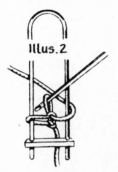

Illus. 2

Step 1: Make a loop at end of yarn (Illus. 1).

Step 2: Insert hook in loop and wind yarn around right prong of staple (Illus. 1).

Step 3: Yarn over hook and draw thru loop, keeping loop at center (Illus. 1).

Step 4: Raise hook to an upright position with hook end down; pass hook thru staple and turn staple to the left (Illus. 2).

Step 5: Insert hook in front loop of left prong (Illus. 3).

Step 6: Yarn over hook and draw loop thru (2 loops on hook), yarn over and draw thru 2 loops—one sc made (Illus. 4).

Note: If staple is filled, remove all but the last 4 loops from staple and continue as before.

EASY WAY TO COUNT LOOPS: If Hairpin Lace Strip requires a large amount of loops, always mark every 25th loop on each side of strip until the necessary amount of loops has been made.

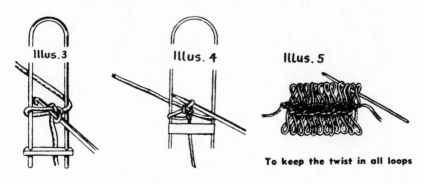

Illus. 3   **Illus. 4**   **Illus. 5**

To keep the twist in all loops

HAIRPIN LACE STOLE

HAIRPIN LACE STOLE

(Stole: 23" x 75", including shell borders)

MATERIALS REQUIRED:
Coats & Clark's "Red Heart" Super Fingering, 3 Ply
1 oz. "Tangle-Proof" Pull-Out Skeins
9 Skeins of No. 1 white
2" Hairpin Lace Staple
#1 Milwards Steel Crochet Hook

STITCH GAUGE:
13 loops = 2"
Width of 2 strips after joining = 4½"

CROCHETING INSTRUCTIONS:

HAIRPIN LACE STRIP (Make 10): Follow steps 1 thru 6 of the basic instructions accompanying the directions for this stole. Repeat Steps 4 to 6 incl until there are 490 loops on each side of strip (see "Easy Way to Count Loops"). Break off and fasten. *Keep the twist in all loops throughout* (see Illus. 5).

HEADING OF FIRST STRIP (Right Side): Make a loop on hook; inserting hook thru first 5 loops, make an sc, * ch 5, sc thru next 5 loops. Repeat from * across, ending with an sc. Break off and fasten. Work across opposite side the same way.

JOINING OF SECOND STRIP: Work as for heading of first strip across one side. Break off and fasten. With right side facing, attach yarn thru first 5 loops on opposite side, sc in same place, ch 2. With Wrong Side of first strip facing, sc in center ch of first ch 5, * ch 2, sc thru next 5 loops on 2nd strip, ch 2, sc in center ch of next ch 5 on first strip. Repeat from * across, ending with an sc thru last 5 loops. Break off and fasten. Join remaining strips the same way.

BORDER: Working across long edge, with Right Side facing, attach yarn to first sc, sc in same place, * ch 1, in center ch of next sp make (tr, ch 1) 3 times; sc in next sc. Repeat from * across.

Working across short edge, * * ch 7, sc in center of hairpin lace strip, ch 7, sc in side of next end, sc on same strip, ch 5, sc in side of sc on next strip. Repeat from * * across, ending with sc in last sc. Work across remaining long and short edges in same way, ending with ch 7, sl st in first sc. Break off and fasten.

With Right Side facing, working along one short edge, attach yarn in first sc and work shell border same as for long edge. Break off and fasten. Work across other short edge the same way.